KITCHENER PUBLIC LIBRARY

D1418578

A Chronology of Weather

Revised Edition

Dangerous Weather

A Chronology
of Weather

Revised Edition

Michael Allaby

ILLUSTRATIONS by Richard Garratt

☑®
Facts On File, Inc.

For Ailsa
—M.A.

To my late wife, Jen, who gave me inspiration
and support for almost 30 years
—R.G.

A Chronology of Weather, Revised Edition

Copyright © 2004, 1998 by Michael Allaby

All rights reserved. No part of this book may be reproduced or utilized in any form or by any means, electronic or mechanical, including photocopying, recording, or by any information storage or retrieval systems, without permission in writing from the publisher. For information contact:

Facts On File, Inc.
132 West 31st Street
New York NY 10001

Library of Congress Cataloging-in-Publication Data

Allaby, Michael.
    A chronology of weather / Michael Allaby; illustrations by Richard Garratt.—Rev. ed.
        p. cm.—(Dangerous weather)
    Includes bibliographical references and index.
    ISBN 0-8160-4792-8 (hardcover)
    1. Weather—History. 2. Weather—Chronology. 3. Natural disasters—Chronology. I. Title.
QC981.A55 2004
363.34'92'09—dc21   2003004000

Facts On File books are available at special discounts when purchased in bulk quantities for businesses, associations, institutions, or sales promotions. Please call our Special Sales Department in New York at (212) 967-8800 or (800) 322-8755.

You can find Facts On File on the World Wide Web at
http://www.factsonfile.com

Text design by Erika K. Arroyo
Cover design by Nora Wertz
Illustrations by Richard Garratt

Printed in the United States of America

VB FOF 10 9 8 7 6 5 4 3 2

This book is printed on acid-free paper.

Contents

Preface

Several years have passed since the first edition of this book was published. Much has happened during those years, and the decision to update the book for a second edition gives me a welcome opportunity to report at least some of them.

There have been more examples of extreme weather, of course. These are included in the "Chronicle of Destruction." Climate research has also intensified in recent years. Concern over the possibility that we may be altering the global climate has stimulated funding agencies to increase the resources available for evaluating the likelihood of global warming and its consequences. I have added the most important discoveries and developments to "A Chronology of Discovery."

My friend and colleague Richard Garratt has drawn all of the illustrations. As always, I am deeply grateful to him for his skill in translating my crude drawings into such accomplished artwork. I am grateful, too, to Frank K. Darmstadt, my editor at Facts On File, for his hard work, cheerful encouragement, and patience.

If this "new, improved" edition of *A Chronology of Weather* encourages you to pursue your study of the weather further, it will have achieved its aim and fulfilled my highest hopes for it. I hope you enjoy reading the book as much as I have enjoyed writing it for you.

—Michael Allaby
Tighnabruaich
Argyll, Scotland
www.michaelallaby.com

Introduction

All of us are affected by the weather, but for most of the time the weather we experience is fairly ordinary. It may be fine or wet, warm or dry, but it is not exceptional. Forecasting it is difficult in detail, but in general it is quite predictable. People will look at you oddly if you try to warn them that the winter will be cold, or that summer is the best time for swimming outdoors because it is warmer then. The average weather conditions over a period of at least several decades—the ordinary, everyday weather—comprise the climate of an area.

Now and again, however, the weather does something extraordinary, and then it can be dangerous. This book lists some of these instances of extreme weather. *A Chronology of Weather* is one of a set of eight books about dangerous weather. The other books in the series describe hurricanes, tornadoes, blizzards, droughts, and floods, one book dealing with each. Two additional books, entitled *Fog, Smog, and Poisoned Rain* and *A Change in the Weather*, describe air pollution and climate change, respectively.

All types of extreme weather can and do cause hardship, destruction, and death. In the past it has done so on a vast scale. Today we are able to limit the harm it does by warning people in advance and providing efficient emergency services that can respond quickly. Even so, extreme weather remains dangerous, because its power is huge and unstoppable. Pollution is unpleasant and harmful to health—our own and the health of some of the animals and plants with which we share the planet—but it differs from extreme weather in one important respect: We are responsible for it, and it is within our power to reduce it. Climate change is entirely natural and occurs constantly, but if certain of our activities are altering the chemical composition of the atmosphere in ways that bring about climate change, we should we aware of what is happening.

Dangerous Weather

Five books in the set describe fully the harm that hurricanes, tornadoes, blizzards, droughts, and floods have caused in the past and are still capable of causing. The books also tell you what is being done to protect lives and property and what you and your family should do to prepare and how to react should one of these monsters strike in your area. Dangerous weather can injure and kill people, but it is possible to survive unharmed. Survival depends on knowing what to expect, making a sensible plan long before the weather emergency occurs, and then, when it does, carrying out your plan without panic. Experts will advise and help you when they are needed. The National Weather Service will keep you informed, and the emergency services will issue instructions.

Dangerous these extremes may be, but the same natural forces that produce our ordinary weather also produce them. They are, after all, simply wind, snow, dry weather, and rain. To understand how they occur, therefore, you need to know something about those natural forces. You need to understand how air moves over the surface of the Earth, what makes the wind blow, how clouds form, what goes on inside a thunderstorm, and why it rains or snows. As you read about dangerous weather, you will also learn about ordinary weather.

Fog, Smog, and Poisoned Rain explains the causes of air pollution and describes its effects. It is not a new phenomenon—in some parts of the world the air was much more seriously polluted in the past—and the book outlines the history of the air we breathe and the steps by which its quality has been improved. Further improvements are still needed, of course, and *Fog, Smog, and Poisoned Rain* explains how these may be achieved.

A Change in the Weather describes how climates have changed in the past to demonstrate that change is a natural state of affairs. It then explains how scientists study past and present climates and how they estimate future changes and their consequences.

A Chronology of Weather

A Chronology of Weather is different from the other books in the Dangerous Weather series; it starts with a general outline of the history of the world's climates over the centuries. Because the weather we experience is much the same from one year to the next, we tend to think it has always been much as it is now. If we imagine, say, a Roman soldier or a medieval knight, we think of them living in a climate just like that of today. This is wrong. The weather then was different. It has changed many times, and it is changing now. After discussing climate change throughout history, the book outlines the way our understanding of the weather and ability to forecast it have developed over the centuries.

The largest part of the book consists of two chronological accounts. One lists some of the major weather disasters by the years in which they occurred. These seem to become more frequent in modern times, but that is because we now have more detailed records. There is no reason to suppose weather disasters happen more often now than they ever have. Look at how many hurricanes, tornadoes, blizzards, droughts, and floods there have been since about 1990 and at the appalling harm they have done and the personal tragedies they have caused, and remember that these years are not special. This is how the weather has behaved during any similar period throughout history, as far back as you care to delve, but we know nothing about those more distant events. Remembering this, try to imagine how terrifying hurricanes and tornadoes must have been to people who had no weather service to warn them they were coming or clear ideas about what caused them.

Notice, too, that no part of the world escapes. Tropical cyclones form only in the Tropics, but they can sometimes survive long enough to cause serious damage and loss of life as far away as Canada and Europe, and those who live in middle latitudes regularly suffer winds of hurricane force and blizzards. The United States has more tornadoes than any other country, but every country experiences some. The chronology also includes major air pollution incidents.

The second account, listing important developments in the understanding of weather and improvements in forecasting, is not limited in the same way by lack of information. Important discoveries and inventions are recorded, and the individuals associated with them often become famous. These advances are also listed by the years in which they occurred and, where appropriate, they include brief biographical details about the persons responsible for them.

Together, these eight books will introduce you to the adventure of exploring our atmosphere and the weather it produces. They may even persuade you to carry your studies further and one day to join the professional meteorologists, with their balloons, instruments, satellites, and powerful computers.

HISTORY OF OUR WEATHER

Weather affects us all. We may want to know whether we can safely invite friends to a picnic next weekend or whether the ground will be dry enough for the game we hope to see or play in a few days' time. It all depends on the weather.

Different people are affected in different ways, of course, and for some it is a more serious matter than being able to plan recreational events. Farmers need to know whether the weather will remain fine long enough for them to plow their fields or bring in the harvest. When you travel by air, the pilot and air traffic controllers have detailed knowledge of the weather conditions along the route you will take. This tells them the height at which it is best to fly, whether they will need to go around large storms that could give you an uncomfortable ride or even damage the airplane, and whether the destination airfield will be clear of fog, low cloud, runway ice, and strong winds. This is information on which lives may depend. Similarly, fishermen, who trust their lives as well as their livelihoods to small boats, need to know whether it is safe to put to sea. Even a large ship can be damaged—and in extreme cases, sunk—if it sails into a hurricane. Sea captains need to know whether there are any severe storms along the routes they plan to follow.

As you know only too well, the weather changes constantly. It changes more often and more dramatically in some parts of the world than in others, but even in the humid Tropics it is not always the same. You might think that in a tropical rain forest it rains every day, but it does not. Sometimes there are dry spells, and the plants are short of water. It rarely rains in a desert, but there are no places where it never rains or snows, and when the desert rains do come, they usually do so in torrents. There are towns in some deserts, and occasionally they are flooded.

It is this changeability that makes weather forecasting so difficult. If the changes were regular, like the phases of the Moon or the movement of the Sun across the sky, we would hardly need weather forecasters at all. We could look up tomorrow's weather, or next month's or even next year's, in a book. Imagine what it would be like to know months or years ahead what the weather will be like on any particular day. Imagine, too, what the consequences might be. Everyone would go on vacation or out for the day at the same time to take advantage of the fine weather. Beaches, scenic areas, and resorts would be even more crowded than they are already!

As the ice retreated

These are only the short-term changes—the changes that take place from one day to the next. Weather also changes on much longer time scales. Weather itself has a history.

If you could travel back in time 10,000 years, you would find a world in which some people were just beginning to domesticate animals and grow plant crops, but most still obtained their food, clothing, fuel, and timber for building by gathering wild plants. They won their meat by fishing and gathering seafood, hunting game, and stealing meat from more formidable hunters such as big cats and wolves.

In the world they inhabited, ice sheets were starting to retreat from a large part of North America, Europe, and Asia. The last ice age was coming to an end. The climate and landscape in what are now Maryland and Virginia were like those you find today in northern Canada and Alaska. What is now Utah's Great Salt Lake formed part of a huge inland sea called Lake Bonneville, covering nearly 20,000 square miles (51,800 km^2) and in places 1,000 feet (300 m) deep. In those days you could have walked from North America across the ice sheet to Greenland, and from there to Europe. The North Sea was mostly dry land. Britain was still joined to the European mainland across the Dover Strait, and Alaska to Siberia across the Bering Strait. Animals and people followed the retreating ice across these land bridges.

Land bridges existed because sea levels were low due to the large amount of water that was frozen and formed the ice sheets. You can still find evidence of those past sea levels. There are places on some coasts where the remains of forests can still be seen offshore. At very low tides they are revealed, not as trees, of course, after all this time, but recognizably as wood. Many present-dry estuaries were once river valleys, drowned as the rising sea flooded low-lying coastal land. High coastal cliffs were once hills some distance from the coast. As the sea advanced, incessant battering from the waves gradually wore away one side.

At other times sea levels were higher, suggesting that the climate has been so much warmer in the past that the polar ice sheets were much smaller than they are now. The ice melted, releasing its water into the oceans. You can find evidence of this, too, along some coasts in the form of *raised beaches*. These are layers of ground, well above the highest level reached by modern tides, containing seashells that must once have lain on the shore.

Moving continents

Still further back in time, beyond the ice ages, there is evidence of climates that were even more dramatically different. Coal is found in many parts of

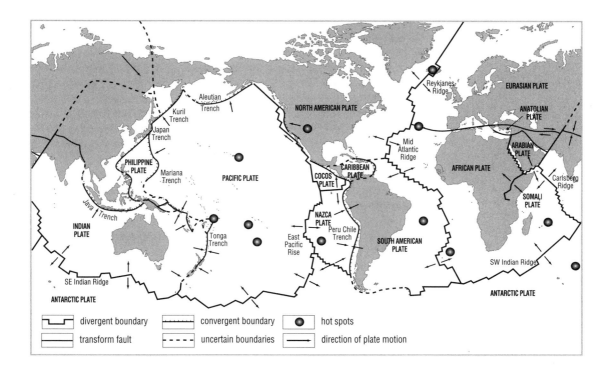

the world. Perhaps there are, or once were, coal mines not far from where you live. Coal is made from partly decayed vegetation, and it forms only in swamps along tropical coasts. What are now coalfields were once tropical coastal swamps. There is coal—lots of it—in Antarctica. That frozen continent was once tropical.

If you live far inland, but the soil is very sandy, your neighborhood may once have been part of a dry, sandy desert or have lain on the seabed. Camels would not have loped across that ancient desert, though, or seals and dolphins swum in those vanished waters. Your local desert or sea existed long before these mammals appeared on Earth.

Big differences such as these were due to more than the changing climate, of course. All the continents of the world are moving. North America and Europe are growing farther apart, for example, as the Atlantic Ocean widens. It is a slow process. The Atlantic is widening by about one inch (25 mm) a year. Over many millions of years, this adds up to a large distance, however, and at the time the coalfields formed, the climate was tropical because the lands in which they are found lay in the Tropics.

Continents move because the Earth's crust of solid rock is broken into sections of varying sizes called *plates*. The plates move in relation to one another. In some places they collide, at *convergent boundaries*. There they may ram into each other, raising mountain chains made from crumpled rock. The Himalayas formed in this way, by collision between the Indian

Plate tectonics. The major plates into which the Earth's crust is divided, with ridges where plates are separating and new rock is being added and trenches where one plate is being subducted beneath its neighbor

and Eurasian Plates. Those plates are still moving, and the Himalayas are still growing taller. Elsewhere, one of the converging plates sinks beneath the other. Some plates are diverging—moving apart—and hot rock from below the crust is rising to the surface to fill the gap with a ridge of submarine mountains. That is what is happening in the Atlantic. Other mountains are really volcanoes that develop above *hot spots*—places where hot rock is rising and pushing against the base of the crust. Because the plates are moving, hot spots sometimes produce strings of mountains as the crustal rock passes over them. The Hawaiian Islands formed in this way. There are also plates that move past one another in opposite directions, along boundaries known as *transform faults*. The map shows the principal plates and their boundaries.

When the Sahara was green

Climates continue to change. After the last ice age ended, the average temperature over much of the world was about 2–5°F (1–3°C) warmer than it is now. There are caves in the central Sahara containing drawings and paintings that were made by people who lived up to 8,000 years ago. What is interesting about these pictures is the way of life they depict. One shows a hippopotamus being hunted by men in canoes. Another shows people driving a herd of cattle. Clearly, what is now the biggest desert in the world was then a much more pleasant place to be, at least in some places, and there is other evidence to corroborate this. Fish bones and old shorelines show that Lake Chad was once a big inland sea. Until about 5,000 years ago, most of the Sahara received enough rain to support grassland vegetation. Rivers ran across it, and they seldom ran dry.

During the whole of this long period of warm, moist weather, average temperatures over Europe and probably over most of the world were about 4°F (2°C) higher than they are now. Already, though, the climate was becoming drier. Some historians believe the rise of civilizations in Egypt and in the valleys of the Rivers Euphrates and Tigris was stimulated by the need to organize food production more efficiently as the rains became lighter and less reliable and large areas of land gradually turned into desert. It was not only the Middle East that was affected. A similar drying of the climate occurred in the Indus valley in northern India and in China.

Since then, the climate has been more variable, but the final years of the warm period coincided with great advances in civilizations throughout the world. Forests and grasslands extended much farther north than they do now, and people lived in regions that are now barely habitable.

The variability of more recent climates involves fluctuations measured in centuries and marked by temperature changes of only a few degrees. This seems small, but it means markedly cooler or warmer summers and longer or shorter winters. Changes of this scale can have a big effect on the way people live. Pictures of the inhabitants of Mycenae, living around 1500 B.C.E., show them naked or very lightly dressed. Some centuries later, the early Greeks wore warm clothing, and there are reports of the River Tiber freezing at Rome around 300 B.C.E. and of snow and ice lasting for some time. Yet, by the first century C.E. the Italian climate was warm, and snow was a very rare sight in Rome. Britain was also enjoying warm weather. When the Romans occupied Britain, they introduced the growing of wine, and by about 300 C.E. British vineyards may have produced sufficiently to satisfy domestic demands, for about then records of wine imports cease.

Vikings in Greenland

After about 400 C.E., the climate changed for the worse, becoming cooler and stormier. In the winter of 859–60, the sea froze along the coast near Venice, and the ice was thick enough to bear the weight of loaded wagons. In 1010–11 even the Nile froze.

Farther north, however, the warm conditions continued for much longer. It was around 980 that Norse settlers led by Erik the Red founded colonies in Greenland. Eventually there were about 3,000 people living there on nearly 300 farms. That does not necessarily mean the weather was especially warm, but another story does. A cousin of Erik's called Thorkel Farserk needed a sheep for the dinner he planned for Erik. The sheep was on an island more than two miles (3.2 km) away, and no boat was available, so Thorkel, not to be denied his party by such a trifling inconvenience, swam out to the island and carried the sheep back. If the story is true, Thorkel would have died if the sea temperature had been lower than 50°F (10°C). Today the sea in those parts is never warmer than 43°F (6°C).

We cannot be certain about Thorkel's swim, but we do know that cereals were being grown in Norway up to about the year 1000, although within a century cooler weather was reducing the farmed area. Warm conditions lasted until about 1300 farther south, however, and the English were producing high-quality wine, with summer temperatures up to 2°F (1°C) higher than those of today. It was warmer still in central Europe.

In North America, the period from about 700 to 1200 was relatively warm and moist. Forests were replacing grasslands, and people were farming along the river valleys into the Great Plains. By about 1150, almost every habitable area was occupied. Some of the inhabitants lived in towns with stone buildings several stories high, and it was in this period that the cliff homes of Mesa Verde were built. People made roads, signaling stations, and channels to carry water to their homes and fields. That was the peak, however, and as the climate became drier, people crowded together along riverbanks. In time, the farms and towns were abandoned. Few remained after 1300.

The Little Ice Age

All over the Northern Hemisphere, climates were cooling. It was a gradual change that began around 1300 and continued until the weather reached its coldest at the end of the 17th century. Between 1690 and 1699, average temperatures in England were 2.7°F (1.5°C) cooler than they are now. This was the Little Ice Age. Alpine glaciers advanced, and European settlers, just starting to arrive in North America, encountered severe weather with long, hard winters. There was ice around the edges of Lake Superior in June 1608, and land in the north that is now free of snow in summer remained covered by snow and ice throughout the year.

We are still living with some of the consequences of the Little Ice Age. It brought such harsh conditions in Scotland that famines and food shortages were common, triggering the start of an emigration of Scots people to many parts of the world, many young men finding work as professional soldiers. It was said that in 1700 there was hardly an army in Europe that did not have some Scottish officers. Then, in 1612, the Scottish king, James VI, who had become James I of England following the union of the two crowns, giving him powers in Ireland, evicted Irish farmers from the more fertile and sheltered lands of Ulster and "planted" Scottish farmers in their place. This helped relieve the hardship in Scotland and at the same time increased his control of the Irish. By the end of the 17th century, the Scottish population of Northern Ireland had reached 100,000 and was still rising rapidly.

The Little Ice Age eased slowly, and there were warm years as well as cold ones, but it did not really end until the latter part of the 19th century. That is when average temperatures began to rise once more, and it is possible that the climatic warming scientists believe has occurred since then is part of this recovery.

The greenhouse effect

Most climatologists now believe that the present climatic change is being accelerated by our release of certain gases into the atmosphere. This, they suggest, will lead to significant global warming due to an enhanced green-house effect.

Enhanced greenhouse warming occurs because although all atmospheric gases are transparent to incoming shortwave solar radiation, some partially absorb the long-wave heat radiated from the land and sea surface after it has been warmed by the Sun. The heat these *greenhouse gases* absorb raises the temperature of the air. Water vapor is by far the most important greenhouse gas, but the greenhouse gases our activities release are carbon dioxide and nitrous oxide, released by burning carbon-based fuels, and methane, released by bacteria in the digestive systems of cattle and in the mud of rice paddies. Chlorofluorocarbon (CFC) compounds, formerly used in refrigerators, freezers, air conditioners, and the making of foam plastics, also absorb long-wave radiation, but these compounds are being phased out, and so their importance is decreasing. If the scientists are right and we continue to release these gases, by the year 2100 the average temperature may rise by about 2.5–10°F (1.4–5.8°C) above its present value.

Warming by this amount would give us climates as warm as those of 8,000 years ago. There have been warm periods since then, but none so warm as is now being predicted, and no warming has ever happened so fast. It is still too soon to know whether the prediction is accurate, and revised calculations suggest that the world will grow warmer by no more than 1.8–2.9°F (1–1.6°C) by the end of the 21st century. Warming by this amount would have little effect. Nevertheless, we would be foolish to ignore the warning. It may turn out to be untrue, but by no means is it impossible.

Today may have been fine and warm. Yesterday may have been cool and wet. Weather changes from day to day and season to season, but it also changes from decade to decade and over the centuries. In the past, people have lived with weather that was markedly different from the weather we experience now. The story of our climate is fascinating, and paleoclimatologists, the scientists who use evidence they find in pollen grains, tree rings, and traces of chemicals stored deep below the ice sheets to reconstruct what past climates were like, are gradually unraveling it.

Climate has a history, and like all histories it is continuing. Little by little we are learning to read some of it, but its story has not yet come to an end.

HISTORY OF THE SCIENCE OF WEATHER

People have always been interested in the weather. This is not surprising. Crops grow or wither according to the sunshine and rain they receive, and the weather determines the amount and condition of the pastures on which farmers graze their animals. Even today, in many parts of the world bad weather can mean a failed harvest and famine.

Violent weather has always brought more immediate disaster. Prolonged heavy rain saturates the ground and causes floods in which thousands sometimes die. Countless sailors have perished in storms at sea. Severe hailstorms have flattened crops, hurricanes and tornadoes have destroyed everything in their paths, and blizzards have not only buried and frozen people, they did the same to the livestock on which the survivors would depend for food. One October night in 1995, a snowslide, triggered by days of fierce storms, swept down a hillside and engulfed 19 homes in the village of Flateyri, Iceland, killing 20 people. On December 25, 1974, a cyclone destroyed 90 percent of the buildings in Darwin, Australia. Such catastrophes have occurred throughout history, and until very recently, they have unleashed their violence without warning.

It is small wonder that in ancient times most people believed the weather was controlled by gods who used it to reward or punish humans. Little provocation was needed to make bad-tempered gods start hurling thunderbolts in all directions, yet in better moods those same gods could send rain to make crops grow and sunshine to ripen them. In the Old Testament, God "commandeth, and raiseth the stormy wind" and "maketh the storm a calm" (Psalm 107).

Despite the capriciousness of the gods, people noticed that particular kinds of weather were often associated with winds from certain directions. In the first century B.C.E., a Greek astronomer called Andronicus of Cyrrhus designed what may have been the world's first weather forecasting device. It was built in Athens, and much of the structure is still standing. It is called the "Tower of the Winds," or *horologion*. The tower has eight sides. At the top of each side, there is the engraved figure of the god associated with the wind from that direction. Boreas, the north wind, is a man wearing a cloak and blowing through a twisted seashell. Kaikas, the northeast wind, is a man carrying a shield from which he is pouring small, round objects that perhaps are hailstones. Apeliotes, a young man holding a cloak filled with grain and fruit, is the east wind. Euros, the southeast wind, is an old man wrapped in a cloak to keep him warm. Notos, the south wind, is a man producing a shower of water by emptying an urn. Lips is a boy pushing a ship and depicts the southwest wind. Zephyros, the west wind, is a young man carrying flowers. Skiron, the northwest wind, is a man with a beard carrying a pot filled with charcoal and hot ashes. A

The Tower of the Winds, probably the world's first weather station and forecasting center

sundial was also attached to each side of the tower. At the top of the tower was the figure of Triton, with the upper body of a man and the lower body of a fish. Triton was free to turn in any direction, and he carried a rod—a wind vane. As the figure turned in the wind, the rod indicated the direction from which the wind was blowing, and Athenians could know what weather to expect. They knew that Boreas blew strongly, Zephyros gently, and Notos had wet breath and brought rain. While they were checking the forecast, passersby could also read the time from whichever sundial was exposed to the Sun. The drawing shows the tower without Triton.

The gods depicted on the Tower of the Winds were meant only as reminders to people familiar with their names and attributes. As early as the fifth century B.C.E., the idea was developing among educated Greeks that the weather is produced by natural forces and not by supernatural beings. The tower reflected this: It is the winds that bring the weather, not the gods.

This outlook was derived principally from Aristotle (384–322 B.C.E.), who taught that if we seek to understand natural phenomena we should observe them directly and intently and then draw conclusions from our observations. This was a radical departure from the prevailing custom of trusting in traditional descriptions and explanations. Aristotle wrote on many topics, and his *Meteorologica*, written in about 340 B.C.E., is the earliest known book on the scientific study of weather. It also gives us the word *meteorology* (literally, "discourse on lofty matters"). In *Meteorologica*, he drew on earlier Egyptian and Babylonian ideas and theories. Aristotle believed that the weather is confined to the region between the surface of the Earth and the Moon. He suggested that some of the water vapor that rises into the sky during the day remains fairly low and sinks again at night to form dew or, if it freezes, hoarfrost. He noted that hailstorms are most common in spring and autumn, and he devised theories to account for most meteorological phenomena.

Today, a meteorologist is a scientist who studies weather, the conditions we experience day by day. Climate is the kind of weather that occurs over a very large area, such as a continent or even the entire world, over a long period. Scientists who study climate are called climatologists. Some climatologists called paleoclimatologists specialize in the reconstruction of climates in prehistoric times.

Weather lore

Although Aristotle was a keen observer, neither he nor his followers had the instruments with which to make accurate measurements, and they performed no experiments. They simply tried to find natural explanations for what they saw. Other writers described particular weather conditions, especially winds, and their effects. The Roman writer Pliny (ca. 23–79 C.E), for example, wrote that the coldest winds are from the north, southerly and southwesterly winds are damp, and northwesterly and southeasterly winds are usually dry. He was describing the winds that affect Italy, of course, just as the Tower of the Winds referred to the winds and weather Athenians experienced.

This is "weather lore." It allows people to predict the weather by noting present conditions and recalling what has usually followed them in the past. We still use it when we predict, often correctly, that a red sky at sunset heralds a fine day tomorrow and that bad weather follows a red sky at dawn. Weather lore extended much further, however, into predictions based on observations of plants and animals. Some are reliable, because many plants and insects are sensitive to changes in temperature and humidity, but others are not. It is hard to see why a rooster crowing at sunset should herald rain by dawn, but this used to be believed in parts of England.

Until suitable instruments were invented, this was as much as meteorologists could achieve. A vast amount of observations were accumulated and sometimes mixed with superstition and astrological interpretations, but from the time of Aristotle the scientific study of the weather made no significant advance until the 17th century.

Invention of instruments

In 1643, Evangelista Torricelli (1608–47), an assistant to Galileo, tried to discover why it is impossible to pump water from a well more than 33 feet (10 m) deep. He thought that the air might have weight and that the pressure it exerted forced water to rise, but that the weight of the air was sufficient to raise water only to this height. To test this, he sealed a glass tube at one end, filled it with mercury, and then inverted it with the open end below the surface in a dish of mercury. He found the mercury fell to a height of about 30 inches (76 cm), proving his supposition had been correct.

Later, Torricelli noticed that the height of the mercury column varied when the weather changed, and he interpreted this to mean that the weight of the air, and therefore the pressure it exerted, was not constant. He had invented the mercury barometer, and it was not long before changes in the height of the mercury were linked to changing weather.

Some years later, Robert Hooke (1635–1709), the English physicist and instrument maker, equipped barometers with a scale reading "change," "rain," "much rain," "stormy," "fair," "set fair," and "very dry." This made it simpler for people to understand barometer readings, and Hooke's scale, or one derived from it, is used to this day on many household barometers.

In 1687 the French physicist Guillaume Amontons (1663–1705) invented the hygrometer, which measures the relative humidity of the air. The Swiss physicist Horace de Saussure (1740–99) invented the hair hygrometer in 1783. This is the type of hygrometer most widely used today.

The air thermoscope, invented by Galileo, was the first attempt to make a thermometer.

There was still no way to measure temperature. Galileo (1564–1642) invented a thermometer based on the expansion of air. Galileo's instrument, shown in the illustration, comprised a vertical tube with a bulb at one end and open at the other. The open end was immersed below the surface of a colored liquid. As the air in the bulb at the top expanded and contracted with changes in temperature, the colored liquid moved up and down in the tube. Unfortunately, Galileo was unaware that the volume of a mass of air varies according to atmospheric pressure. Consequently, his thermometer—called the "air thermscope"—was very inaccurate.

Several other scientists made more accurate thermometers in the years that followed. Their efforts culminated with the first mercury thermometer, invented in 1714 by Daniel Gabriel (or Gabriel Daniel) Fahrenheit (1686–1736), who also devised the temperature scale that bears his name. The most widely used alternative temperature scale also bears the name of the man who devised it, the Swedish astronomer and physicist Anders Celsius (1701–44). In the first version of his scale, water freezes at 100° and boils at 0°. The scale was reversed later.

Together with the rain gauge, which had been known since ancient times, the barometer, hygrometer, and thermometer allowed meteorologists to make accurate atmospheric measurements. The next major advance occurred on October 15, 1783. On that day François Pilâtre de Rozier (1757–85) made the first ascent in a tethered hot-air balloon, paving the way for the first free flight, by Pilâtre de Rozier and the Marquis d'Arlandes, on November 21. The two aviators rose from the gardens of the Château la Muette, near Paris, France, and flew over the city for a distance of 5.6 miles (9 km). The success of balloon flight gave scientists access to the upper air, allowing them to study its composition and physical characteristics for the first time.

Scientific understanding of atmospheric processes increased steadily, but it was still very difficult to study conditions that occurred simultaneously at places hundreds of miles apart. The reason is obvious. In those days no message could travel faster than the speed of a galloping horse. By the time observations taken many miles apart had been collected at a central point it would be several days after the recorded events. Forecasting was impossible.

The telegraph and the first weather forecasts

Efficient collection of records became possible in 1844. That was the year Samuel Morse (1791–1872) persuaded the U.S. Congress to finance the construction of a telegraph line between Baltimore and Washington. Morse invented the telegraph and the binary code—Morse code—it used, and it was highly successful. Within 20 years France, followed by the United States, Britain, and other countries, had established weather stations that reported their measurements and observations by telegraph to centers for analysis and forecasting. Modern meteorology may be said to have begun around the middle of the 19th century.

Although the weather experienced at a particular place may seem to be very local, the weather system producing it often extends halfway across a continent or ocean and from the surface all the way to the tropopause, at a height of 5–10 miles (8–16 km). Meteorologists, who study weather systems and their movement and use the information they gather to forecast the weather over the coming few days, now rely on a worldwide network of stations that record and forward measurements every few hours.

Surface weather stations form a network covering the world, although not very evenly. There are enough stations in North America and Europe to provide a reliable picture of conditions everywhere, but they are spread very thinly in parts of Asia, Africa, and South America, and even more thinly over the oceans.

Weather stations measure wind strength and direction, temperature, humidity, air pressure, cloud type and amount, and visibility. Some take measurements each hour, just before the hour; others manage only to take measurements every six hours, and all weather stations, no matter where they are in the world, report their measurements in Universal Time. Universal Time (UT) is the same as the time at Greenwich, England, so all weather stations report at the same hours. This makes it easier to build up a picture of the situation over the whole world at a particular time, even though it means station (UT) time may be quite different from local time.

Weather balloons

Some stations measure conditions only at ground level, but others also sample the upper atmosphere, using balloons called *radiosondes*. *Sonde* is the French word for a soundingline, used to measure the depth of water beneath a ship. The weather balloons are called radiosondes because they take soundings (measurements) and transmit them by radio to receiving stations. Radiosondes measure atmospheric conditions above ground level to a height of about 80,000 feet (24.4 km), in the middle of the stratosphere. Balloons were first used for this purpose in 1927.

To make sure that measurements from around the world can be combined to produce a comprehensive picture of atmospheric conditions at a particular time, every participating weather station, no matter where it is, releases one radiosonde at midnight and a second at noon Universal Time every day. The U.S. National Meteorological Center, in Washington D.C., receives about 2,500 sets of radiosonde data every day.

The balloon itself is spherical, about five feet (1.5 m) in diameter, and filled with hydrogen. Beneath it is a cable nearly 100 feet (30 meters) long with a package of instruments attached to its lower end. The cable must be this long to ensure that air movements around the balloon do not interfere with instrument readings. The standard instrument package comprises a very sensitive thermometer, a hygrometer to measure humidity, and a barometer to measure air pressure. There are also timers, switches to turn the instruments on and off at predetermined times, a radio transmitter, batteries to supply power, and a parachute to return the instruments safely to the ground.

After it is released, the radiosonde climbs steadily, at about 15 feet (4.5 m) per second. As it rises, its hydrogen expands, and when it reaches a height of about 80,000 feet (24.4 km), the balloon bursts and its instruments parachute to the ground, from where they are recovered and returned to the weather station from which they were launched. During its flight, the radiosonde broadcasts its measurements to the ground station.

In addition to its instruments, the radiosonde carries a radar reflector immediately below the balloon. This strongly reflects radar pulses and allows the movement of the radiosonde to be tracked from the ground. Before radar was invented, balloons were tracked visually, but, of course, they disappeared from view as soon as they entered cloud.

As it ascends, the radiosonde moves horizontally with the wind, which usually changes direction and speed in different layers of air. Balloons that are tracked by the signals received from their radar reflectors to study winds at very great heights are sometimes called "rawinsondes" (for radar wind-sounding). Such tracking provides accurate information on the wind speed and direction in each atmospheric level through which the device passes. In years to come rawinsondes will probably broadcast their precise locations using the Global Positioning System.

Weather satellites

Since the first weather satellite (*TIROS-1*) was launched in 1960, satellites have played an increasingly important part in tracking weather systems. They transmit instrument measurements to ground stations, as well as photographs taken in one or more visible-light wavelengths or in the infrared.

Weather satellites are positioned in two types of orbit: geostationary and polar. Those in geostationary orbit, also known as geosynchronous orbit and Clarke orbit (because the writer Sir Arthur C. Clarke first suggested the orbit), remain in a fixed position relative to the Earth's surface.

A satellite remains in orbit because its forward speed balances the rate at which it is drawn downward by gravity. If it moved more slowly, the satellite would fall, and if it moved faster, it would leave its orbit, either entering a higher orbit or leaving Earth altogether. The satellite is in free fall, but it does not descend because of its forward motion. If the satellite orbits above the equator at a height of approximately 22,370 miles (36,000 km), equal to about 5.6 times the radius of the Earth, traveling in the same direction as the Earth's rotation, it takes precisely 24 hours, as measured by the position of the stars, to complete one orbit. The Earth takes the same length of time to complete one rotation. Consequently, the satellite remains above the same point on the Earth's surface. At this height the instruments on the satellite have a field of view spanning almost an entire hemisphere, and it takes about 20 minutes for them to scan the whole of it. The diagram shows the geostationary orbit.

Although a satellite in geostationary orbit has such a wide view that you might think one or two would be sufficient, in fact there are many satellites monitoring the atmosphere in this orbit. The *Applications Technology Satellite-1* (*ATS-1*) was the first to be launched, in December 1966. It was a U.S. satellite. The ATS series was replaced in 1974 by the first in the Synchronous Meteorological Satellite (SMS) series, and the first Geostationary

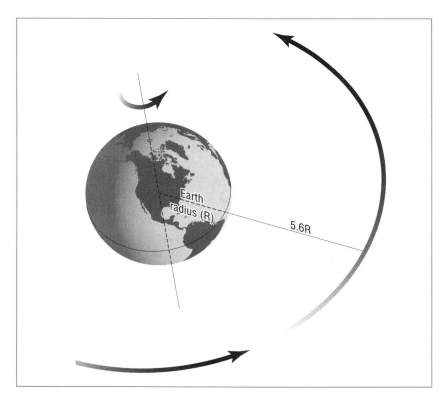

Geostationary orbit.
The satellite remains
over the same place
on the equator.

Operational Environmental Satellite *(GOES-1)* was launched on October 16, 1975.

A total of 12 GOES satellites have been launched (although one launch failed). Two are operational at any time. One, orbiting at 75° W, observes eastern North America, the western Atlantic Ocean, and western South America. The other, at 135° W, observes western North America, the eastern North Pacific Ocean as far as Hawaii, and the eastern South Pacific. Both satellites transmit data at half-hour intervals.

The European Space Agency is responsible for the Meteosat and Meteosat Second Generation satellites. The Japanese operate a series of five Geostationary Meteorological Satellites (GMS) and two Multifunctional Transport Satellites (MTSat). The Indian government operates the series of 11 Indian National Satellites (INSat). Russia operates the Geostationary Operational Meteorological Satellite (GOMS) series, which has been renamed Elektro. China has two Feng Yun (FY) satellites.

Satellites images show the distribution of clouds, but they reveal little about what is happening below the cloud tops. This should change as a result of CloudSat, a project forming part of the NASA Earth System Pathfinder Mission. The CloudSat spacecraft is due to be launched in 2004 on a Delta rocket from Vandenberg Air Force Base, in California, and it will spend two years measuring the heights and thicknesses of clouds, as well as the amount of water and ice they contain and the way they develop. The spacecraft, carrying very advanced equipment including radar especially designed to study clouds, will fly as part of a formation of other satellites. These will include the Aqua and Aura satellites operated by NASA, the French Space Agency's PARASOL satellite, and the CALIPSO satellite, operated jointly by NASA and the French Space Agency.

Satellites in polar orbits travel around the Earth about every 102 minutes, passing close to the North and South Poles. The illustration shows a typical polar orbit. Polar orbiting satellites circle at a height of about 530 miles (850 km)—approximately one-seventh the radius of the Earth. Some travel in Sun-synchronous orbits that are fixed in relation to the position of the Sun. Sun-synchronous orbits cross the meridians (lines of longitude) at an angle, so successive passes carry the satellite over every point on the Earth's surface.

The U.S. TIROS-1—the Television and InfraRed Observation Satellite—was the first weather satellite to enter polar orbit. A total of 10 TIROS satellites completed the series, and in 1966 the first of nine Environmental Science Services Administration (ESSA) satellites was launched, using a TIROS operating system. The U.S. also operated the Nimbus satellites, launched between 1964 and 1978. Currently the U.S. uses the National Oceanic and Atmospheric Administration (NOAA) Advanced TIROS-N and National Polar-Orbiting Environmental Satellite System (NPOESS) series of satellites. Russian polar-orbiting weather satellites all belong to the Meteor series, whose first successful launch was in 1969. There are also three Chinese Feng Yun satellites.

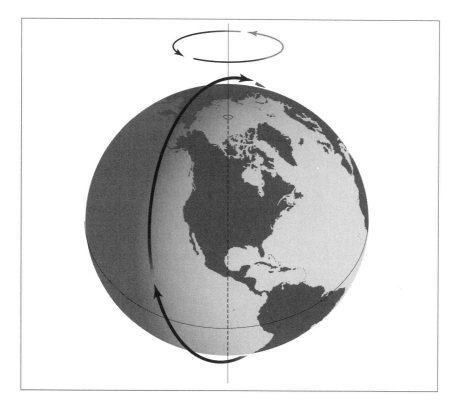

Polar orbit. The satellite's orbit carries it over or close to the North and South Poles.

Information from satellites and surface stations is sent to centers where it is fed into supercomputers for processing. It is from these supercomputers that the weather maps are compiled from which those appearing in newspapers and on television are derived. If you have the necessary equipment you can receive data and pictures from weather satellites.

The World Meteorological Organization is the United Nations agency responsible for coordinating meteorological and climatological studies throughout the world. In the United States, the National Oceanic and Atmospheric Administration, part of the U.S. Department of Commerce, operates the National Weather Service. In Britain, the Meteorological Office produces and issues weather forecasts and other relevant information.

The weather forecasts we receive daily are only part of the service these organizations provide. They also produce specialized forecasts for ships, airlines, fishermen, farmers, climbers, and others.

A CHRONICLE OF DESTRUCTION

5,000 Years of Dangerous Weather

ca. 3200 B.C.E.

- The Euphrates River flooded, inundating the city of Ur (in modern Iraq) and the surrounding countryside. In 1929, archaeologists discovered evidence of the flood in the form of a layer of flood deposits 8 feet (2.4 m) thick.

ca. 2200 B.C.E.

- Drought, with intermittent fierce storms, caused deserts to spread and harvests to fail over large parts of the Mediterranean region and the Near and Middle East. This caused the collapse of the empire of Akkad, the Old Kingdom of Egypt (during which the greatest of the pyramids were built), several Bronze Age cities in Palestine, civilizations in Crete and Greece, and the cities of Mohenjo-Daro and Harappa in the Indus valley. Dust deposits, falling water levels in lakes, and ocean sediments provide evidence of the drought.

245 C.E.

- Floods inundated thousands of acres in Lincolnshire, England.

ca. 300

- Drought in central Asia coincided with local wars that led nomads to invade northern China, causing the collapse of the Tsin dynasty. Refugees fleeing south stimulated cultural development in southern China, Korea, and Japan.

ca. 520

- The whole of Cantref y Gwaelod, a county bordering Cardigan Bay in west Wales, was inundated when a severe storm breached a dike.

678

- A drought began in England and lasted three years.

1099

- A storm surge along the coasts of England and the Netherlands caused 100,000 deaths.

1103

- Severe gales on August 10 caused severe damage to crops in England.

1140

- A tornado caused extensive damage in Wellesbourne, Warwickshire, England.

1246

- Severe drought began in the southwestern United States and lasted until 1305, being most intense from 1276 to 1299.

1276

- Drought began in England and lasted until 1278.

1281

- A typhoon from the China Sea destroyed most of a fleet of Korean ships carrying a Mongol army on its way to invade Japan. The wind, which saved the Japanese from foreign conquest, was believed to be a "divine wind" (*kamikaze*) sent by the gods.

1305

- Drought in England caused the hay crop to fail, and many farm animals died. Mortality was also high among humans, due partly to a smallpox epidemic.

1333

- The Arno River in Italy overflowed on November 4, causing 300 deaths.

1353

- Drought in England, lasting from March to the end of July, caused some famine. The drought continued into the following year.

1421

- An estimated 100,000 people drowned on April 17 when the sea broke through dikes at Dort, Netherlands.

1558

- A tornado struck the area around Nottingham, England, on July 7. All houses and churches were destroyed within a mile of the city, a child was lifted to 100 feet (30 m) and dropped, trees were thrown more than 200 feet (61 m), and five or six people were killed.

1592

- On December 16–17, the River Niger overflowed, flooding the city of Timbuktu, capital of the kings of Mali and Songhay, causing the population to flee. Unusually heavy rains in Guinea, near the source of the river, caused the floods.

1638

- On Sunday, October 21, a tornado accompanied by ball lightning struck the church at Widecombe-in-the-Moor, on Dartmoor, in southwest England, during the morning service. Different accounts recorded between five and 50 people killed.

1642

- The Yellow River in China flooded when dikes were deliberately broken during a peasant revolt led by Li Tzu-cheng in the hope of inundating and capturing the besieged city of Kaifeng. About 900,000 people were killed.

1654

- Severe drought, lasting several years in the Midi of France, led people at Périgueux to visit the shrine of St. Sabina and ask her to intervene and bring rain.

1666

- Drought in England reduced the flow of water in the Thames so seriously it threatened to ruin boatmen. By September, wooden structures in London were so dry that a small spark could ignite them (that is when the Great Fire of London occurred).

1674

- A blizzard on the border of England and Scotland began on March 8 and lasted 13 days.
- A severe gale on December 21 uprooted entire forests in Scotland.

1703

- Hurricane-force winds along the English Channel swept the southern coast of England on November 26 and 27, destroying 14,000 homes and killing 8,000 people. Eddystone Lighthouse (off Plymouth) was destroyed, and 12 warships sank. Damage in London was estimated at £2 million (about $3.6 million at today' exchange rates).

1726

- Floods in southern England in March raised the level of the Thames and inundated Salisbury Cathedral.

1730

- Drought began in England and lasted until June 1734.

1740

- A hurricane struck London on November 1.

1757

- On November 12, the River Liffey overflowed, causing extensive damage in Dublin.

1762

- A blizzard in England lasted 18 days in February, killing nearly 50 people.

1780

- A prolonged Caribbean storm, known simply as "the Great Hurricane," swept through the West Indies in October. The British fleet, anchored at Barbados, suffered severe damage, as did a Spanish fleet in the Gulf of Mexico, nearly 2,000 miles (3,200 km) distant.

1813–1814

- Smog in London lasted from December 17 to January 2.

1824

- Ice jamming the River Neva in Russia caused flooding in St. Petersburg and Kronshtadt. Ten thousand people drowned.

1829

- On August 3, 4, 27, and 29, there was severe flooding in Morayshire, Scotland, known as the "Moray Floods," when the rivers Spey and Findhorn overflowed. Many lives were lost.

1831

- A hurricane struck Barbados, killing 1,477 people and causing extensive damage to buildings and ships moored in the harbor.

1852

- Heavy rains brought widespread flooding in central England in September, turning the Severn valley into a continuous "sea."

1853

- Heavy rain brought widespread flooding in England in summer, destroying crops and killing many sheep.

1854

- During the Crimean War, a hurricane on November 14 devastated the British fleet, moored off Sevastopol because the Russians had mined the harbor. Winter supplies for the army were lost, resulting in severe deprivation among the troops.

1865

- In June, a tornado moved through Viroqua, Wisconsin, demolishing 80 buildings and causing more than 20 deaths.

1873

- Winter smog in London caused 1,150 deaths.

1875

- The River Thames rose on November 15, some said by more than 28 feet (8.5 m), causing widespread flooding in London.

1876

- The Bakarganj cyclone formed in the Bay of Bengal and moved north. Coinciding with the high monsoon river level of the Ganges, it caused flooding on islands in the Ganges Delta and on the mainland in which 100,000 people drowned in half an hour.

1879

- On Sunday, December 28, the Tay Bridge, carrying the rail line across the Firth of Forth, was destroyed by a storm just as the evening mail train was crossing on its way from Edinburgh to Dundee. One theory holds that it was struck by two tornadoes simultaneously. The train fell into the river, far below. The number of passengers is uncertain, but between 75 and 90 people lost their lives.

1881

- A typhoon in China on October 8 killed an estimated 300,000 people.

1887

- The Yellow River, China, burst its banks in September and October, causing extensive flooding in Honan, Shantung, and Hebei (Chihli) Provinces, beginning with a breach in the dikes near Chengchou. Flood water flowed through 1,500 or more towns and villages and covered an area of about 10,000 square miles (25,900 km²). Estimates of the number of fatalities ranged from 900,000 to 2.5 million.

1888

- From January 11 to 13, Montana, the Dakotas, and Minnesota experienced the most severe blizzard these states had ever known.
- Following a mild winter, a blizzard with winds gusting to 70 MPH (113 km/h) struck the eastern United States from Chesapeake Bay to Maine from March 11 to 14. Temperatures fell close to 0°F (–18°C), an average of 40 inches (1,016 mm) of snow fell over southeastern New York and southern New England, and more than 400 people died, 200 of them in New York City.
- On March 28, a storm and storm surge caused great damage in Wellington, New Zealand.

1891

- On February 7, severe blizzards, continuing for several days, caused many deaths in Nebraska, South Dakota, and other U.S. states.

• Between March 9 and 13, more than 60 people died in blizzards in southern England, and near-hurricane-force winds destroyed about 14 ships in the English Channel, with heavy loss of life.

1892

• On January 6, a cyclone caused many deaths in Georgia and neighboring states.

1894

• The River Thames overflowed on November 15 between Oxford and Windsor, England, causing extensive flooding and severe damage.

1900

• A category 4 hurricane struck Galveston, Texas, on September 8, killing 6,000 people, injuring more than 5,000, and destroying half the buildings in the town.

1903

• On June 14, a thunderstorm, lasting from 4 P.M. to 5 P.M., brought heavy rain to the Willow Creek basin in the Blue Mountains foothills, sending a flash flood through Heppner, Oregon (population 1,400), and killing 247 people.

1919

• A category 4 hurricane struck the Florida Keys, killing 900 people.

1922

• On January 15, a hurricane, with torrential rain, struck the area around Tamanrasset, Algeria. The rain continued into the following day, floods sweeping away huts and gardens beside a wadi (an ordinarily dry river channel) and destroying the wall of the Père de Foucauld fort. The collapsing wall buried 22 people, killing eight and injuring eight more.

1925

• A series of tornadoes, possibly seven in all, developed over Missouri in March and crossed Illinois and Indiana, traveling 437 miles (703 km), one moving more than 120 miles (193 km) in three hours. Altogether, 689 people were killed. On March 18, at Annapolis, Maryland, passenger trains were overturned, and 50 motor cars were lifted, carried over rooftops, and dropped in the fields beyond.

1927

- The Mississippi River flooded in April, following heavy rain that began in August 1926. High water levels in the main river caused backwater to raise the levels of several tributaries, which also flooded. Eventually, floodwaters covered more than 25,000 square miles (647,500 km²) in seven states. In places they were 18 feet (5.5 m) deep and 80 miles (129 km) across. The worst-affected states were Louisiana, Arkansas, and Mississippi. The floods finally receded in July. Officially, the death toll was given as 246, but it may have been much higher, and nearly 650,000 people lost their homes.

1928

- A category 4 hurricane struck Lake Okeechobee, Florida, causing floods that killed 1,836 people.

1930s

- Drought over most of North America was most severe in the Great Plains, especially in Kansas and the Dakotas. Between 1933 and 1935 soil, exposed by plowing and reduced to fine dust by the weather, began to blow away in a series of dust storms. The most severe storms, in 1934 and 1935, carried soil to the Atlantic coast, and erosion affected 80 percent of the Great Plains. After this the most severely drought-stricken area became known as the "Dust Bowl." About 150,000 people migrated from the region. Other droughts occurred in the Great Plains between 1825 and 1865 and in 1863–64, 1881, 1894–95, 1910, 1936, 1939–40, the 1950s, and the 1960s.

1930

- On December 1–5, a valley fog mixed with industrial pollutants blanketed the Meuse Valley, Belgium, killing 60 people and making several hundred ill.

1931

- In China, the Yellow River overflowed between July and November, flooding about 34,000 square miles (8.8 million km²). An estimated 1 million people died from drowning and in the famine and epidemics that followed, and 80 million were made homeless.
- The Yangtze River in China rose 97 feet (30 m) after heavy rain. More than 3.7 million people died, most from the subsequent famine, and the cost of damage was estimated at $1.4 billion.

1935

- A category 5 hurricane struck the Florida Keys on Labor Day, generating winds of 150–200 MPH (240–320 km/h) and killing 408 people.

1937

- The Mississippi River flooded in January, after heavy rains in the Ohio River basin caused it to flood and to discharge a huge amount into the Mississippi, raising the level 63 feet (19 m) at Cairo, Illinois. Water flowed back into the tributaries of both rivers. The floodwaters covered about 12,500 square miles (323,750 km²) and destroyed 13,000 homes, and 137 people died. Damage was estimated at about $418 million.

1938

- A category 3 hurricane struck New England, killing 600 people.
- The Yellow River in China flooded on June 9 when Kuomintang forces broke the dikes, hoping to cause a small, local flood that would check a Japanese advance on Chengchou. The river flowed out of control, submerging more than 9,000 square miles (233,100 km²). The flood caused 500,000 deaths, and 6 million people lost their homes.

1944

- A U.S. naval fleet in the Philippine Sea inadvertently sailed directly into Typhoon Cobra, with winds of up to 130 MPH (209 km/h) and waves up to 70 feet (21 m) high. Three destroyers sank, 150 carrier-borne aircraft were destroyed, and 790 sailors were killed.

1948

- In October, smog due to pollution at Donora, Pennsylvania, killed 17 people and made about 6,000 ill.

1950

- On November 24, air polluted by hydrogen sulfide at Poza Rica, Mexico, killed 22 people and made 320 ill.

1952

- Following heavy rain on already saturated land on Exmoor, in southwest England, amounting to 9 inches (229 mm) in 24 hours, on the night of August 15 the West and East Lyn Rivers overflowed, cut a new channel, and inundated the coastal village of Lynmouth, depositing about

224,000 tons (203,000 tonnes) of debris, including large boulders, on the shore. In all, 34 people died, 93 homes were destroyed, and repairing the damage cost an estimated $2 million.

- In the U.S. Midwest, the Nishnabotna River, a tributary of the Missouri, overflowed, inundating more than 66,000 acres (26,700 ha) of farmland.
- On December 5–9, smog covered London, killing at least 4,000 people.

1953

- On the night of January 31, a storm surge driven by winds of more than 100 MPH (160 km/h) moved southward through the North Sea causing floods in which nearly 2,000 people lost their lives along the coasts of England, the Netherlands, and Belgium. It was the worst natural disaster of the 20th century in Britain.
- A typhoon caused extensive damage in Nagoya, Japan. One million people were made homeless, and 100 died.

1954

- A typhoon struck the island of Hokkaido, Japan, killing 1,600 people.
- Hurricane Hazel, formed in the Lesser Antilles, struck Haiti on October 12, killing an estimated 1,000 people. It reached Myrtle Beach, South Carolina, on October 15, devastating coastal towns, producing a 17-foot (5-m) storm surge, and killing 19 people. It then crossed North Carolina, Virginia, Maryland, Pennsylvania, and New York State, killing 76 people. Winds of more than 100 MPH (160 km/h) were recorded at La Guardia and Newark Airports. Total damage in the U.S. amounted to $250 million. Hazel continued into Canada, killing 80 people, leaving 4,000 homeless, and causing $100 million of damage. On October 18 Hazel moved into the Atlantic, eventually producing heavy rain and strong winds in Scandinavia.
- China's Yangtze River overflowed. About 30,000 people died, most from the subsequent famine.
- Severe thunderstorms on August 17 filled dry creeks and ravines at Farahzad, Iran, sending a wall of water 90 feet (27 m) high crashing through a shrine where 3,000 people were worshiping. A mullah shouted a warning, but more than 1,000 people died.
- On December 8, a severe tornado struck west London, England, during the afternoon rush hour. It made a track 100–400 yards (90–366 m) wide extending 9 miles (14.5 km) through Chiswick, Gunnersbury, Acton, Golders Green, and Southgate, causing extensive damage.

1955

- During the day and night of August 18, almost 8 inches (203 mm) of rain fell on land drained by the Quinebaug River in Connecticut. The land was already saturated by previous intense rain, and on the morning of August 19 a series of dams broke, releasing flash floods on the town of Putnam (population 8,200), to the south. Roads, bridges, railroad embankments, and one-quarter of all the buildings in Putnam were destroyed. Water entered a warehouse containing 20 tons (18 tonnes) of magnesium, which ignited in a series of explosions. The waters receded a week later. Damage was estimated at $13 million, but thanks to rapid evacuation and efficient emergency services no lives were lost.

- Hurricanes brought rains to the eastern United States that caused flooding in southern New England, southeastern New York, eastern Pennsylvania, and New Jersey. Damage was estimated to cost $686 million, and 180 people died.
- The Macquarie, Castlereagh, Namoi, Hunter, and Gwydir Rivers, in New South Wales, Australia, flooded. Nearly 40,000 people were made homeless, and 50 died.

1956

- Extremely heavy rains in Australia caused rivers to flood, forming a continuous "sea" 40 miles (64 km) wide between the towns of Hay and Balranald.
- Hurricane Audrey, category 3, reached the U.S. Gulf Coast near the Louisiana-Texas border on June 27 with winds of 100 MPH (160 km/h) and a 12-foot (3.7-m) storm surge. Nearly 400 people died.

1957

- Hurricane Diane brought heavy rain to the United States in August, a few days after Hurricane Connie had saturated the ground. More than 190 people died, and damage cost $1.6 billion.

1959

- Typhoon Vera struck the island of Honshu, Japan, in September, destroying 40,000 homes. It killed nearly 4,500 people and left 1.5 million homeless.
- A hurricane killed 2,000 people on the west coast of Mexico.
- A cyclone from the Bay of Bengal left 100,000 people homeless on the islands of the Ganges Delta and the adjacent mainland.

1961

- Typhoon Muroto II caused a 13-foot (4-m) storm surge and flooding in Osaka, Japan, in September, killing 32 people.
- In September, the most powerful hurricane ever experienced in the region struck Galveston, Texas. There was extensive wind damage and flooding,

but the sea wall erected in the aftermath of the 1900 hurricane held back the worst of the storm surge waves. Fewer than 50 people died.

1962

- In December, smog in London killed 700 people.

1963

- Rocks and scree (loose rocks) on the slopes of Mount Toc, Italy, which were destabilized when a reservoir was filled behind an 860-foot (262-m) dam at the junction of the Vaiont and Piave Rivers, moved calamitously after heavy rains throughout the summer. At 10:41 P.M. on October 9, 314 million cubic yards (7,121.5 million m³) of rock fell into the reservoir. This caused a wave 330 feet (100 m) higher than the dam wall to release a wall of water into the valley below. The wave was 230 feet (70 m) high when it reached the town of Longarone, 1 mile (1.6 km) downstream. It killed almost all the inhabitants, then flooded the villages of Pirago, Villanova, and Rivalta. In all, 2,600 people died.

1964

- On March 27, earthquakes in Alaska caused tsunamis along the U.S. Pacific coast.

1966

- The Arno River in Italy overflowed on the night of November 3 after prolonged heavy rain, flooding Florence, in places to a depth of 20 feet (6 m). There was extensive damage to historic buildings and art treasures, 35 people died, and 5,000 were made homeless.

1968

- Chicago was brought to a standstill for several days when 24 inches (610 mm) of snow fell, driven by winds up to 50 MPH (80 km/h).

1969

- Hurricane Camille, category 5, struck Mississippi and Louisiana on August 17 and 18. It killed about 250 people on the coast and caused $1.42 billion of damage. As Camille weakened and headed south, then east over the Blue Ridge Mountains of Virginia, its winds gathered moist Atlantic air and funneled it through the narrow valleys of the Rockfish and Tye Rivers. There it encountered an advancing cold front, with thunderstorms. The resulting 18 inches (457 mm) of rain, starting at

9:30 P.M., flooded 471 square miles (12,199 km²) in Nelson County, Virginia. Flash floods destroyed or damaged 185 miles (298 km) of road and deposited mud and debris, in some places to a depth of 30 feet (9 m), and 125 people died by drowning or by being crushed by boulders. The floods subsided after 80 days.

- On October 24, severe flooding in Tunisia left more than 300 people dead and 150,000 homeless.

1970

- In November, one of the worst natural disasters of the 20th century occurred when a cyclone moved north through the Bay of Bengal and devastated Bangladesh, killing about 500,000 people.

1972

- Hurricane Agnes, category 1, struck Florida and New England in June, causing $2.1 billion of damage.
- Torrential rain in the Black Hills of South Dakota caused extensive flooding throughout the state on June 10. Many hundreds of people died.
- Seasonal rains failed in the Ethiopian highlands from June to September, and crops could not be planted in the worst-affected provinces. This led to the loss of 80 percent of the cattle in those provinces and many camels. In September 1973 it was estimated that 100,000 to 150,000 people had died.

1973

- On January 10, a tornado with 100 MPH (160 km/h) winds, lasting three minutes, destroyed buildings, killed 60 people, and injured more than 300 in San Justo, Argentina.
- Hurricane-force winds struck the coasts of Spain and Portugal on January 17. At least 19 people died.
- Severe storms brought snow, sleet, and freezing rain to the southeastern United States from February 8 to February 11. On February 10, Macon, Georgia, had 16.5 inches (419 mm) of snow and ended with a total of 23 inches (584 mm), and the storms brought an average of 16 inches (406 mm) to parts of Georgia and the Carolinas. Charleston, South Carolina, had 7.1 inches (180 mm). Communications were disrupted, traffic halted, and crops killed.
- The Caratinga River, Brazil, flooded on March 26. Thousands of people were made homeless, and at least 20 died. Damage was estimated at $16 million.
- Floods in late March and early April devastated towns and countryside in Tunisia. About 6,000 homes were destroyed, 10,000 cattle were killed, and about 90 people died.

- A storm lasting 24 hours on April 9 generated huge waves on Lake Michigan. These pounded 28 miles (45 km) of lakefront, causing damage estimated at $600,000. The storm killed 26 people.
- Typhoon-force winds and rain struck Faridpur District, Bangladesh, on April 12, killing up to 200 people, injuring about 15,000, and leaving 10,000 homeless.
- The Mississippi River and its tributaries flooded near St. Louis, Missouri, on April 29, submerging almost 1,000 square miles (25,900 km²) and causing at least 16 deaths.
- Tornadoes and rainstorms affected 11 states in the southeastern and south central United States on May 16–28. Alabama and Arkansas were declared disaster areas, and 48 people died.
- Intense rain caused flooding on July 8 in the towns of San Pedro Itzican, Ocotlán, and Mazcola, on the shores of Lake Chapala, Mexico, killing at least 30 people.
- Heavy rains on July 14–15 caused floods and resulting landslides in the Italian Riviera, killing 14 people.
- Although no estimate could be made of the number of deaths, after seven years of drought Senegal, Mauritania, Mali, Upper Volta, Niger, and Chad were threatened with one of the worst famines of the century, alleviated by food and other supplies from many parts of the world.
- Unusually heavy monsoon rains along the Himalayas caused rivers to overflow in August in Pakistan, Bangladesh, and the Indian states of Uttar Pradesh, Assam, and Bihar. Entire towns were inundated, thousands of square miles of farmland was submerged, food stores, roads, railroads, and bridges were destroyed, and damage came to hundreds of millions of dollars. Thousands of people were killed and millions made homeless.
- Prolonged rain in August caused floods in Iripuato, Mexico, that killed about 200 people and left 150,000 homeless. Damage was estimated at more than $100 million.
- Heavy rains in October caused flash floods in states from Nebraska to Texas, killing at least 35 people.
- Intense rain from October 19 to 21 caused flash floods in Granada, Almería, and Murcia, Spain. At least 500 people died, and damage was estimated at $400 million.
- Typhoons struck Vietnam on November 10 and 11, bringing rains that destroyed bridges and buildings and ruined crops. At least 60 people died, and 150,000 had to leave their homes.
- A typhoon and heavy monsoon rain caused flooding in many towns along the Cagayan Valley, Philippines, on November 18 to 24, killing 54 people.
- A cyclone struck the coast of Bangladesh on December 9, capsizing at least 200 fishing boats. Of the 1,000 people missing, many were feared drowned.

- Flooding caused by heavy rain in Qafseh, Tunisia, on December 13 killed 45 children.
- Blizzards and low temperatures from Maine to Georgia on December 17 caused at least 20 deaths.

1974

- Floods in eastern Australia in January caused 17 deaths and left about 1,000 people homeless.
- Rains and tidal surges caused flooding in Situbondo, in East Java, Indonesia, in January, killing 19 people and leaving about 2,000 homeless.
- Prolonged storms caused flooding in eastern Australia in late January. In Queensland at least 15 people died, and damage was estimated at more than $100 million.
- Heavy rain in northwestern Argentina caused flooding in February over half of Santiago del Estero Province and severe flooding in 10 other provinces. At least 100 people died, and more than 100,000 had to leave their homes.
- Intense rainfall caused rivers to overflow in Natal, South Africa, during the night of February 10, sweeping away homes. More than 50 people died.
- Torrential rains in late March, following months of drought, caused flooding in Tubarão, Brazil (population 70,000). The Tubarão River rose 36 feet (11 m) in a few hours and overflowed, virtually destroying the city. It was estimated that between 1,000 and 1,500 people died, and 60,000 were left homeless.
- In early April, heavy rain caused severe flooding at Grande Kabylie, Algeria. At least 50 people died, and 30 were injured.
- Thunderstorms and a total of 148 tornadoes developed on April 3, from Michigan to Alabama and Georgia, and in 16 hours, 10 minutes, traveled a combined distance of 2,598 miles (4,180 km), eventually entering Canada, killing 323 people, injuring 6,000, and causing more than $600 million of damage. The small town of Guin, Alabama, was almost totally destroyed, and in Xenia, Ohio, nearly 3,000 buildings were damaged or destroyed and 34 people killed.
- Heavy rains in early May caused flooding in northeastern Brazil. About 200 people died.
- A series of tornadoes crossed Oklahoma, Kansas, and Arkansas during the night of June 8. Altogether, 24 people were killed.
- Hurricane Dolores, accompanied by heavy rain, devastated an area housing poor people on the outskirts of Acapulco, Mexico, on June 17. At least 13 people died, 35 were injured, and 16 were unaccounted for.
- A typhoon with heavy rain struck southern Japan on July 6 and 7, killing 33 people, injuring about 50, and leaving 15 unaccounted for.
- Flooding in Bangladesh and northeastern India in August caused at least 900 deaths, and an additional 1,500 people died in Bangladesh from a

cholera epidemic that followed the floods. In Bangladesh most of the grain crop was destroyed.

- Monsoon rains caused extensive flooding in August in Luzon, Philippines. At least 94 people died, and more than 1 million needed disaster relief.
- A cyclone struck West Bengal, India, on August 15, killing at least 20 people and injuring about 100.
- Monsoon rains caused flooding along the Irrawaddy River, Burma, on August 20, inundating nearly 2,000 villages and washing away roads and railroads. At least 12 people died, and 500,000 were left homeless and stranded.
- Hurricane Fifi, category 3, struck Honduras on September 20 with 130-MPH (209-km/h) winds and heavy rain. An estimated 5,000 people were killed and tens of thousands left homeless.
- A small river flooded on November 19 in Silopi, Turkey, trapping members of a nomadic tribe camped nearby and killing 33 of them.
- A 12-foot (3.7-m) storm surge swept over low-lying islands in the southeastern Bay of Bengal on November 29 in the wake of a cyclone that passed the previous day. The wave killed 20 people.
- Cyclone Tracy destroyed 90 percent of the city of Darwin, Australia, on December 25, killing more than 50 people.

1975

- Prolonged drought in East Africa, starting in 1974 and lasting until June 1975, affected about 800,000 people in the Ogaden region of Ethiopia and the adjacent area of Somalia and caused the death of an estimated 40,000 people.
- Widespread flooding following heavy rain in southern Thailand in January killed 131 people.
- A blizzard with 50-MPH (80-km/h) winds and temperatures below 0°F (−18°C) swept through the central United States in early January, killing 50 people.
- A tornado destroyed a shopping mall in Mississippi on January 10, killing 12 people and injuring about 200.
- A tropical storm caused 30 deaths in January on land and off the coast of Mindanao, Philippines.
- The Nile flooded on February 20 and 21, inundating 1,000 acres (405 ha) in Egypt and destroying 21 villages. At least 15 people died.
- Monsoon rains caused flooding in northwestern India in July. About 400 square miles (10,360 km²) were inundated, 14,000 homes were destroyed or badly damaged, and 300 people died.
- Typhoon Phyllis struck the island of Shikoku, Japan, in August, killing 68 people. A week later it was followed by Typhoon Rita, which killed 26, injured 52, and left three unaccounted for.

- Floodwater inundated San'a, Yemen Arab Republic, in August, killing 80 people.
- Monsoon rains caused floods up to 10 feet (3 m) deep in the town of Bulandshahr, in Uttar Pradesh State, India, in September. At least 30 people drowned.
- Hurricane Eloise, category 4, with winds up to 140 MPH (225 km/h) and heavy rain, struck Puerto Rico on September 16, causing widespread damage and killing 34 people. It then moved to Hispaniola (killing 25 people), Haiti, and the Dominican Republic, then reached Florida, where 12 people died. It finally moved to the northeastern United States, where damage was so severe that a state of emergency was declared.
- Hurricane Olivia struck Mazatlán, Mexico, on October 24, killing 29 people.

1976

- Hurricane-force winds of more than 100 MPH (160 km/h; hurricane category 3) struck northern Europe on January 2 and 3, killing 26 people in England, 12 in Germany, and 17 in Denmark, Belgium, the Netherlands, Sweden, Austria, France, and Switzerland combined.
- A tornado struck at least 12 villages in Faridpur District, Bangladesh, on April 10, killing 19 people and injuring more than 200.
- Rains associated with Typhoon Olga caused widespread flooding in Luzon, Philippines, in May. At least 600,000 people were made homeless, 215 were killed, and damage was estimated at $150 million.
- Floods covering millions of acres followed prolonged heavy rain in Mexico in July, causing an estimated 120 deaths and leaving hundreds of thousands homeless.
- In July, an accident at a factory manufacturing the herbicide 2,4,5-T at Seveso, Italy, released a cloud of gas containing dioxin; all 700 inhabitants were evacuated, more than 600 animals were destroyed, and all the topsoil in a 5-mile (8-km) radius was removed and incinerated.
- The Ravi River, in northern Pakistan, overflowed on August 10, causing flooding that affected about 5,000 villages and killed more than 150 people.
- Earthquakes caused tsunamis in the Philippines on August 17 in which more than 6,000 people died.
- A tropical storm struck Hong Kong on August 25, killing at least 11 people, injuring 62, and leaving about 3,000 homeless.
- Floodwaters demolished an earth dam in Baluchistan Province, Pakistan, on September 5, causing floods that inundated more than 5,000 square miles (129,500 km²) and swept away entire villages.
- Typhoon Fran, category 3, struck southern Japan on September 8 to 13 with 100-MPH (160-km/h) winds and 60 inches (1,524 mm) of rain, killing 104 people, leaving 57 missing, and making an estimated 325,000 homeless.

- Hurricane Liza, category 4, with 130-MPH (209 km/h) winds and 5.5 inches (140 mm) of rain, struck La Paz, Mexico, and on October 1 destroyed a 30-foot (9-m) earth dam. A 5-foot (1.5-m) wall of water swept through a shantytown, killing at least 630 people and leaving tens of thousands homeless.
- Heavy rain caused flooding in Trapani, Sicily, on November 6, in which 10 people died.
- Heavy rain caused widespread flooding in eastern Java, Indonesia, in November, killing at least 136 people.
- Heavy rain caused widespread flooding in Aceh, Sumatra, Indonesia, on December 20, killing at least 25 people.

1977

- Heavy rain caused two rivers to overflow in southwestern Brazil in January. The floods caused 60 deaths and left about 3,500 people homeless.
- States of emergency were declared in New York, New Jersey, and Ohio on January 28 due to blizzards and freezing temperatures. Several other states declared disaster areas.
- A cyclone with heavy rain struck Madagascar in February, destroying more than 230 square miles (5,960 km²) of rice fields and 30,000 homes and killing 31 people.
- Blizzards throughout the northeastern states of the United States on February 1 caused more than 100 deaths.
- A blizzard in the central United States in March blocked 100 miles (160 km) of interstate highway in South Dakota and killed nine people in Colorado, four in Nebraska, and two in Kansas.
- A tornado struck Madaripur and Kishorganj, Bangladesh, on April 1, killing more than 600 people and injuring 1,500.
- Tornadoes and floods in the United States on April 4 affected West Virginia, Virginia, Alabama, Mississippi, Georgia, Tennessee, and Kentucky, killing 40 people and causing damage estimated to cost $275 million.
- A cyclone, category 3, with 100-MPH (160-km/h) winds struck northern Bangladesh on April 24, killing 13 people and injuring nearly 100.
- A tornado at Moundou, southeastern Chad, on May 20 killed 13 people and injured 100.
- Floods following heavy rain in Khorramabad, Iran, on May 23 killed 13 people.
- Floods in Iran on June 4, following heavy rain in the northwest of the country, killed at least 10 people.
- A cyclone struck Oman in June, destroying 98 percent of the buildings on the island of Masirah, killing two people and injuring more than 40. Three days later, heavy rain caused flooding in Dhofar Province, where more than 100 people were killed and about 15,000 farm animals were carried away by the floodwater.

- Severe flooding followed heavy rain in southwestern France in July, killing 26 people and causing widespread damage to crops, livestock, and property.
- Flooding and landslides caused by heavy rain in and around Seoul, South Korea, in July killed at least 200 people, injured more than 480, and left 80,000 homeless.
- Overnight rain caused flooding in Johnstown, Pennsylvania, on July 20. About 70 people died, 30 were missing, and damage was estimated at $200 million.
- Typhoon Thelma, category 4, with winds up to 120 MPH (193 km/h), struck Kao-hsiung, Taiwan, on July 25, killing 31 people and destroying nearly 20,000 homes.
- A typhoon struck Taipei, Taoyuan, and Nan-tou, Taiwan, on July 31, killing at least 38 people.
- Following 12 inches (305 mm) of rain, flash floods struck Kansas City, Missouri, on September 13. At least 26 people died, and damage was estimated at more than $100 million.
- Flooding followed 16 hours of continuous heavy rain in Taipei, Taiwan, in September, killing at least 14 people.
- Widespread flooding in northwestern Italy in October caused 15 deaths and caused damage estimated at $350 million in Genoa and parts of Piedmont, Liguria, and Lombardy.
- After 2.7 inches (69 mm) of rain fell in 15 hours on November 2 and 3, the Kifissos and Ilissos Rivers in Greece rose 6.5 feet (2 m) and caused flooding in Athens and Piraeus, killing 26 people.
- Prolonged heavy rain caused the collapse of a dam near Toccoa, Georgia, on November 6, releasing a 30-foot (9-m) wall of water that killed at least 39 people and injured 45.
- Flash floods and landslides in Palghat, Kerala, India, on November 8 killed at least 24 people and injured three.
- Five days of heavy rain caused floods and landslides in northern Italy on November 10. Genoa and Venice were inundated. At least 15 people died and thousands were left homeless.
- A cyclone in Tamil Nadu, India, killed more than 400 people on November 12.
- A typhoon struck the northern Philippines on November 14, killing at least 30 people and leaving nearly 50,000 homeless.
- A cyclone and storm surge struck Andhra Pradesh, India, on November 19, washing away 21 villages and severely damaging 44 more. An estimated 20,000 people died, and more than 2 million were made homeless.

1978

- Rainstorms, high tides, and 75-MPH (121-km/h) winds (hurricane category 1) caused extensive flooding and property damage along the east coast of the United Kingdom on January 12, killing 17 sailors when three ships sank and seven other people.

- Floods in southeastern Colombia caused 20 deaths on January 13.
- Floods in Rio de Janeiro, São Paulo, and Paraíba, in southeastern Brazil, killed 26 people and left thousands homeless on January 13 to 17.
- A blizzard on January 25 and 26 brought winds gusting to 100 MPH (160 km/h), about 31 inches (787 mm) of snow, and temperatures down to −50°F (−45°C) in Ohio, Michigan, Wisconsin, Indiana, Illinois, and Kentucky. More than 100 people died, and damage was estimated at millions of dollars.
- Severe flooding in East Java, Indonesia, on January 26 to 30 caused 41 deaths.
- Flooding on January 28 to 30 caused 26 deaths in Transvaal, South Africa.
- A blizzard with winds of 110 MPH (177 km/h) and 18-foot (5.5-m) tides brought 50 inches (1,270 mm) of snow to Rhode Island and eastern Massachusetts on February 5 to 7. At least 60 people died.
- Severe flooding caused by heavy rain released a wall of water 20 feet (6 m) high along a canyon in southern California on February 10. It destroyed the resort of Hidden Springs and caused the ports of Los Angeles and Long Beach to be closed. Zoo animals escaped when their cages were demolished, and 25 people were missing and feared dead.
- A storm caused flooding and mudslides in southern California and northern Mexico on March 5. Five people were killed in California and 20 in Mexico, and 20,000 people were left homeless.
- A tornado lasting about two minutes caused severe damage in northern Delhi, India, on March 17, killing 32 people and injuring 700.
- The Zambezi River flooded in Mozambique on March 27, killing at least 45 people and leaving more than 200,000 homeless.
- A tornado in Orissa State, India, on April 16 killed nearly 500 people and injured more than 1,000.
- A tornado in West Bengal, India, in April was believed to have killed 100 people.
- Floods in Sri Lanka on May 15 killed 10 people and left thousands homeless.
- Floods in West Atjeh, North Sumatra, Indonesia, on May 16 caused 21 deaths.
- In mid-June, a week of torrential rain caused floods in South Korea in which 17 people died, 10 were missing, and 2,000 were left homeless, and the damage was estimated at $400,000.
- Heavy monsoon rains caused widespread summer flooding in India. Nearly 900 people died, hundreds of thousands were made homeless, the fall rice crop was almost completely destroyed, and damage was estimated at $100 million.
- Floods along the border between Afghanistan and Pakistan on July 10 caused at least 120 deaths.
- On July 26, monsoon floods in six Indian states caused nearly 190 deaths.

- Floods in central Texas due to rainfall at nearly one inch (25 mm) per hour caused more than 25 deaths on August 1.
- The Hab River in Pakistan overflowed in August, causing floods that killed more than 100 people.
- Flooding and mudslides in the northern Philippines in August killed 45 people and left thousands homeless.
- Typhoon Rita, category 4, struck the Philippines on October 26. Nearly 200 people were killed, 60 were not accounted for, and about 10,000 homes were destroyed.
- Monsoon rains caused floods in Kerala and Tamil Nadu, southern India, in November in which at least 144 people died.
- A cyclone struck Sri Lanka and southern India on November 23, killing at least 1,500 people. It destroyed more than 500,000 buildings and flooded about 45 villages.

1979

- A blizzard on February 19 caused 13 deaths in New York and New Jersey.
- Heavy rain caused floods and landslides in Flores Island, Indonesia, in March, killing 97 people, injuring 150, and leaving 8,000 homeless.
- Cyclone Meli struck Fiji on March 27, killing at least 50 people and destroying about 1,000 homes.
- A tornado with winds up to 225 MPH (362 km/h) moved through the Red River Valley on the border between Texas and Oklahoma on April 10. As it passed through Wichita Falls, Texas, it killed 59 people and injured 800.
- A typhoon struck the Philippines on April 16 and 17, killing at least 12 people and causing damage estimated at $3.5 million.
- A cyclone struck Andhra Pradesh and Tamil Nadu, India, on May 12 and 13, killing more than 350 people.
- Floods following heavy rain at Balikpapan, Borneo, Indonesia, on June 13 caused 13 deaths.
- Floods up to 14 feet (4.25 m) deep at Montego Bay, Jamaica, in June, caused by heavy rain, killed at least 32 people and left 25 unaccounted for.
- A flash flood at Valdepeñas, Spain, on July 2 killed at least 22 people.
- A tsunami 6 feet (1.8 m) high, caused by the collapse of the volcano Gulung Werung, struck Lomblem Island, Indonesia, on July 18, killing 539 people.
- Heavy rain swelling the Machhu River, at Morvi, India, caused an earth dam to collapse on August 11, sending a wall of water 20 feet (6 m) high through the town and killing up to 5,000 people.
- Tornadoes forming in the midwestern and New England states of the United States moved eastward, crossing the Atlantic and reaching the Irish Sea in August, during the Fastnet Race between England and Ire-

land. Of 306 yachts entering the race, only 85 finished. Twenty-three vessels sank or were abandoned, and 18 people died.

- Typhoon Judy brought intense rain that caused flooding in southern South Korea on August 25 and 26, in which nearly 60 people died and about 20,000 were made homeless.
- Hurricane David, category 5, with winds up to 150 MPH (241 km/h), struck the Caribbean and the East Coast of the United States in late August and early September, affecting the Dominican Republic, Dominica, Puerto Rico, Haiti, Cuba, the Bahamas, Florida, Georgia, and New York. Altogether, more than 1,000 people were killed, and the damage was estimated at billions of dollars. It remained at category 5 for 36 hours.
- Hurricane Frederic struck 100 miles of the U.S. coast in Florida, Alabama, and Mississippi in early September. About 8 people were killed. The swift evacuation of nearly 500,000 people saved many lives.
- The Brahmaputra River overflowed on October 13, causing widespread flooding in Assam, India. At least 13 people drowned.
- Two tsunamis, up to 10 ft (3 m) high, caused by an undersea landslide, struck a 60-mile (96-km) stretch of the French Mediterranean coast on October 16. Eleven people were swept away and presumed dead in Nice and one in Antibes.
- A severe storm caused flash floods on October 17 near Groblersdal, South Africa. The Elands River overflowed, and a large dam broke, carrying away at least 20 people.
- Typhoon Tip, with winds up to 190 MPH (306 km/h), caused widespread damage throughout Japan on October 19. At least 36 people died. (On October 12 surface pressure in the eye of Tip was 870 mb; this is the lowest surface pressure ever recorded.)
- A blizzard with 70-MPH (113-km/h) winds and heavy falls of snow affected Colorado, Nebraska, and Wyoming on November 21, killing at least 10 people.
- The Playonero River overflowed on November 25, sending flood water and mud through the towns of El Playón and Lebrija, Colombia, killing 62 people.

1980

- Cyclone Hyacinthe struck the island of Réunion in the Indian Ocean in January, killing at least 20 people.
- Floods and huge mudslides followed prolonged heavy rain in California, Arizona, and Mexico in February, causing 36 deaths and damage estimated at $500 million.
- A blizzard on March 2 caused at least 36 deaths in North Carolina, South Carolina, Ohio, Missouri, Tennessee, Pennsylvania, Kentucky, Virginia, Maryland, and Florida.

- Heavy rain caused floods and landslides in several parts of Turkey on March 27 and 28, killing at least 75 people.
- Heavy rain caused floods, mudslides, and rock slides in central Peru in April, leaving at least 90 people missing and feared dead.
- Cyclone Wally struck Fiji in April, causing floods and landslides that killed at least 13 people and left thousands homeless.
- Tornadoes passed through Kalamazoo, Michigan, on May 13, killing five people and injuring at least 65.
- Floods in Gujarat State, India, in July in which 37 dams overflowed caused 11 deaths.
- Typhoon Joe struck North Vietnam on July 23, killing more than 130 people and making about 3 million homeless.
- Monsoon floods in India in July and August inundated 7,500 square miles (194,250 km²), killed at least 600 people, and caused damage estimated at more than $131 million.
- Hurricane Allen, category 5, with winds of 175 MPH (282 km/h) gusting to 195 MPH (314 km/h), struck Barbados, St. Lucia, Haiti, the Dominican Republic, Jamaica, Cuba, and the southeastern United States in August. More than 270 people died, most of them in Haiti.
- Two Chinese cities were flooded in August when the Dongting Hu (lake), fed by the Yangtze River, overflowed. Thousands of people died.
- Monsoon rains caused flooding and landslides in West Bengal, India, in August and September, killing nearly 1,500 people.
- Heavy rain caused a dam to burst above Arandas, Mexico, causing floods on September 1 to 3 in which at least 100 people were dead or missing.
- Typhoon Orchid struck South Korea on September 11, killing seven people and causing more than 100 fishermen to be lost at sea.
- Typhoon Ruth struck Vietnam on September 15 and 16, killing at least 164 people.
- Heavy rain caused flash floods in Orissa, India, in September. The floods burst a dam, flooding two towns to a depth of 10 feet (3 m). About 200 people drowned, and at least 300,000 were marooned.
- The Guaire River, near Caracas, Venezuela, overflowed in September, causing floods that brought the city to a standstill and killed at least 20 people.
- Floods in northwestern Bangladesh in September killed 655 people.
- A cyclone struck Maharashtra State, India, in September, killing at least 12 people and injuring 25.
- Widespread monsoon floods in Thailand in October killed 28 people.

1981

- The Buffels River in South Africa overflowed on January 24 and 25, sending a wall of water 6 feet (1.8 m) high through the town of Laingsburg and killing at least 200 people.

- Drought in northeastern Brazil ended in March and early April with 10 days of continuous rain that caused floods in which 30 people drowned and about 50,000 were left homeless.
- Floods in Colombia lasting a week in April killed 65 people and left 14,000 homeless.
- A tornado at Noakhali, Bangladesh, on April 12 killed about 70 people, injured 1,500, and destroyed 15,000 homes.
- A tornado passed through four villages in Orissa State, India, on April 17, killing more than 120 people, injuring hundreds, and destroying 2,000 homes.
- Prolonged heavy rain caused floods and mudslides in Venezuela in April in which at least 27 people died.
- Floods in Khorasan Province, Iran, on May 3 killed or injured 100 people.
- Floods and mudslides in Java, Indonesia, in May killed 127 people, left 170 unaccounted for, and injured 38.
- Shoal Creek, near Austin, Texas, overflowed because of flash floods on May 25, sending flood water through the city, killing 10 people, and leaving eight missing.
- Typhoon Kelly struck the central Philippines on July 1, causing floods and landslides and killing about 140 people.
- Monsoon rains caused China's Yangtze River and its tributaries to flood on July 12 to 14. About 1,300 people were killed or missing and more than 28,000 injured, and 1.5 million were left homeless. Damage was estimated at $1.1 billion.
- Flash floods in northern Nepal on July 13 killed nearly 100 people.
- Typhoon Maury struck northern Taiwan on July 19, causing floods and landslides and killing 26 people.
- Floods in Assam, Uttar Pradesh, and Rajasthan, India, on July 19 killed about 500 people and left 100,000 homeless.
- The Salamina River, Colombia, overflowed on August 17, flooding the town of Saravena and leaving 150 people dead or missing.
- Floods in Sichuan Province, China, killed 15 people in August.
- Typhoon Tad, category 1, with winds up to 80 MPH (129 km/h), struck central and northern Japan on August 23, killing 40 people and leaving 20,000 homeless.
- Typhoon Agnes struck South Korea on September 1, bringing 28 inches (711 mm) of rain in two days and leaving 120 people dead or missing.
- Floods in El Eulma, Algeria, on September 3 killed 43 people.
- Winds up to 80 MPH (129 km/h; hurricane category 1) struck the United Kingdom on September 21, killing at least 12 people.
- Typhoon Clara struck Fujian Province, China, on September 21, destroying 130 square miles (3,367 km²) of rice crops.
- Flash floods in Nepal on September 29 left about 500 people dead or missing.
- Floods and landslides in Sichuan Province, China, in October killed 240 people.

- Storms caused floods in northern Mexico on October 7, in which 65 people died.
- A blizzard in Michigan and Minnesota on November 19 and 20 caused at least 17 deaths.
- Typhoon Irma, category 5, with winds of 140 MPH (225 km/h), struck the Philippines on November 24, causing great destruction in the coastal towns of Garchitorena and Caramoan. More than 270 people died, and 250,000 were left homeless. Damage was estimated at $10 million.
- Monsoon rains caused flash floods in Thailand in December in which at least 37 people died.
- Floods and mudslides in Brazil on December 3 killed more than 40 people.
- A typhoon struck Bangladesh and India on December 11, killing at least 27 people.

1982

- Five cyclones—Benedict, Frida, Electra, Gabriel, and Justine—struck Madagascar between January and March. More than 100 people were killed and 117,000 left homeless.
- Floods on January 4 killed 90 people in Nariño Province, Colombia.
- Floods and landslides on January 5 caused 15 deaths in Rio de Janeiro, Brazil.
- Blizzards in western Europe from January 9 to 12 caused at least 23 deaths. Wales was completely cut off from England by snowdrifts 12 feet (3.7 m) deep.
- The Chuntayaco River, in western Peru, burst its banks along a 60-mile (96-km) stretch on January 23 and 24, carrying away 17 villages. At least 600 people died, and 2,000 were missing.
- Floods in Santa Cruz, Bolivia, in March caused widespread damage to crops. About 50 families were missing, presumed drowned.
- Typhoons Mamie and Nelson struck the Philippines in March, killing at least 90 people and leaving 17,000 homeless.
- Heavy rain caused floods and landslides in Cuzco Province, Peru, in April. About 200 people were believed killed.
- Tornadoes moved through Ohio, Texas, Arkansas, Mississippi, and Missouri on April 2 and 3, killing 31 people, 10 of them in the city of Paris, Texas, and 14 in Arkansas.
- A blizzard on April 6 killed 33 people in the northern United States.
- A cyclone, category 4, with 124-MPH (199-km/h) winds, struck Burma on May 4, killing 11 people and leaving 7,200 families homeless.
- Tornadoes moved through Kansas, Oklahoma, and Texas on May 11 and 12, killing at least seven people. Damage at Altus Air Force Base, in Oklahoma, was estimated at $200 million.
- Severe flooding in Guangdong Province, China, in May killed at least 430 people and destroyed about 46,000 homes.

- Severe flooding in May killed 75 people in Nicaragua and 125 in Honduras and caused $200 million of damage.
- Flooding in Hong Kong on May 29 killed at least 20 people.
- A tornado at Marion, Illinois, killed at least 10 people on May 29.
- Monsoon rains caused flooding in Sumatra, Indonesia, on June 3, killing at least 225 people and leaving about 3,000 homeless.
- Winds of up to 137 MPH (220 km/h; hurricane category 5) struck Orissa, India, on June 4, killing 200 people and leaving about 200,000 homeless.
- Flooding in Connecticut on June 5 and 6 killed at least 12 people.
- Winds up to 90 MPH (145 km/h; hurricane category 2) in Paraña and São Paulo, Brazil, on June 26 and 27 killed at least 43 people and injured 500.
- Floods in Fukien Province, China, in June killed 75 people.
- Monsoon rains caused floods and landslides in southern Japan in July that killed 245 people and left 117 unaccounted for.
- A typhoon struck the coast of South Korea on August 12 and 13, causing flash floods and landslides and leaving 38 people dead, 26 missing, 100 injured, and 6,000 homeless.
- Typhoon Cecil struck South Korea in August, killing at least 35 people, with 28 unaccounted for, and caused more than $30 million of damage.
- Monsoon flooding in Orissa, India, in September caused at least 1,000 deaths and left 5 million people marooned on high ground and roofs and dependent on supplies dropped by air. Eight million people were displaced and more than 2,000 cattle killed.
- Typhoon Judy, category 3, with winds of 110 MPH (177 km/h), struck Japan on September 11 and 12, killing 26 people, injuring 94, leaving eight missing, and causing extensive damage.
- Floods and mudslides in El Salvador on September 17 to 21 killed at least 700 people, injured 18,000, and left 55,000 homeless. In Guatemala the storms that caused the floods killed 615 people.
- Hurricane Paul, category 4, with winds of 120 MPH (193 km/h), struck Sinaloa, Mexico, on September 30, leaving 50,000 people homeless.
- A hurricane struck Nghe Tinh Province, Vietnam, in October, killing hundreds of people and leaving nearly 200,000 homeless.
- Drought in Indonesia, lasting four months, led to outbreaks of cholera and dengue fever in October, in which more than 150 people died.
- A category 4 typhoon, with winds of 120 MPH (193 km/h), struck the provinces of Isabela, Kalinga-Apayao, and Cagayan, Philippines, on October 14 and 15, killing 68 people and leaving tens of thousands homeless.
- A category 4 hurricane, with winds of 125 MPH (201 km/h), struck Gujarat, India, on November 8, killing at least 275 people and destroying 30,000 homes.

- Flooding in Arkansas, Illinois, and Missouri in December killed 20 people, left four missing, and caused at least $500 million of damage.
- Blizzards, storms, and tornadoes struck the western United States in December, killing 34 people.

1983

- Flooding in Ecuador in January caused 30 deaths and caused about $90 million of damage.
- The Arrucadas River in Brazil overflowed on January 3, flooding the city of Belo Horizonte and killing 40 people.
- A blizzard on February 11 and 12 delivered at least 2 feet (610 mm) of snow to every city in the northeastern United States and caused at least 11 deaths.
- On February 16, bush fires known as the Ash Wednesday fires blazed out of control in Australia. A total of about 180 fires burned approximately 1,384 square miles (3,585 km²). More than 2,000 homes were destroyed, 75 people died, and hundreds were injured.
- Blizzards near Alayh, Lebanon, from February 18 to 22 killed 47 people. Many froze while trapped in their cars.
- The Pirai River, in Santa Cruz, Bolivia, overflowed in March, leaving 96 people dead or missing.
- Flooding in Guangdong Province, China, in March killed at least 27 people.
- Floods and mudslides in Peru and Bolivia on March 20 and 21 killed at least 260 people and left hundreds missing.
- A cyclone struck West Bengal, India, in April, killing 76 people, injuring about 1,500, and leaving 6,000 homeless.
- A tornado in Fujian Province, China, on April 11 killed 54 people.
- A cyclone on April 12 caused damage in about 21 coastal villages near Calcutta, India, killing at least 50 people, injuring 1,500, and leaving 6,000 homeless.
- Floods and landslides in Piura and Tumbes, Peru, on April 14 killed 37 people.
- A tornado struck Khulna, Bangladesh, on April 26, killing 12 people and injuring 200.
- A flash flood near Chepén, Peru, on April 30 swept over a road bridge, knocking several vehicles into the Chaman River. At least 50 people drowned.
- Flooding occurred in May when major rivers in northern France and southern Germany overflowed. Altogether, 25 people died.
- Flooding in May in the basins of the Paraguay and Paraná Rivers in Argentina, Brazil, and Paraguay killed 23 people and caused damage estimated at $338 million.
- Tornadoes in central Vietnam in May killed more than 76 people.

- At least 59 tornadoes, with storms that produced flash floods, moved through Texas, Tennessee, Missouri, Georgia, Louisiana, Mississippi, and Kentucky from May 18 to 20. At least 24 people died, and 350 homes were destroyed in Houston, Texas.
- A tsunami caused by a Richter magnitude 7.7 earthquake struck northern Honshu, Japan, on May 26, killing at least 58 people.
- Widespread flooding and landslides in Ecuador in June killed at least 300 people.
- Floods and landslides in Taiwan on June 5 killed 24 people.
- Flooding in Gujarat, India, in June left at least 935 people dead or missing.
- The Yangtze River in China overflowed in late June and early July, causing extensive flooding that was believed to have caused hundreds of deaths.
- Floods and landslides in Masuda, Japan, on July 23 killed 82 people.
- Flooding in Banggai, Indonesia, in July killed 11 people and left 2,000 homeless.
- Flooding in Bangladesh in August killed 41 people.
- Hurricane Alicia, category 4, with winds of 115 MPH (185 km/h), struck southern Texas on August 18, causing extensive damage in Galveston and Houston. At least 17 people died, and damage was estimated at $1.6 billion.
- Flooding on August 26 in the Basque region on the border between France and Spain left 33 people dead and 13 missing.
- Monsoon rains in India in September killed more than 400 people.
- Flooding in Papua New Guinea in September killed 11 people and caused $11.9 million of damage.
- Typhoon Forest struck the Japanese islands of Honshu, Kyushu, and Shikoku on September 29, bringing up to 19 inches (483 mm) of rain and leaving 16 people dead, 22 missing, and 30,000 homes flooded.
- Flooding in Bangladesh in September killed 61 people, six of whom died from snakebites while climbing trees away from the water.
- Flooding in southern Arizona in late September and early October left a number of towns under several feet of water and caused 13 deaths.
- Flooding in Uttar Pradesh, India, on October 14 killed 42 people.
- A cyclone struck Bangladesh on October 15, destroying 1,000 homes in Chittagong and killing at least 25 people.
- Widespread flooding in Thailand in October caused 18 deaths and extensive damage in Bangkok.
- Hurricane Tico struck the coast of Mazatlán, Mexico, on October 20, killing 105 fishermen whose boats were lost at sea.
- A blizzard on November 28 in Wyoming, Colorado, South Dakota, Nebraska, Kansas, Minnesota, and Iowa killed at least 56 people.
- Monsoon rains in Malaysia in December caused at least 10 deaths from drowning and necessitated the evacuation of 15,000 people.

1984

- Gales and snowstorms crossed northern Europe from January 12 to 16, causing at least 22 deaths in the United Kingdom.
- A hurricane struck Swaziland on January 30 and 31, killing at least 13 people.
- Cyclone Domoina struck Mozambique, South Africa, and Swaziland from January 31 to February 2, causing severe flooding that killed at least 124 people and left thousands homeless.
- On February 4, blizzards in the United States killed at least 33 people.
- On February 7, blizzards in western Europe killed 13 people.
- In February, monsoon rains in Java, Indonesia, killed 26 people.
- Blizzards from Missouri to New York on February 28 caused at least 29 deaths.
- Blizzards in the eastern United States on March 9 killed 23 people.
- Blizzards in New England on March 14 killed at least 11 people.
- Blizzards and thunderstorms in the western United States from March 19 to 23 killed 27 people.
- Tornadoes in North Carolina and South Carolina on March 28 killed more than 70 people.
- A cyclone, category 5, with winds of 150 MPH (241 km/h), struck Mahajanga, Madagascar, on April 12, destroying about 80 percent of the town and killing at least 15 people.
- Tornadoes in Water Valley, Mississippi, on April 21 killed 15 people.
- A tornado in Oklahoma on April 26 killed 11 people, destroyed more than half the buildings in Morris, and killed three people elsewhere in the state.
- Tornadoes and thunderstorms, with serious flooding in Appalachia and Kentucky, Louisiana, Tennessee, Ohio, Maryland, and West Virginia from May 6 to 9 killed at least 14 people and left 6,000 homeless.
- Floods and landslides in Bangladesh and India from May 13 to 16 killed at least 136 people.
- Floods caused by overnight rain in Tulsa, Oklahoma, on May 27 killed at least 12 people and left thousands homeless.
- Flooding in Rio Grande do Sul, Brazil, in May killed 17 people and left nearly 10,000 homeless.
- Floods in the northeastern United States in late May and early June caused 18 deaths and left thousands of people homeless.
- Flooding in northeastern India in June killed at least 38 people.
- Monsoon floods in Bangladesh and India in June killed an estimated 200 people.
- Flooding and landslides in Taipei, Taiwan, on June 3 caused 25 deaths.
- Storms with 49 tornadoes caused extensive damage in the Great Plains and midwestern states on June 8. Barneveld, Wisconsin, was totally demolished, and nine people died.

- Tornadoes in Russia on June 9 and 10 caused widespread damage and hundreds of deaths in the towns of Ivanovo, Gorky, Kalinin, Kostroma, and Yaroslavl.
- Flooding in South Korea from July 4 to 7 killed at least 14 people and left nearly 2,000 homeless.
- Floods and landslides around Recife, Brazil, in July killed at least 13 people and left 1,000 homeless.
- Floods in Seoul, South Korea, from August 31 to September 3 left 81 people dead and 36 missing and caused more than $7 million of damage.
- Typhoon Ike struck the Philippines on September 2 and 3, killing more than 1,300 people and leaving 1.12 million homeless.
- Typhoon Ike struck the coast of Guangxi Zhuang, China, on September 6, causing widespread damage and killing 13 people whose fishing boats were lost at sea.
- Floods and landslides in Nepal in September killed more than 150 people.
- Floods in central Vietnam in October killed 33 people and left more than 38,000 families homeless.
- A tornado at Maravilha, Brazil, on October 9 killed at least 10 people.
- Typhoon Agnes, category 5, with winds of 185 MPH (298 km/h), struck the central Philippines in November, killing at least 300 people, leaving 100,000 homeless, and causing $40 million of damage.
- Flooding in Colombia in November killed at least 40 people.
- Hurricane-force winds caused widespread damage on November 24 in England, Germany, the Netherlands, France, and Belgium, and at least 14 people died.
- On December 23, an accident at a Union Carbide pesticide factory in Bhopal, India, released methyl isocyanate, killing at least 3,000 people and injuring hundreds of thousands.

1985

- Flooding in Brazil in January killed at least 71 people and left thousands homeless.
- Flooding in Algeria on January 5 killed at least 26 people.
- Cyclones Eric and Nigel struck Viti Levu, Fiji, on January 22, killing 23 people.
- Monsoon rains in Indonesia on February 21 caused a landside in Lombok, killing at least 11 people, and floods in Java that killed 10.
- Floods in northeastern Brazil in April killed 27 people.
- A cyclone with a 10–15 foot (4–4.5-m) storm surge struck islands at the mouth of the Meghna (Ganges) River in Bangladesh on May 25. Authorities set the death toll at 2,540, but it might have been as high as 11,000.
- Floods inundated Buenos Aires, Argentina, on May 30 and 31, killing at least 14 people and forcing 90,000 to leave their homes.

- Tornadoes crossed Pennsylvania, Ohio, New York, and Ontario, Canada, on May 31, killing at least 88 people and almost destroying several towns in Pennsylvania.
- Floods in Guangxi Province, China, on June 6 killed 64 people.
- Monsoon rains caused floods and landslides in western India in June, leaving at least 46 people dead and 25,000 homeless.
- Monsoon rains caused flooding in the northern Philippines in June, leaving at least 65 people dead and more than 100,000 homeless.
- Typhoon Irma struck Japan on July 1, causing 19 deaths and extensive damage in Numazu and Tokyo.
- Monsoon floods in Punjab, India, in July killed 87 people.
- A typhoon struck Zhejiang Province, China, on July 30, killing 177 people and injuring at least 1,400.
- Dikes failed and the Yalu River, near the border between North Korea and China, overflowed in late July and early August, causing floods that destroyed two villages near Dandong, China, and killing 64 people.
- Typhoons and heavy rain in China killed more than 500 people in August and left 14,000 homeless.
- Typhoon Pat, category 4, with winds of up to 124 MPH (199 km/h), struck Kyushu, Japan, on August 30, leaving 15 people dead and 11 missing.
- Two typhoons struck Thailand in October, causing floods in which 16 people died.
- Typhoons struck Bangladesh on October 16 and 17, killing 12 people.
- Floods in India on October 18 and 19 caused 78 deaths.
- Typhoon Dot struck Luzon, Philippines, on October 19, destroying 90 percent of the buildings in the city of Cabanatuan, killing at least 63 people, and causing $5.3 million of damage.
- A tropical storm caused floods in Louisiana in October, leaving seven people dead and eight missing, and causing $1 billion in damage.
- Floods in West Virginia, Virginia, Maryland, and Pennsylvania, following 20 inches (508 mm) of rain in 12 hours, killed at least 49 people.
- A blizzard in the northwestern United States in November killed at least 33 people.
- Hurricane Kate struck Cuba and Florida from November 19 to 21, killing at least 24 people.
- Blizzards in Michigan, South Dakota, Iowa, Minnesota, and Wisconsin in December killed 19 people.
- Floods in Saudi Arabia in December left 32 people dead and 31 missing.

1986

- Floods and landslides in Sri Lanka in January killed 43 people.
- Monsoon rains caused floods and landslides in Indonesia in January in which 19 people died.
- Lake Titicaca in Peru overflowed its banks in March, flooding the city of Puno and leaving at least 12 people dead and 28 missing.

- Cyclone Honorinnia struck Madagascar on March 17, destroying 80 percent of the buildings in Toamasina and leaving 32 people dead and 20,000 homeless.
- Hurricane-force winds struck western Europe on March 24, leaving at least 17 people dead and 19 missing.
- A cyclone struck Rajasthan, India, on May 16, killing 11 people.
- Typhoon Namu struck the Solomon Islands on May 19, killing more than 100 people and leaving more than 90,000 homeless.
- Floods in central Chile in June killed 10 people and left 35,000 homeless.
- Typhoon Peggy struck the northern Philippines on July 9, causing floods, mudslides, and extensive damage. More than 70 people were killed. Two days later, in southeastern China, Typhoon Peggy caused widespread flooding. More than 170 people died, at least 1,250 were injured, and more than 250,000 homes were destroyed.
- A typhoon struck Taiwan on August 22, leaving 22 people dead, 9 missing, and more than 110 injured.
- Hurricane Charley struck the British Isles on August 25, causing at least 11 deaths.
- Monsoon rains caused flooding in Andhra Pradesh, India, in August in which more than 200 people died.
- A typhoon struck Vietnam on September 4, killing 400 people and injuring 2,500.
- Typhoon Abby struck Taiwan on September 19, killing 13 people and causing $80 million of damage.
- Floods in and around Manila, Philippines, on October 6 killed 14 people and forced nearly 60,000 to leave their homes.

1987

- A blizzard from Maine to Florida on January 22 caused at least 37 deaths.
- Floods inundated São Paulo, Brazil, in January, causing at least 75 deaths.
- Floods and mudslides in Peru in February destroyed part of the town of Villa Rica and killed more than 100 people.
- Floods in the Republic of Georgia in February left 30 people dead and six missing.
- Cyclone Uma struck Vanuatu on February 7, killing at least 45 people.
- The area around Lima, Peru, was flooded on March 9 when dams weakened by rain collapsed. More than 100 people died, and 25,000 were left homeless.
- A tornado at Saragosa, Texas, on May 22 killed 29 people.
- Floods in central Chile from July 12 to 16 caused 16 deaths, 12 of them when a bridge north of Santiago was destroyed.
- A flash flood at Le Grand-Bornand, France, on July 14, caused when the Borne River broke its banks, washed away a vacation campsite, killing at least 30 people.

- Typhoon Thelma struck South Korea on July 15, causing floods, landslides, and mudslides. At least 111 people died, and 257 were missing.
- Floods and landslides in northern Italy on July 18 killed at least 14 people, 12 of them at a mountain hotel that was destroyed.
- Floods and landslides in Chungchong Province, South Korea, on July 21 and 22 left 100 people missing, feared dead.
- The Boojhan River in Iran overflowed on July 24, causing floods in which at least 100 people died.
- Seoul, South Korea, was flooded on July 27, and at least 74 people died.
- Typhoon Alex struck Zhejiang Province, China, on July 28, triggering a huge landslide. There was widespread damage, and at least 38 people died.
- A tornado in Heilongjiang Province, China, on July 31 caused extensive damage in 14 towns and left 16 people dead, 13 missing, and more than 400 injured.
- Five tornadoes, with 60-MPH (96-km/h) winds, struck a trailer park and nearby industrial center at Edmonton, Alberta, Canada, on July 31 and killed more than 25 people.
- Floods in Bangladesh in August killed more than 1,000 people.
- Floods near Maracay, Venezuela, in September killed about 500 people.
- Floods in Natal Province, South Africa, from September 25 to 29 left 174 people dead, 86 missing and more than 50,000 homeless and caused $500 million of damage.
- Heavy rain caused rock and mud to slide down on Villa Tina, an area of Medellín, Colombia, on September 27, leaving at least 175 people dead and 325 missing, believed buried beneath rubble.
- Floods in northern Bihar, West Bengal, Uttar Pradesh, and Assam, India, in September killed more than 1,200 people.
- Hurricane-force winds struck England on October 15, killing 13 people and causing $1 billion of damage.
- Typhoon Lynn struck Taiwan on October 24, destroying 200 homes.
- Cyclone-force winds in Andhra Pradesh, India, from November 3 to 6 killed at least 34 people.
- Typhoon Nina, with a storm surge, struck the Philippines on November 26, killing 500 people in Sorsogon Province, Luzon.
- Blizzards in the midwestern United States from December 12 to 16, generating tornadoes in Arkansas, caused 73 deaths.
- Floods and landslides in Sulawesi, Indonesia, on December 25 killed at least 92 people.
- Floods in Minas Gerais, Brazil, in December killed at least 12 people.

1988

- Blizzards in the midwestern and eastern United States from January 2 to 8 killed at least 33 people.
- Mud and rocks, flowing after heavy rain, killed at least 30 people in Huanoco Province, Peru, on February 3.

- Floods, landslides, and mudslides in Rio de Janeiro State, Brazil, in February killed more than 280 people and injured 600.
- Flash floods in the Orange Free State, South Africa, on February 22 killed at least 12 people.
- Floods in Kenya on April 23 and 24 killed at least 13 people.
- Flash floods in Fujian Province, China, on May 22 killed 72 people and injured 200.
- Floods in southeastern China in May caused at least 149 deaths.
- Floods in Cuba in June killed at least 21 people.
- Flash floods at Ankara, Turkey, on June 12 killed 13 people.
- Flash floods in Zhejiang Province, China, on July 29 and 30 left 264 people dead and 50 missing, feared drowned.
- Floods in Sudan in August, caused when the Nile burst its banks, killed at least 90 people and left 2 million homeless.
- Monsoon rains left 75 percent of Bangladesh inundated by floods in late August and September. More than 2,000 people died, and many more suffered waterborne diseases. At least 30 million people were left homeless.
- Floods in southern China in September killed at least 170 people and left 110,000 homeless.
- Hurricane Gilbert, category 5, struck the Caribbean and Gulf of Mexico from September 12 to 17. Its winds exceeded 155 MPH (249 km/h), and its core surface pressure fell to 888 mb—the lowest surface pressure ever recorded in the Western Hemisphere. It caused extensive damage in Jamaica, moved to the Yucatán Peninsula, Mexico, killing about 200 people in Monterrey, and caused $10 billion in damage. It killed at least 260 people and generated nearly 40 tornadoes in Texas.
- Flash floods in the village of Darbang, western Nepal, on September 22 killed at least 87 people.
- Flash floods in southern Ethiopia in September killed at least 81 people and left 2,240 homeless.
- Widespread floods in northwestern India in late September and early October killed an estimated 1,000 people.
- Floods in northern Vietnam from October 10 to 18 killed at least 27 people.
- Hurricane Joan struck the Caribbean coast from October 22 to 27, causing severe damage in Nicaragua, Costa Rica, Panama, Colombia, and Venezuela and killing at least 111 people. The storm weakened and became Tropical Storm Miriam, which then struck El Salvador, where it left 3,000 people homeless.
- Typhoon Ruby struck the Philippines on October 24 and 25, causing flooding and mudslides, killing about 500 people, and causing $52 million of damage.
- Typhoon Skip struck the Philippines on November 7, killing at least 129 people.

- Monsoon rains caused floods in southern Thailand in November and December in which more than 400 people died.
- A cyclone struck Bangladesh and eastern India on November 29, killing up to 3,000 people.
- Floods and landslides in Java, Indonesia, in December killed at least 40 people.

1989

- Cyclone Firinga, category 4, with winds of more than 125 MPH (201 km/h), struck Réunion Island on January 28 and 29, killing at least 10 people and leaving 6,000 homeless.
- Floods in central Peru killed 57 people in February.
- Hurricane-force winds in Spain on February 25 and 26 killed at least 12 people.
- Floods in Yemen in March killed at least 23 people.
- Floods, landslides, and avalanches caused by heavy rain killed more than 50 people in the Republic of Georgia on April 19.
- A tornado in Bangladesh on April 26 struck more than 20 villages and left up to 1,000 people dead, 12,000 injured, and nearly 30,000 homeless.
- Tornadoes and floods in the United States on May 6 killed 23 people and injured more than 100 in Texas, Virginia, North Carolina, Louisiana, South Carolina, and Oklahoma.
- Typhoon Cecil struck Vietnam on May 25 and 26, destroying 36,000 homes and leaving 140 people dead and 600 missing.
- A cyclone struck Bangladesh and eastern India on May 27, killing 200 people.
- Typhoon Brenda struck southern China in May, killing 26 people.
- Monsoon rains caused floods in Sri Lanka in June, killing 300 people and leaving 125,000 homeless.
- Floods in Sichuan Province, China, in June and July killed more than 1,300 people.
- Floods and landslides in Ecuador in June killed 35 people and left about 30,000 homeless.
- Blizzards in western China in June and July killed at least 67 people.
- Typhoon Gordon struck Luzon, Philippines, on July 16, killing 33 people.
- Typhoon Irving struck Thanh Hoa Province, Vietnam, on July 24, killing at least 200 people.
- Typhoon Judy struck South Korea in July, killing at least 17 people.
- Monsoon rains in July caused floods in which 81 people died in South Korea, 750 in India (and 2,000 missing), 17 in Pakistan, 200 in Bangladesh, and 1,500 in China.
- Typhoon Sarah struck Taiwan on September 11, breaking a Panamanian ship in half and killing 13 people.

- Typhoon Vera struck Zhejiang Province, China, on September 16, leaving 162 people dead, 354 missing, and 692 injured.
- Hurricane Hugo, category 5, with winds up to 140 MPH (225 km/h) and gusts up to 220 MPH (354 km/h), struck the Caribbean and East Coast of the United States on September 17 to 21. It reached Guadeloupe, killing 11 people, and Dominica in the Leeward Islands (Lesser Antilles) on September 17, then St. Croix, St. John, St. Thomas, and smaller islands in the U.S. Virgin Islands, and Puerto Rico on September 19. Ten people died on Montserrat, six in the Virgin Islands, and 12 in Puerto Rico. Hugo then turned north and weakened to category 4, striking Charleston, South Carolina, on September 21, killing one person when a house collapsed, and Charlotte, North Carolina, on September 22, where one child died, crossed the Blue Ridge Mountains, and in the afternoon crossed Virginia, killing two people, and Pennsylvania. Winds of 81 MPH (130 km/h) were recorded in Virginia. Awendaw, South Carolina, was hit by a tidal surge, and tornadoes forming part of the storm caused damage on several islands and also in North Carolina. Almost everyone in Montserrat was made homeless, and in Antigua 99 percent of homes were destroyed. In St. Croix, 90 percent of the population was left homeless; in Puerto Rico and Folly Beach, South Carolina, the figure was 80 percent. Hugo caused damage costing $10.5 billion in the United States.
- Typhoon Angela struck the Philippines in October, killing at least 50 people.
- Three typhoons struck Hainan Province, China, from October 2 to 13, killing 63 people and injuring more than 700.
- Typhoon Dan struck the Philippines on October 10, killing 43 people and leaving 80,000 homeless.
- Typhoon Elsie struck the Philippines on October 19, killing 30 people and leaving 332,000 homeless.
- Typhoon Gay struck Thailand on November 4 and 5, killing 365 people and damaging or destroying 30,000 homes.
- A cyclone struck southern India on November 9, killing 50 people.
- A tornado in Huntsville, Alabama, on November 15 killed 18 people and destroyed 119 homes.
- Floods in Brazil in December left 35 people dead and 200,000 homeless.

1990

- A cyclone struck Madagascar in January, killing at least 12 people.
- Floods in Tunisia from January 20 to 24 killed 30 people and left more than 9,500 homeless.
- Hurricane-force winds struck Europe on January 25, killing 45 people in the United Kingdom, 19 in the Netherlands, 10 in Belgium, eight in France, seven in Germany, and four in Denmark.

- Floods and landslides in Java, Indonesia, on January 27 and 28 killed more than 130 people.
- Hurricane-force winds struck France and Germany on February 3, killing 29 people and tearing tiles from the roof of Chartres Cathedral.
- Hurricane-force winds struck Europe on February 26, killing at least 51 people.
- Flooding in Kenya and Tanzania in March and April killed 140 people and left 25,000 Tanzanians homeless.
- Flooding in Rio de Janeiro, Brazil, on April 18 killed 11 people.
- Flooding in Russia in May, caused when melting snow made the Belaya River overflow, inundated 130 villages and killed 11 people.
- Floods in Texas, Oklahoma, Louisiana, and Arkansas in May killed 13 people.
- A cyclone struck Andhra Pradesh, India, on May 9, killing at least 962 people and leaving thousands unaccounted for.
- Tornadoes in Indiana, Illinois, and Wisconsin on June 2 and 3 killed 13 people.
- A flash flood in Shadyside, Ohio, on June 14 demolished homes and killed at least 26 people.
- Floods in Hunan and Jiangxi Provinces, China, in June destroyed 16,000 homes and killed more than 100 people.
- Floods in Turkey on June 20 killed 48 people.
- Typhoon Ofelia struck the Philippines, Taiwan, and China on June 23 and 24, killing a total of 57 people.
- Floods in Yunnan Province, China, in July killed 108 people.
- Floods in Bangladesh in July killed 26 people.
- Floods around Lake Baikal, Siberia, in July caused extensive damage and an unknown number of deaths.
- Floods and landslides in Kyushu, Japan, on July 2 killed 24 people.
- A typhoon struck Guangdong and Fujian Provinces, China, in August, killing 108 people.
- A hurricane struck Mexico in August, causing floods in which 23 people drowned.
- Typhoon Yancy struck the Philippines and China in August, killing 216 people in Fujian and Zhejiang Provinces, China, and 12 in the Philippines.
- Floods in the Chitwan National Park, Nepal, in August drowned 20 people.
- A tornado at Plainfield, Illinois, on August 28 killed 29 people and injured 300.
- Typhoon Abe struck Zhejiang Province, China, on August 31, killing 48 people.
- Floods and landslides in Seoul, South Korea, on September 11 and 12 left 83 people dead and 52 missing.
- Typhoon Flo struck Honshu, Japan, on September 16 and 17, killing 32 people.
- Flash floods in Chihuahua, Mexico, on September 22 and 23 left 45 people dead, 30 missing, and 5,000 homeless.

- Floods in Bangladesh in September killed 14 children.
- Storm surges in the Bay of Bengal in October left 50 people dead and at least 3,000 fishermen missing in Bangladesh.
- A typhoon struck Vietnam on October 23, killing 15 people and leaving thousands homeless.
- Typhoon Mike struck the Philippines on November 14, leaving 190 people dead, 160 missing, and 120,000 homeless.

1991

- Floods in Pakistan in February killed 24 people.
- Iraqi forces retreating at the end of the Persian Gulf War set fire to 613 oil wells, storage tanks, and refineries in Kuwait. A pall of black smoke covered the entire region for several months.
- Floods in Mulanje, Malawi, on March 10 killed more than 500 people and left 150,000 homeless.
- A tornado at Sripur, Bangladesh, on April 10 destroyed a textile mill, killing 60 people and trapping 100 beneath debris.
- More than 70 tornadoes in Kansas on April 26 killed 26 people and injured more than 200.
- A cyclone with a storm surge producing waves 20 feet (6 m) high struck coastal islands in Bangladesh on April 30, killing at least 131,000 people and leaving 5,000 fishermen unaccounted for.
- A tornado at Tungi, Bangladesh, on May 7 killed 100 people.
- A tornado at Sirajganj, Bangladesh, on May 9 killed 13 people.
- Floods in Bangladesh in May killed more than 100 people and left more than 1 million homeless.
- Floods in China from May to August killed at least 1,800 people.
- Flash floods in Jowzjan Province, Afghanistan, in June killed up to 5,000 people.
- Floods in Sri Lanka in June killed 27 people.
- Floods and landslides in India and Bangladesh in July killed at least 80 people.
- Typhoon Amy struck southern China on July 20 and 21, killing at least 35 people.
- Prolonged heavy rain caused a dam to burst near Onesti, Romania, on July 28, killing more than 100 people.
- Monsoon rains caused a dike to burst in Maharashtra State, India, on July 30, inundating 52 villages and leaving 475 people dead and 425 missing.
- Floods in Cameroon and Chad in August killed at least 41 people.
- Hurricane Bob struck the East Coast of the United States from August 18 to 20, killing 16 people.
- Typhoon Gladys struck South Korea on August 23, bringing 16 inches (406 mm) of rain to Pusan and Ulsan, killing 72 people, and leaving 2,000 homeless.

- Floods in Cambodia in September killed 100 people.
- Floods in Bangladesh in September killed 250 people.
- Floods in West Bengal, India, from September 7 to 14 killed 40 people.
- Floods in Vietnam in September killed 17 people.
- Typhoon Mireille, category 4, with winds up to 133 MPH (214 km/h), struck Kyushu and Hokkaido, Japan, on September 27, killing 45 people.
- Typhoon Ruth, category 5, with winds up to 143 MPH (230 km/h), struck Luzon, Philippines, on October 27, killing 43 people.
- Floods in the Philippines on November 5, caused by Tropical Storm Thelma, left 3,000 people dead.
- Floods in southern India in November killed 125 people.
- Typhoon Val, category 5, with winds up to 150 MPH (241 km/h), struck Western Samoa from December 6 to 10, leaving 12 people dead and 4,000 homeless.
- Floods in Texas on December 21 and 22 killed 15 people.

1992

- Floods and mudslides in Rio de Janeiro, Brazil, on January 5 killed 25 people.
- Blizzards in southern Turkey from February 1 to 7 caused avalanches and snowslides that killed 201 people.
- Floods in Los Angeles and Ventura Counties, California, in February killed eight people and caused $23 million of damage.
- Floods in Jiangxi Province, China, in March killed 29 people.
- Floods in Tajikistan from May 13 to 15 killed at least 200 people.
- Heavy rain caused the Paraguay, Paraná, and Iguaçu Rivers to overflow in May and June, causing floods in Argentina, Brazil, and Paraguay that inundated hundreds of towns, killing 28 people and requiring the evacuation of 220,000.
- Floods in Fujian and Zhejiang Provinces, China, in July killed more than 1,000 people.
- Monsoon rains caused flooding in southern Pakistan in July and August, killing 56 people and leaving thousands homeless.
- Hurricane Andrew, category 5, with winds up to 164 MPH (264 km/h), struck the Bahamas, then moved to Florida and Louisiana from August 23 to 26. Homestead and Florida City, Florida, were almost destroyed. In Florida, the hurricane killed 38 people, destroyed 63,000 homes, and caused $20 billion of damage. In Louisiana it left 44,000 people homeless and caused $300 million in damage. It was the most costly hurricane in U.S. history.
- Tropical Storm Polly caused a storm surge with 20-foot (6-m) waves at Tianjin, China, on August 30 and 31, killing 165 people along the southeastern coast and leaving more than 5 million homeless.
- Tsunamis caused by an undersea earthquake struck the western coast of Nicaragua on September 1, killing 105 people and injuring 489.

- Flash floods near Gulbahar, Afghanistan, on September 2 destroyed villages and killed up to 3,000 people.
- Monsoon rains caused the Indus River to overflow its banks, causing floods in Pakistan and India from September 11 to 16. More than 2,000 people died in Pakistan and at least 500 in India.
- Flash floods in Manila, Philippines, on September 15 killed 10 people.
- Flash floods in the Ardèche, Vaucluse, and Drôme regions of France on September 22 left 80 people dead and 30 missing.
- Floods and landslides in Kerala, India, in October killed 60 people and left thousands homeless.
- Floods and mudslides in southern India in November killed 230 people and left thousands homeless.
- Floods in Ukraine in November killed 17 people.
- Floods in Albania in November, caused when the Mati River overflowed, killed 11 people.
- From November 21 to 23, up to 45 tornadoes across 11 states in the United States, from Texas to Ohio, killed 25 people.
- A cyclone, with heavy rain and snow, struck the northeastern United States on December 10 and 11, killing 17 people and causing $10 million of damage in Atlantic City.

1993

- Cyclone Kina, category 4, with winds up to 115 MPH (185 km/h), struck Fiji on January 2 and 3, killing 12 people.
- Floods and mudslides in Tijuana, Mexico, and southern California from January 7 to 20 killed 30 people and left 1,000 homeless.
- A tornado lasting five minutes in the Sylhet and Sunamganj districts of Bangladesh on January 8 killed 32 people and injured more than 1,000.
- Floods in Java, Indonesia, in February killed 60 people, destroyed many homes, and required about 250,000 people to be evacuated.
- Floods in Ecuador in February caused great damage and an unknown number of deaths.
- Floods in Iran in February killed about 500 people and caused about $1 billion of damage.
- A blizzard in the eastern United States from March 12 to 15 killed approximately 270 people, as well as four in Canada and three in Cuba, and caused $1 billion of damage.
- A tornado in West Bengal, India, on April 9 destroyed five villages and killed 100 people.
- Floods and landslides in Colombia on April 26, caused when the Tapartó River overflowed, killed up to 100 people.
- Floods and mudslides in Santiago, Chile, on May 3 killed 11 people.
- Floods in the midwestern United States from June to August, caused when the Missouri and Mississippi Rivers overflowed, killed 50 people and caused $12 billion of damage in Illinois, Iowa, Kansas,

Minnesota, Missouri, Nebraska, North Dakota, South Dakota, and Wisconsin.

- Floods in Dhaka, Bangladesh, in June killed nearly 200 people.
- Monsoon rains caused floods in Himachal Pradesh State, India, in July in which at least 175 people died.
- Hurricane Calvin struck Mexico on July 6 and 7, killing 28 people.
- Monsoon rains caused floods in Bangladesh, Nepal, and India in July and August, killing thousands of people.
- Floods and landslides in Hunan and Sichuan Provinces, China, in July killed 120 people.
- Floods and mudslides in Japan in July and August left 40 people dead and 22 missing.
- Tropical Storm Bret caused floods and mudslides in Venezuela on August 8 in which at least 100 people died.
- Typhoon Yancy, category 4, with winds up to 130 MPH (209 km/h), struck Kyushu, Japan, in September, killing 41 people.
- Floods and mudslides in Nicaragua, Honduras, and Mexico in September killed a total of at least 42 people.
- For 10 days at the end of October and beginning of November, wildfires raged in the Los Angeles Basin of California, fanned by a Santa Ana wind. The fires burned more than 300 square miles (777 km²).
- Mudslides in northern Honduras from October 31 to November 2 destroyed 1,000 homes and killed 400 people.
- Typhoon Kyle struck Vietnam on November 23, killing at least 45 people.
- A cyclone struck southern India in December, killing 47 people.
- Hurricane-force winds struck the United Kingdom in December, killing 12 people.
- Floods and mudslides in Dabeiba, Colombia, on December 17 left 22 people dead, 35 injured, and several missing.
- Mudslides at Oran, Algeria, on December 25 killed 12 people and injured 46.
- Typhoon Nell struck the Philippines on December 25 and 26, killing at least 47 people.
- Floods in Malaysia in December killed 14 people.
- Floods in Belgium, France, Germany, Luxembourg, the Netherlands, and Spain in December killed at least seven people.

1994

- Floods and landslides in the Philippines on January 7 left 15 people dead and 30 missing.
- Floods in Colombia in February killed 19 people and destroyed 1,400 homes.
- Cyclone Geralda, category 5, with winds up to 220 MPH (354 km/h), struck Madagascar from February 2 to 4, leaving 70 people dead and

500,000 homeless. In the port of Toamasina, 95 percent of the buildings were destroyed.

- Floods and mudslides in Peru in February killed 50 people and left 5,000 homeless.
- Tornadoes on March 27 killed 42 people in Alabama, Georgia, North Carolina, South Carolina, and Tennessee.
- A cyclone struck Nampula Province, Mozambique, in March, killing 34 people and leaving 1.5 million homeless.
- A cyclone, category 5, with winds up to 180 MPH (290 km/h), struck Bangladesh on May 2, killing 233 people.
- Floods in Guangdong and Guangxi Provinces, China, in June killed up to 400 people.
- On June 3, earthquakes sent a series of tsunamis onto the east coast of Java, Indonesia. More than 200 people were killed while they slept at Banyuwangi.
- Monsoon rains caused floods in India in June and July in which about 500 people died.
- Floods in the Philippines in July killed 68 people.
- A typhoon, category 1, with winds up to 85 MPH (137 km/h), struck Taiwan in August, killing 10 people.
- Typhoon Fred struck Zhejiang Province, China, on August 20 and 21, killing about 1,000 people and causing more than $1.1 billion of damage.
- Floods in Baluchistan Province, Pakistan, on August 26 killed 24 people when their minibus was swept away by the waters.
- Floods in Moldova on August 27 and 28 killed at least 50 people.
- Floods in Niger in August killed 40 people.
- Floods in Algeria on September 23 killed 29 people.
- Floods at Houston, Texas, from October 16 to 19 killed 10 people.
- Typhoon Teresa struck Luzon, Philippines, on October 23, killing 25 people.
- Floods in northern Italy on November 4 and 5 killed about 100 people.
- Tropical Storm Gordon struck the Carribbean, Florida, and South Carolina from November 13 to 19, killing 537 people and causing at least $200 million of damage.
- A cyclone struck northern Somalia in November, killing 30 people.

1995

- In January, violent storms caused floods in much of California. At least 11 people died, and the damage was estimated at $300 million.
- In late January and early February, heavy rain and melting snow combined to make the Rhine, Main, Mosel, Meuse, Waal, and Nahe Rivers overflow, causing widespread floods in Belgium, France, Germany, and especially the Netherlands. About 30 people died, and damage was estimated at more than $2 billion.

- In early March, California suffered further floods, in which at least 12 people died.
- On March 27, heavy rain triggered a mudslide in Afghanistan. A village was destroyed, killing 354 people and injuring 64.
- In early May, floods and landslides in northern Sumatra, Indonesia, killed at least 55 people and made about 17,500 homeless.
- On May 17, a heavy rainstorm and tidal surge combined to kill nearly 100 people in southeastern Bangladesh.
- In late May, rains washed away a feeding center in Angola, killing 33 people, 25 of them children.
- On June 3, a tornado lasting about 20 minutes near Dimmitt, Texas, destroyed a home, lifted automobiles from the ground, and removed a section of asphalt more than 475 square yards (397 m²) in area from a highway and dropped it about 220 yards (201 m) from its original position. The tornado produced winds of more than 155 MPH (249 km/h) and a downdraft of more than 56 MPH (90 km/h) at the eye. This was the first tornado to be studied using new radar equipment that revealed more detail of its internal structure than had been observed previously.
- In June, pre-monsoon rains caused widespread flooding and landslides in Bangladesh and Nepal. At least 50 people were killed in Bangladesh and 60 in Nepal.
- In June and July, heavy rains caused flooding in Hunan, Hubei, and Jiangxi Provinces, China. At least 1,200 people died, and about 5.6 million were stranded. About 900,000 homes were destroyed and 4 million damaged, requiring the relocation of 1.3 million people.
- On July 13, flash floods triggered a mudslide at Senirkent, Turkey. About 200 homes were destroyed, and at least 50 people died.
- In mid-July, more than 150 people died in widespread floods in Bangladesh and nearly 600 people died in floods in Pakistan.
- In mid-July, prolonged heavy rain caused a landslide that descended on a village in southwestern China during the night and buried it while everyone was asleep, killing 26 people.
- In mid-July, Typhoon Faye struck South Korea. At least 16 people died, and 25 were missing.
- In North Korea, flooding began in late July that continued for months, rendering 100,000 families homeless and affecting 5 million people, nearly 25 percent of the population. On September 11 the World Health Organization of the United Nations announced it had provided $100,000 to meet the immediate health needs of flood victims.
- On August 17, heavy rain caused flash floods in the Atlas Mountains, Morocco, killing more than 230 people and leaving about 500 missing.
- In early September, monsoon rains caused the deaths of at least 40 people in northern India.
- Further flooding in Morocco in early September killed 31 people.

- Hurricane Luis, category 4, with winds gusting to more than 140 MPH (225 km/h), struck Puerto Rico and the U.S. Virgin Islands on September 4 to 6. At least 15 people were killed.
- Hurricane Ismael struck Mexico on September 14, killing at least 107 people, many of them fishermen at sea, in the northwestern Pacific states.
- In mid-September, floods affected 52 of the 76 provinces of Thailand. At least 62 people died.
- Hurricane Marilyn struck the U.S. Virgin Islands and Puerto Rico on September 15 to 16, with winds of more than 100 MPH (160 km/h), leaving nine people dead and 100 injured or missing and destroying 80 percent of the houses on St. Thomas.
- In late September and early October, five days of heavy rain caused widespread flooding in Bangladesh. More than 100 people died, and more than 1 million were trapped in their homes.
- On October 1, Tropical Storm Sybil struck the Philippines, causing damage in 29 provinces and 27 cities. It triggered floods, landslides, and volcanic mudflows. More than 100 people were killed, and 100 were missing and feared killed.
- Hurricane Opal, category 4, with winds of 150 MPH (241 km/h), formed over the Yucatán Peninsula of Mexico on September 27. By the end of the month it was classed as a tropical storm but became a hurricane by October 2. It killed 50 people in Guatemala and Mexico and 13 in the United States, although it had weakened to category 3 by the time it reached Florida on October 4. It then moved into North Carolina, Georgia, and Alabama. The damage it caused was due mainly to a storm surge producing 12-foot (3.7-m) storm-surge waves and breaking waves. Damage was estimated at more than $2 billion.
- Hurricane Roxanne, category 3, with 115-MPH (185-km/h) winds, struck the island of Cozumel, off the Mexican coast, in October, killing 14 people in Mexico and driving tens of thousands from their homes.
- Following days of fierce storms and blizzards, before dawn on October 26 a snowslide engulfed 19 homes and killed 20 people in the fishing village of Flateyri, Iceland.
- Tropical Storm Zack struck the Philippines in late October, causing severe flooding, capsizing a ship sailing between islands, and killing at least 59 people. In all, at least 100 people died, and 60,000 had to leave their homes.
- Typhoon Angela, category 4, struck the eastern Philippines on November 3 with winds of 140 MPH (225 km/h). It killed more than 700 people, destroyed 15,000 homes, and left more than 200,000 people homeless. Damage to crops, roads, and bridges amounted to $77 million.
- On November 11–12, heavy snow triggered snowslides and mudflows in Nepal, killing at least 49 people.
- On December 25, flash floods caused by prolonged heavy rain killed at least 130 people in Natal Province, South Africa.

- In late December, extreme cold and blizzards affected Europe and Asia from Britain to Kazakhstan and Bangladesh. More than 350 people died, many of them in Moscow, where people froze while drunk.
- In late December, about 60 people died in floods in Brazil caused by heavy rain.

1996

- From January 6 to 9, the worst blizzards in 70 years swept the eastern United States. At least 23 people died as snow driven by 25–35-MPH (40–56-km/h) winds affected Alabama, Indiana, Kentucky, Maryland, Massachusetts, New Jersey, New York, North Carolina, Ohio, Pennsylvania, Rhode Island, Virginia, Washington, D.C., and West Virginia. States of emergency were declared in Kentucky, Maryland, New Jersey, New York City, Pennsylvania, Virginia, and West Virginia. President Clinton designated nine states as disaster areas. No mail was delivered in New York City on January 9, and the United Nations building was closed.
- On May 13, a tornado with 125-MPH (201-km/h) winds killed more than 440 people and injured more than 32,000 in Bangladesh. Lasting less than half an hour, it destroyed 80 villages, striking hardest in the Tangail district, 45 miles (72 km) north of Dhaka. Of those killed, at least 120 were in the village of Bashail, some of them students at a boarding school that collapsed. Further, 55 people died in Rampur, and there were deaths in Gopalpur, Kalihati, Shafiur, Mirzapur, and Ghatail.
- On June 3, a 60-acre (24-ha) brushfire in Alaska turned into a huge wildfire when it ignited forest-floor moss that had dried as a result of drought and was driven by 25-MPH (40-km/h) winds. Firefighters suspected the fire had been started by fireworks. By June 6 it had grown into 60 separate wildfires covering more than 40,000 acres (16,188 ha), and these were still burning at the end of the month.
- On June 16, a cyclone and heavy rainfall caused extensive flooding in the southern Indian states of Andhra Pradesh, Tamil Nadu, and Karnataka. Telephone and power lines were brought down, thousands of people were driven from their homes, and at least 100 died. More than 190 people, most of them fishermen, were reported missing.
- On June 19, storms brought severe flooding in Tuscany, Italy. Mudslides caused rivers to burst their banks, and bridges were swept away. Fornovalasco and Cardoso were the worst-affected villages, inundated by the river Vezza. More than 1,000 inhabitants were evacuated from the two villages on June 20. The main rail line between Rome and Genoa was blocked by a mudslide. By June 21, 11 bodies had been recovered, and 30 people were missing.
- In late June, drought led to wildfires in Nevada, New Mexico, Utah, and Arizona. The Nevada fire, started by boys playing with gasoline 60 miles (96 km) south of Reno, burned about 4,000 acres (1,619 ha). On June

23, between 3,000 and 4,000 people were evacuated from their homes but were allowed to return the following day. In Arizona, the fires burned more than 31,500 acres (12,748 ha) of forest. In Utah, 30,000 acres (12,141 ha) were burned, and 360 acres (146 ha) of the Santa Fe National Forest in the Jemez Mountains, about 45 miles (72 km) northwest of Albuquerque, New Mexico, were destroyed. By July, as the drought continued, drinking water was becoming scarce in parts of Texas. On July 27, the Nevada fires were brought under control with the help of steady drizzle, but lightning ignited more fires in Utah, damaging 8,000 acres (3,238 ha) of the Dixie National Forest. A fire in Idaho burned 13,000 acres (5,261 ha) of brush, and in Colorado a 5,340-acre (2,161-ha) fire was brought under control. By late August, 84,000 fires had burned a total of 4.8 million acres (1.9 million ha) in nine western states. More fires began in Oregon on August 26, adding to others already burning and affecting 100,000 acres (40,470 ha) in the state, and fires were still raging in California, Washington, Idaho, Utah, Nevada, Montana, and Wyoming. By the end of August, nearly 20,000 firefighters were battling blazes across the western states.

- At the end of June, the Orinoco River burst its banks when its level rose in some places by 10 feet (3 m) following two weeks of rain. More than 10,000 acres (4,047 ha) of lands cultivated by Amazonian tribes was flooded, and on June 28 the governor of Amazonas State, Venezuela, declared a state of emergency.

- Two weeks of monsoon rains in late June and early July caused the Ganges and Brahmaputra Rivers to burst their banks, flooding nearly one-third of Bangladesh and affecting 3 million people. On July 7, the Jamuna River inundated 50 villages, displacing nearly 70,000 people in Sirajganj, 65 miles (105 km) northwest of Dhaka. Lack of safe drinking water led to outbreaks of typhoid and diarrhea affecting more than 1,000 people. The rains and flooding continued for more than a month, killing at least 115 people, and nearly 6 million lost their homes and crops. The same monsoon rains caused 82 deaths in Nepal and 78 in India.

- Heavy rain, beginning in late June and continuing into August, caused widespread flooding in 11 provinces of central and southern China. In Lin'an and Tonglu, southwest of Hangzhou, the capital of Zhejiang Province, the water was 20 feet (6 m) deep on July 8. More than 1,500 people died, and the floods were estimated to have destroyed at least 2.5 million acres (1 million ha) of crops and injured or damaged the property of 20 million people. By mid-July the Yangtze and other rivers in central China were still rising, and Dongting Lake overflowed, flooding 39 counties and cities in Hunan, in places to a depth of 20 feet (6 m). About 8 million troops, police, reservists, officials, and military academy students were mobilized to rescue more than 650,000 people. The cost of the floods was estimated at about $12 billion. The floods started receding on July 25 but returned in early August. Mongolia also suffered floods, killing 41 people, and the capital, Ulan Bator, was inundated when two rivers overflowed.

- Starting on July 6, snowstorms affected large areas of eastern South Africa, leaving thousands of travelers and many hikers stranded. More than 3,000 people were trapped at Harrismith, where 6-foot (1.8-m) drifts blocked a pass. By July 10 the death toll had reached 44, including two boys in Lesotho. By July 11, 96 hikers had been rescued by helicopter from the Drakensberg Mountains, where they had been stranded since July 6, and roads reopened. South of Johannesburg 91 people were rescued. In villages in the Maluti Mountains of Lesotho, more than 100,000 people were trapped. Temperatures fell to 10°F (–7°C) at Lady Grey, Free State Province, south of Johannesburg. The weather bureau in Pretoria said it was the heaviest and most sustained snowfall since 1962, and in some parts of Free State Province it was the first snowfall in 50 years.

- On July 7, two people died in flooding in the area around Lake Maggiore, in northern Italy, one a woman of 67 in a landslide near Omegna, the other a German canoeist who was swept away near Cannobio. By July 8, the main road into Omegna was underwater and strewn with debris. The floods were caused by heavy storms.

- On July 8, Hurricane Bertha reached the U.S. Virgin Islands with torrential rain and winds up to 103 MPH (166 km/h), crossing St. Thomas, but coming only to within 45 miles (72 km) of Puerto Rico, where winds reached 85 MPH (137 km/h) and 5–8 inches (127–203 mm) of rain fell, triggering flash floods and mudslides. Bertha crossed the British Virgin Islands, where roofs were torn from buildings, power lines were brought down, and buildings were flooded by heavy rain, then moved on to St. Kitts and Nevis and Anguilla. On July 10 Bertha reached the Bahamas with 20-foot (6-m) waves and 100-MPH (160-km/h) winds. On July 12, the hurricane reached the Carolina coast and moved north, eventually to Delaware and New Jersey. By July 11 Bertha had caused six deaths in Puerto Rico and the Virgin Islands and one in Florida. Radio calls were received from a Venezuelan ship adrift off Puerto Rico near the eye of the storm with 42 people on board and only 14 lifejackets, and the U.S. Coast Guard conducted a search. Bertha was initially classified as a category 1 hurricane, but was later upgraded to category 2 and on July 9, as its winds reached 115 MPH (185 km/h), category 3. It was large, with a diameter of 460 miles (740 km), and its winds reached hurricane force 115 miles (185 km) from the eye.

- On July 12, a severe storm caused flash flooding at Buffalo Creek, Colorado, destroying two roads and a bridge, as well as several buildings.

- On July 13, monsoon rains caused floods in north Bengal and a landslide in West Bengal state. The flood swept 14 people to their deaths and left nearly 100,000 marooned, and 37 died in the landslide.

- By mid-July, monsoon rains had caused floods that inundated 60 villages in Assam State, India. The state government set up 120 relief camps to accommodate 1.5 million people.

- In mid-July, a tornado destroyed electrical and communications equipment and several hundred houses in the cities of Jiangyan and Taixing, in Jiangsu Province, China. Many farmers were killed or injured by collapsing houses. The tornado killed 21 people and injured more than 200.
- On July 18, Typhoon Eve crossed the Satsuma peninsula on the southern tip of Kyushu, the southernmost island of Japan, with maximum wind speeds of 119 MPH (191 km/h), later weakening.
- In Quebec, after two days in which 11 inches (279 mm) of rain fell, more than ordinarily falls in the whole of July, on July 21 rivers burst, causing widespread flooding in the Saguenay River region, about 200 miles (320 km) north of Montreal. At least eight people died. About 100 houses were destroyed as well as several other buildings in La Baie, where 12,000 residents had to leave their homes and were not allowed to return for some days for fear that nearby dams might burst. About 3,000 were accommodated in tents at a military base at Bagotville, and two tents were also provided for 40 cats and dogs. The Quebec government created a $200-million relief fund, but that amount was believed to be a conservative estimate of the cost of the flooding.
- On July 23, Tropical Storm Frankie moved from the Gulf of Tonkin to the Red River Delta, Vietnam, bringing winds of 56 MPH (90 km/h) and 4.5–8 inches (114–203 mm) of rain. After two days the storm abated, leaving 41 people dead and many missing.
- On July 25, Typhoon Gloria, with winds gusting to 106 MPH (170 km/h), caused damage in the Philippines and caused at least 30 deaths. It was the sixth major storm to strike the islands in 1996. The next day, Gloria, downgraded to a tropical storm, reached Taiwan and the southeast coast of China on July 26, killing three people.
- Five days of heavy rain in late July delivered up to 20 inches (508 mm) of rain on rice-growing areas in North and South Korea, some parts of North Korea receiving nearly 29 inches (737 mm). United Nations officials reported that at least 230 people died in North Korea. Rivers flooded, there were landslides, and in South Korea 64 people died, 44 of them soldiers buried by mud inside their barracks and posts. The South Korean border towns of Yonchon and Munsan were flooded to roof level, and about 50,000 people had to leave their homes in an area north of Seoul. Damage was estimated at $600 million. In North Korea the floods followed heavy flooding in 1995 and destroyed 20 percent of the country's annual food production, threatening famine.
- Typhoon Herb, with winds of 121 MPH (195 km/h), reached Taiwan on July 31, bringing 44 inches (1,118 mm) of rain in 24 hours at Mount Ali, southern Taiwan, and flooding thousands of homes. The typhoon killed at least 41 people, and 34 were missing. It was the worst storm to strike Taiwan in 30 years. It then crossed the Taiwan Strait to China, reaching Pingtan, in Fujian Province, on August 1, with winds of 87 MPH (140 km/h).

- On July 7, monsoon rains triggered landslides in northeastern Nepal, in an area 55 miles (88 km) northeast of Katmandu. Dozens of homes were destroyed in the village of Jhagraku, and at least 40 people died.
- On July 7, after two days of heavy rain, a campsite in the Spanish Pyrenees was destroyed by floodwater, mud, and rocks. At least 100 people were killed.
- On August 14, Typhoon Kirk crossed southwestern Honshu, Japan, with winds of 130 MPH (209 km/h) and up to 12 inches (305 mm) of rain. On August 15, it returned and crossed the northern part of the island, but with winds of only 56 MPH (90 km/h). Kirk then moved to northeastern China, causing floods that inundated 845 villages along the Yellow River.
- By mid-August, two weeks of heavy rain in the far east of Russia had flooded eight towns and 126 villages along the Ussuri, Ussurka, and Malinovka Rivers, killing four people. Roads, bridges, and crops were destroyed, power and telephone lines brought down, and 3,500 buildings damaged. The damage was estimated to cost $140 million.
- On August 20, Tropical Storm Dolly, with winds of 30 MPH (48 km/h), strengthened to hurricane force when its wind speed measured 75 MPH (121 km/h) as it reached Punta Herrero on the Caribbean coast of Mexico. It then weakened but regained hurricane force as it moved back over the sea and headed toward northeastern Mexico and Texas.
- In August, North Vietnam suffered severe storms, with a waterspout offshore from Hau Loc on August 14. The storm destroyed many fishing boats and together with flooding due to heavy rain killed 53 people. More than 1,000 homes were destroyed by flash floods and mudslides, leaving 10,000 people homeless near the border with Laos. On August 21 Hanoi was threatened with flooding as the level of the Red River rose 1.6 feet (49 cm) above the flood-warning mark. The following day it burst its banks at a dike about 30 miles (48 km) northwest of Hanoi, causing 80,000 people to flee their homes in the city, which was under several feet of water. Tropical Storm Niki, downgraded from a typhoon, struck just south of Haiphong on August 23, sinking four cargo ships and leaving one person dead.
- On September 1, Hurricane Edouard headed toward Cape Cod, and a state of emergency was declared in Massachusetts. Hurricane winds had by then weakened from 140 MPH (223 km/h) to 100 MPH (160 km/h). Edouard had already battered New Jersey, killing two people. Hurricane Fran was then 290 miles (467 km) northeast of Puerto Rico in the Caribbean, with winds of 80 MPH (129 km/h) and expected to strengthen, and Gustav was west-southwest of the Cape Verde Islands.
- In late August, prolonged heavy rain caused widespread flooding in northern Bangladesh. The Padma River overflowed, and some low-lying outskirts of the city of Rajshahi (population 2 million) were under 2 feet (60 cm) of water. Rice crops were damaged in Rajshahi, Chapainawabgani,

Dinajpur, and Sherpur. At least 500,000 people were affected, 100,000 had to leave their homes, and 20 died.

- On September 2, following two hours of heavy rain, flash floods destroyed rail lines and bridges in and around al-Geili, north of Khartoum, Sudan. Thousands of people were made homeless, and 15 died.
- On September 6, Hurricane Fran, category 3, with winds of 115 MPH (185 km/h) gusting to 125 MPH (201 km/h) extending to 145 miles (233 km) from the eye, passed Cape Fear, North Carolina, shortly before 8 P.M., heading north. By midnight winds had dropped to 100 MPH (160 km/h), and the eye had disappeared. Nevertheless, the hurricane produced tornadoes and a storm surge of up to 12 feet (3.7 m) and in some places 16 feet (4.9 m). More than 500,000 people were ordered to evacuate coastal areas of South Carolina, and evacuation was also ordered in all or part of eight counties in North Carolina. By the following day, Fran had swept through North and South Carolina, Virginia, and West Virginia, causing 34 deaths and damage preliminarily estimated at $625 million, but expected to rise. President Clinton declared major disasters in North Carolina and Virginia, and state governors declared emergencies in Virginia, West Virginia, and North Carolina. The flooding caused by the hurricane was followed by a second wave of heavy rain in eastern North Carolina, causing the Neuse River to rise about 13 feet (3.9 m). Roads were closed, creeks and rivers overflowed, and 1,000 people were evacuated from their homes in Kinston. Then, on September 16, a wave of heavy rain and tornadoes swept the southeastern part of the state, causing more damage, some of it about a mile from Kinston.
- On September 7, Tropical Storm Hortense delivered heavy rain over Martinique, causing flooding and bringing down power lines. It then headed for the British Virgin Islands and Puerto Rico, with forecasts of up to 10 inches (254 mm) of rain and winds of 60 MPH (96 km/h) extending 100 miles (160 km) from the center. By September 10, strengthened to a category 1 hurricane, it delivered up to 20 inches (508 mm) of rain on Puerto Rico, causing flash floods, mudslides, and damage estimated to cost $155 million. Then the hurricane moved to the Dominican Republic. It killed 16 people and left dozens missing there and in Puerto Rico, then headed for the Bahamas and Turks and Caicos Islands.
- On September 10, Typhoon Sally passed Hong Kong and crossed the coast of Guangdong, China, with winds of up to 108 MPH (174 km/h). More than 130 people were killed, thousands were injured, nearly 400,000 homes were destroyed, and more than 30 fishing boats were sunk.
- In September, tropical storms caused floods in central Vietnam in which 17 people died and 114,000 had to leave their homes.
- On September 22, Typhoon Violet crossed Japan, with winds of 78 MPH (125 km/h) gusting to 116 MPH (187 km/h) and 10.4 inches (264 mm) of rain in Tokyo. By September 23, it had weakened to a tropical storm and was moving into the Pacific. At least seven people were killed,

most in the Tokyo area. In Honshu, Violet caused about 200 landslides, destroyed more than 80 homes, and flooded more than 3,000.

- In late September, Typhoon Willie struck the Chinese island of Hainan, killing at least 38 people and leaving 96 missing. In the capital, Haikou, 70 percent of the streets were flooded. Some parts of the island had more than 15 inches (381 mm) of rain. Three of the fatalities were in the county of Wenchang, where the typhoon breached breakwaters and swept away 53 fishing boats and 43 houses. The Niandu River inundated 95,000 acres (38,446 ha) of farmland around Qiongshan city.
- More than a week of heavy rain in September caused widespread flooding in Bosnia. A state of emergency was declared in several regions, and roads, power, and telephone lines were damaged.
- On September 25, Tropical Storm Isidore formed in the eastern Atlantic and strengthened. It was traveling west-northwest at about 21 MPH (34 km/h), with winds of up to 65 MPH (105 km/h), and was expected to strengthen further.
- On September 28, Typhoon Zane crossed Taiwan, triggering mudslides and killing two people. It then moved to Okinawa.
- On September 29, the Cambodian government declared a state of emergency after floods caused by heavy monsoon rains inundated 100 homes and damaged nearly 30,000 acres (12,141 ha) of farmland. The following day, floodwaters entered Phnom Penh. At least 11 people died, and the floods affected 3 million. Across the border in Laos, the floods and landslides were the worst in living memory. At least 30 people died, and rice fields and homes were devastated. By October 2, the Mekong River in Vietnam was flooding along the Cambodian border. Levels continued to rise, and by October 7, 21 people had died in Vietnam, 200,000 homes had been flooded, and more than 24,700 acres (9,996 ha) of crops had been inundated.
- Heavy rains brought flooding to Matamoros, Mexico, starting on October 4. By the following day, the city streets were under 3 feet (91 cm) of water. More than 1,500 people were made homeless in the area, and two died.
- Tropical Storm Josephine reached the Florida coast of the United States on the night of October 7, bringing winds of 70 MPH (113 km/h) and up to 5 inches (127 mm) of rain, as well as triggering tornadoes. The storm produced a storm surge of 6–9 feet (1.8–2.7 m).

1997

- Heavy rains and snowstorms caused severe flooding in California, Idaho, Nevada, Oregon, and Washington during the last week of December 1996 and the beginning of January. A state of emergency was declared in more than 90 counties, and at least 125,000 people were evacuated from their homes. At least 29 people died.
- A cold wave swept across Europe in early January, claiming at least 228 lives.

- On February 18, heavy rains caused a mudslide in southern Peru that buried the villages of Cocha and Pumaranra, killing up to 300 people.
- In late February and early March, Bolivia experienced the heaviest rains for nearly 30 years in the tropical lowlands. Approximately 100,000 farmers lost their crops, and at least 16 people were killed.
- At the same time, heavy rains caused extensive flooding along parts of the Ohio River in Indiana, Kentucky, Ohio, Tennessee, and West Virginia. Many small towns were inundated, necessitating the evacuation of thousands of people, and at least 30 people died.
- In early March, tornadoes caused widespread damage and killed at least 25 people in Arkansas.
- In early March, Cyclone Gavin caused widespread damage in Fiji and killed at least 26 people.
- Strong winds and heavy rain killed 21 people in Saudi Arabia in late March.
- In late April, heavy rains and flooding caused landslides that killed 13 people on Pohnpei Island, Federated States of Micronesia.
- On May 2, a sandstorm in Egypt killed 12 people and injured 50.
- In May, heavy rain caused flooding in Guangdong Province, China, in which 177 villages were inundated, at least 110 people died, and more than 1,300 were injured.
- A cyclone devastated coastal regions of southeastern Bangladesh on May 19. More than 600,000 homes were damaged or destroyed. At least 100 people were killed, and nearly 10,000 were injured.
- On May 27–29, several tornadoes crossed Texas from Waco to Austin, damaging about 1,000 acres (400 ha) of farmland and destroying 60 homes. Thirty people died, 27 of them in Jarrell, 40 miles (64 km) north of Austin, where on May 29 one tornado with winds of 260 MPH (418 km/h) leveled a 5-mile (8-km)-long, half-mile (800-m)-wide area.
- In late May, heavy rain caused floods in the Philippines in which at least 29 people died.
- In June, three weeks of incessant rain in central Chile caused floods in which 18 people died and 45,000 were left homeless.
- Monsoon rains from June to August caused floods and landslides in India in which at least 945 people died and crops were damaged on 3.8 million acres (1.55 million ha) of farmland.
- Between June and December, more than 500 people died in Irian Jaya, Indonesia, and at least 70 in Papua New Guinea due to famine caused by drought, frosts, and forest fires triggered by El Niño.
- On June 23, 11 people died in storms in western Ukraine and Belarus.
- Between late June and early August, central Europe suffered the worst floods in 200 years. Hundreds of thousands of people were driven from their homes as hundreds of towns were inundated, and more than 100 people died in Poland and the Czech Republic.
- At the same time, heavy rains caused floods in Myanmar in which at least 13 people died and thousands were left homeless.

- Tornadoes and thunderstorms in southern Michigan on July 2 destroyed 339 homes and businesses, killed 16 people, and injured more than 100.
- On July 5, torrential rains in northeastern Iran caused flash floods that drowned 11 people, washed away hundreds of homes, and damaged pastures and farmland.
- On July 10, rains triggered a mudslide in Izumi, Japan, that demolished a 45-foot (14-m) concrete barrier and destroyed 16 houses, killing 19 people.
- Floods in southeastern Bangladesh on July 13 killed at least 57 people and left around 250,000 homeless.
- A landslide caused by heavy rain killed more than 30 people in Guizhou Province, China, on July 18.
- July floods caused by a week of heavy rainfall devastated southern China, killing 56 people, stranding thousands more, and inflicting more than $220 million in property damage.
- In Villa Angel Flores, Mexico, a small tornado swept up toads from a nearby pond and dropped them like rain on the town on July 8.
- On August 4, Typhoon Victor, with winds up to 75 MPH (121 km/h), struck Guangdong and Fujian Provinces in southern China, killing 49 people and destroying 10,000 homes.
- Typhoon Winnie struck Taiwan, eastern China, and the Philippines on August 18–19, with winds of 92 MPH (148 km/h) and heavy rain. At least 37 people died in Taiwan, 140 in Zhejiang and Jiangsu Provinces of China, where tens of thousands of homes were destroyed, and 16 in the Philippines, where 60,000 people had to abandon their homes.
- Floods caused by storms killed 28 people in southern Thailand in late August.
- An unusually strong El Niño caused drought in Indonesia that caused seasonal fires to burn out of control in September in Sumatra, Kalimantan, and Java. Smoke covered much of southern Asia. The fires continued until spring of 1998.
- On September 27, a cyclone injured hundreds of people and killed at least 60 in Bangladesh.
- On October 8–10, Hurricane Pauline devastated Acapulco, Mexico, and many villages in the states of Oaxaca and Guerrero with winds of up to 115 MPH (185 km/h) and waves up to 30 feet (9 m), killing 217 people and leaving 20,000 homeless.
- On October 12, a tornado at Tongi, Bangladesh, killed at least 25 people who had gathered to worship on the banks of the Turag River and injured thousands.
- From mid-October to late November, torrential rain caused the worst flooding in more than 30 years in Somalia, Ethiopia, and Kenya. Crops were destroyed, more than 2,000 people died, and about 800,000 lost their homes.

- In late October, snowstorms in Colorado, Kansas, Nebraska, Missouri, Iowa, Wisconsin, and Michigan closed roads and airports and caused power failures. At least 16 people died.
- On October 31, heavy rain triggered mudslides that buried several houses in Ribeira Quente, on the island of São Miguel, in the Azores, killing at least 16 people.
- Cyclone Martin struck the Cook Islands in early November, killing at least 18 people.
- Typhoon Linda, category 1, with winds up to 75 MPH (121 km/h), struck Vietnam, Cambodia, and Thailand. Thousands of homes were destroyed. In Vietnam 464 people were killed and 3,218 were missing, and more than 20 people died in Cambodia and Thailand.
- Rain and mudslides killed 25 people in Ecuador in November and left approximately 10,000 homeless.
- At least 29 people died in eastern Uganda on November 23 when heavy rain triggered floods and landslides.
- On December 1, a storm struck about 35 villages in northern India, killing at least 44 people and injuring 100.

1998

- Powerful winds and high waves across northern Spain and southern France on January 2 caused widespread damage and killed at least 18 people.
- An unexpected cold spell killed more than 130 people in northern Bangladesh in early January.
- In January, Peru suffered its worst floods for 50 years, due to torrential rains caused by El Niño. Around 70 people were killed and 22,000 left homeless.
- On January 5–11, an ice storm in Quebec, Ontario, and New Brunswick and parts of Maine, New Hampshire, Vermont, and New York caused at least 20 deaths and left 3 million homes without power, some for more than two weeks.
- In mid-January, floods killed at least 86 people in Kenya.
- On February 23, tornadoes in central Florida killed at least 42 people, injured more than 260, and destroyed hundreds of homes.
- Flash floods in Baluchistan, Pakistan, on March 3–4 killed 300 people, with another 1,500 missing and presumed dead, and left approximately 25,000 people homeless.
- On March 20, tornadoes killed at least 14 people and injured 80 in northern Georgia, and killed two people and injured 22 in North Carolina.
- In late March, a cyclone struck several villages in West Bengal and Orissa, India, killing at least 200 people and leaving 10,000 homeless.
- In early April, floods killed 100 people in Iran.
- On April 8–9, tornadoes killed 39 people in Mississippi, Alabama, and Georgia.

- On April 16, two tornadoes killed at least 10 people in Kentucky, Tennessee, and Arkansas.
- In late April, flooding along the basin of the Paraná River in Argentina and Paraguay killed 18 people and forced about 100,000 to leave their homes.
- In May, dry conditions due to El Niño caused fires to burn out of control in Mexico. (Rural people use fire to clear the land prior to planting.) The fires covered about 1,875 square miles (4,856 km²) in the states of Oaxaca, Guerrero, Yucatán, Campeche, and Morelos. Smoke covered Mexico City and spread to the southern United States.
- In early May, a river of mud swamped the town of Sarno, Italy, killing at least 135 people.
- In late May and early June, the worst heat wave in 50 years killed at least 2,500 people in India.
- A cyclone struck southern Bangladesh on May 22, killing at least 25 people and injuring more than 100.
- In June and July, 110 people died in a heat wave in Texas.
- Flooding along the Yangtze River in China from June to August affected an estimated 230 million people, cost 3,656 lives, and caused damage estimated at $20 billion.
- On June 9, a powerful cyclone struck Gujarat, India, leaving more than 100 people missing and feared dead.
- Floods killed 21 people in Romania in mid-June.
- In late June, thunderstorms, floods, and tornadoes claimed at least 21 lives across the midwestern and eastern United States from Wisconsin to West Virginia and in the Appalachian Mountains as far north as Vermont.
- In July, at least 115 people died in floods in Uzbekistan and Kyrgyzstan.
- In July and August, floods in South Korea killed 234 people, left 91 missing, and rendered more than 121,000 homeless.
- Between mid-July and mid-September, monsoon rains in Bangladesh caused floods to cover more than two-thirds of the country. More than 30 million people were made homeless, and at least 1,000 died.
- On July 17, a tsunami destroyed several villages and killed at least 2,500 people in Papua New Guinea.
- In late July, floods in eastern Slovakia killed at least 21 people.
- In early August, a heat wave in Cyprus killed 48 people.
- In August, floods killed at least 30 people in Yemen.
- Between mid-August and early September floods and landslides in northern and eastern India killed at least 1,000 people.
- On August 23–24, flooding along the Rio Grande in southern Texas and northern Mexico left 16 people dead and more than 60 missing.
- On August 26, a mudslide enveloped several mountain villages in northern Guatemala, killing at least 25 people and forcing 4,000 from their homes.
- Typhoon Rex, category 4, with winds of up to 132 MPH (212 km/h), failed to cross any coast, but in late August it passed close to Honshu,

Japan, bringing torrential rain that caused floods and mudslides in which 13 people died, 30 were injured, and 40,000 had to leave their homes.

- In early September, floods in Chiapas, Mexico, killed at least 185 people and left some 25,000 homeless.
- The Nile River in Sudan flooded in September and October, killing at least 88 people. The floods destroyed more than 120,000 homes and left at least 200,000 people homeless.
- Hurricane Georges, category 3, struck the Caribbean and U.S. Gulf Coast on September 21–28, with torrential rain and winds of up to 120 MPH (193 km/h). At least 300 people died in the Caribbean, including 250 in the Dominican Republic and 27 in Haiti. Georges then crossed parts of Louisiana, Mississippi, Alabama, and Florida, causing four deaths.
- In late September and early October, Tropical Storm Yanni caused floods in South Korea covering one-quarter of the cropland. At least 27 people died, and 28 were missing.
- In mid-October, Typhoon Zeb struck the Philippines, Taiwan, and Japan. At its peak it reached category 4, with winds of 150 MPH (241 km/h) gusting to 184 MPH (296 km/h). It killed at least 74 people in the Philippines, 25 in Taiwan, and 12 in Japan.
- On October 17–18, heavy rain caused floods that covered one-quarter of Texas. At least 22 people were killed.
- Floods killed 52 people in central Vietnam on October 20–22.
- Hurricane Mitch struck Central America in late October. The most devastating hurricane in 200 years, on October 26 it reached category 5, with winds in excess of 155 MPH (249 km/h) and a central pressure of 906 mb. Mitch remained at category 5 for 33 hours, with sustained winds of more than 180 MPH (290 km/h) for 15 hours. The storm left more than 1.5 million people homeless. It caused 6,500 deaths in Honduras, 1,845 in Nicaragua, 239 in El Salvador, 253 in Guatemala, eight in Costa Rica, and two in Panama. In addition, 12,000 people throughout the region were missing.
- In late October, Typhoon Babs struck the Philippines, killing at least 132 people and leaving about 320,000 homeless.
- In mid-November, floods in the Carpathian Mountains destroyed approximately 30 villages in western Ukraine, killing at least 12 people and driving 8,000 from their homes.
- Cold weather in late November killed at least 71 people across Europe.
- On November 19–23, Typhoon Dawn struck central Vietnam, causing floods that forced 200,000 people to leave their homes. More than 100 people died.
- In mid-December, Tropical Storms Faith and Gil drove thousands of people from their homes in central Vietnam and killed at least 22.
- A tornado on December 15 killed at least 17 people and injured 162 at Umtata, South Africa.

1999

- In early January, blizzards in Illinois, Indiana, Iowa, Kentucky, Michigan, Minnesota, Missouri, Nebraska, Ohio, and Wisconsin killed at least 50 people.
- In mid-January, tornadoes killed eight people in Tennessee and at least six in Arkansas .
- In early February, flash floods killed at least 20 people in the southern Philippines.
- In March, the worst flooding in 40 years destroyed more than 39,500 acres (16,000 ha) of crops in Inhambane Province, Mozambique. Approximately 70,000 people were displaced, and 32 died.
- In mid-April, a heat wave killed at least 40 people in India.
- Tornadoes in Oklahoma and southern Kansas on May 3 killed 44 people, injured more than 500, and destroyed more than 1,500 buildings.
- On May 20, a cyclone struck coastal areas of Thatta and Badin, Pakistan, causing extensive flooding. More than 50,000 people were left homeless, 128 were killed, and 1,000 were missing.
- Floods covering one-tenth of Bangladesh in June and July destroyed more than 133,000 acres (54,000 ha) of crops, and at least 24 people died.
- The Yangtze River in China flooded in late June and July, causing at least 240 deaths.
- At the same time, floods affected more than 2,000 villages in Bihar, India. At least 125 people died, and the damage was estimated at more than $10 million.
- On July 8, two mudslides in Tajikistan killed at least 23 people near Leninabad and five near Jirgital.
- A heat wave in late July and August caused drought in the midwestern and eastern United States, killing at least 500 people and causing more than $1 billion in damage.
- In early August, heavy rain from Typhoon Olga, category 1, caused floods and landslides in the Philippines in which more than 111 people died and about 80,000 were left homeless. Olga crossed South Korea on August 2–4, causing floods that inundated about 86,500 acres (35,000 ha) of cropland. The floods left 31 people dead, 21 missing, and 20,000 homeless.
- Hurricane Floyd formed on September 7 and struck the eastern United States from September 15–17, causing floods and damage in North Carolina, Virginia, Pennsylvania, and New Jersey. At its peak Floyd reached category 4, with winds of 145 MPH (233 km/h). Many towns were flooded, 4 million people were evacuated, and 74 died.
- Typhoon Bart, category 5, with winds of 160 MPH (257 km/h), struck Japan on September 24, killing at least 26 people in Honshu. It also triggered a tornado that injured about 350 people in the town of Toyohashi.
- In early October, floods along the Gulf Coast and through the southern states of Mexico cost at least 222 lives.

- In late October and early November, storms in Vietnam caused floods in which at least 488 people died.
- At the same time, a cyclone struck Orissa, India, destroying many villages and causing widespread flooding. A total of 9,463 people died, and a further 8,000 were missing.
- In mid-November, storms caused floods and mudslides in southwestern France in which at least 27 people lost their lives.
- In early December, floods in central Vietnam cost 114 lives.
- Torrential rains caused flash floods in Durban and Pinetown, South Africa, on December 22–24, leaving 20 people dead and thousands homeless.
- In mid- /to late December, northern Venezuela experienced the worst floods for a century, triggering mudslides that destroyed many towns, including the city of Carmen de Uria. As many as 50,000 people may have been killed.
- Two waves of storms crossing western Europe from December 25–28 killed at least 136 people.

2000

- In early January, a cold wave crossed the Gangetic Plain in India, killing 341 people.
- At the same time, floods and landslides in southeastern Brazil killed at least 28 people and left many thousands homeless.
- A heat wave in Australia on January 20–23 killed 22 people.
- The worst floods for 40 years affected southern Africa from late January to mid-March. In Mozambique, the country most severely hit, about 200,000 homes were destroyed. On February 22, Cyclone Eline, category 5, struck Mozambique with winds of up to 162 MPH (260 km/h). Eline then moved to Madagascar. Tropical Storm Gloria also struck Madagascar, on March 4–5. In all, 492 people died in Mozambique with many more missing, at least 137 died in Madagascar and about 500,000 were left homeless, and at least 70 people died in northern South Africa. Thousands of people were also left homeless in Zimbabwe, Namibia, and Botswana.
- On February 14, tornadoes in Georgia killed 18 people, injured more than 100, and caused widespread damage.
- In mid-May, floods in West Timor, Indonesia, killed at least 140 people and left 20,000 homeless.
- On May 21, at least 21 people died in floods and mudslides in southern Colombia.
- In mid-June, floods triggered by monsoon rains killed at least 20 people in Assam and Arunachal Pradesh, India.
- A heat wave in early July killed more than 50 people in southeastern Europe.

- A heat wave and drought lasting from spring to summer caused about 140 deaths in the south-central and southeastern United States and caused more than $4 billion in damage.
- At the same time, fires fed by drought and driven by high winds damaged nearly 7 million acres (2.8 million ha) in the western United States and caused more than $2 billion in damage.
- A landslide caused by heavy rain destroyed a slum settlement near Mumbai (Bombay), India, on July 12, killing at least 80 people.
- On July 13, a mudslide in Shaanxi Province, China, buried many houses, killing at least 119 people.
- Heavy rain in mid-July caused floods in which around 140 people died in Maharashtra, Gujarat, and Andhra Pradesh, India.
- In late July and early August, torrential rain in northeastern Brazil caused mudslides in which at least 56 people died. More than 100,000 were forced from their homes.
- Between late July and early October, the worst flooding for 40 years occurred in the Mekong Delta of Vietnam, Laos, and Cambodia. At least 315 died.
- On August 22, Tropical Storm Kaemi killed 14 people in Vietnam.
- On August 22–24, floods in Andhra Pradesh, India, killed at least 70 people.
- On August 23, Typhoon Bilis, category 5, with winds of up to 156 MPH (251 km/h), struck Taiwan, killing 11 people, injuring 80, and causing crop damage estimated at $48 million.
- Typhoon Maria struck Guangdong and Hunan Provinces of southern China on September 1, killing at least 47 people and causing $223 million in damage.
- In September and October, monsoon rains caused floods in West Bengal, India, in which more than 900 people died, and in Bangladesh, where about 150 people died and about 5 million were left homeless.
- On September 10, flash floods in southern Italy triggered a mudslide that destroyed a campsite, killing 11 people and leaving four missing and feared dead.
- In mid-September, at least 19 people died in floods and mudslides in Guatemala.
- In mid-October, floods and landslides killed at least 35 people in the Italian and Swiss Alps.
- Monsoon rains caused floods in southeast Asia in late October and November. At least 119 people were killed in Indonesia, 51 in Malaysia, and about 20 in Thailand.
- On November 1–2, Typhoon Xangsane struck Taiwan with winds of 90 MPH (145 km/h), killing at least 58 people, with 31 left missing, and causing more than $2 billion in damage.
- On November 3, floods in the northern Philippines triggered by Typhoon Bebinca killed at least 40 people, with 13 left missing.
- Floods in early December killed at least 30 people in northern Tanzania and left more than 600 homeless.

2001

- From December 31 to January 2, a blizzard in Inner Mongolia, China, followed by freezing weather throughout January, affected 1,640,000 people. At least 39 people and more than 200,000 head of livestock died.
- On January 18, heavy rains triggered a landslide in western Tanzania that destroyed 30 homes in a fishing village. At least 15 people were killed or missing and feared dead.
- From January 20 until late March, heavy rains over the area drained by the Zambezi River caused flooding in Zambia, Zimbabwe, Malawi, and Mozambique. At least 80 people died, and hundreds of thousands were displaced.
- Snow up to 6 feet (1.8 m) deep buried several villages in Khuzistan Province of western Iran on January 30; 28 people who ventured out in search of food were missing and feared dead.
- In early February, heavy rains caused floods and landslides in West Java Province of Indonesia in which at least 94 people died.
- At the same time, more than 500 refugees in refugee camps in Herāt Province, Afghanistan, died of cold.
- Hailstorms and tornadoes over six days in April killed at least three people and caused damage costing at least $1.7 billion in Texas, Oklahoma, Kansas, Nebraska, Iowa, Missouri, Illinois, Indiana, Wisconsin, Michigan, Ohio, Kentucky, West Virginia, and Pennsylvania.
- On May 1, a landslide in southwestern China, caused by heavy rain, made a nine-story apartment building collapse, killing at least 65 people.
- On May 6–7, floods in Tazeh-Qalel, Iran, killed at least 32 people and injured 50.
- On May 9, at least 17 people died in a storm in Bihar, India; some were killed when trees crashed onto their homes.
- Storms and landslides in Bangladesh on May 11 killed at least 31 people and injured about 500.
- Rains and floods in Haiti killed at least 21 people in mid-May.
- On June 6–17, Tropical Storm Allison caused extensive damage, estimated at $5 billion, in the southern and eastern United States. At least 20 people were killed in Texas, two in Louisiana, nine each in Florida and North Carolina, one in Virginia, and six in Pennsylvania.
- On June 23–24, Typhoon Chebi struck Taiwan and Fujian Province, China, killing nine people in Taiwan and at least 73 in Fujian, where a further 87 were missing and feared dead.
- At least 30 people died on June 27 in floods at Limbe, Cameroon.
- In early July, Typhoon Utor killed one person in Taiwan, at least 121 people in the Philippines, and 23 in Guangdong Province, China.
- On July 15, a tropical storm caused floods and landslides in South Korea in which at least 40 people died and 14 were missing. About 34,000 homes were flooded in and around Seoul.

- Monsoon rains triggered flash floods on July 23 in Mansehra, Swat, and Buner districts of Pakistan. Hundreds of homes were destroyed, and at least 150 people were killed.
- Thunderstorms and floods caused widespread damage in southeastern Poland in late July. At least 26 people died when the Vistula River overflowed.
- On July 30, Typhoon Toraji caused floods and landslides in Hualien and Nantou Provinces, Taiwan, in which 77 people died and 133 were missing and presumed dead.
- On August 1, torrential rains triggered floods and landslides on Nias Island, Indonesia. More than 70 people were killed, and at least 100 were missing.
- From August 10 to 12, northeastern Iran suffered the worst floods in 200 years. Some 10,000 people were displaced, 181 died, at least 168 were missing, and the cost of damage was estimated as $25 million.
- Flash floods on August 11 killed approximately 86 people in Phetchabun Province, Thailand.
- In late August, floods killed at least 28 people in Nepal.
- From September 16 to 19, Typhoon Nari caused floods, mudslides, and extensive damage in Taiwan, killing at least 94 people.
- Hurricane Iris struck southern Belize on October 8–9, destroying at least 3,000 houses, leaving 12,000 people homeless, and killing 22.
- A storm in southern India killed at least 31 people on October 17.
- On November 7, Tropical Storm Lingling struck the Philippines with winds up to 56 MPH (90 km/h), killing at least 68 people.
- Torrential rain caused flooding in northern Algeria on November 9–17 in which 750 people died and at least 1,500 homes were destroyed, leaving about 24,000 people homeless.
- In late December, at least 52 people died, more than 30 were missing, and about 2,000 were forced from their homes when rains and mudslides struck Rio de Janeiro State, Brazil.

2002

- In January, heavy rain and extremely cold weather in Mauritania killed at least 25 people.
- In late January, winds swept across northern Europe with speeds of nearly 124 MPH (200 km/h). Eight people died in Britain, three in Germany, and four in Poland.
- Prolonged heavy rain triggered landslides and floods in February on Java in Indonesia. At least 150 people were killed.
- On February 19, the most destructive storm in the city's history struck La Paz, Bolivia, causing flash floods and mud slides in which 69 people died, at least 100 were injured, and hundreds were rendered homeless.
- Between May 9 and May 15, at least 1,030 people died during a heat wave in Andhra Pradesh, India.

- In early June, a heat wave in northeastern Nigeria killed more than 60 people in the city of Maiduguri in Borno State.
- In early June, at least 205 people died in floods across northwestern China. The worst-affected area was south of the city of Xian, where 20 inches (508 mm) of rain fell in two days.
- In June floods, inundated about 70 villages in the Stavropol and Krasnodar regions of southern Russia and in the republics of Karachay-Cherkessia, North Ossetia, Ingushetia, and Chechnya. At least 53 people died, and 75,000 were made homeless.
- Between June and mid-August, monsoon rains caused flooding in parts of Nepal, India, and Bangladesh. At least 422 people died and thousands were made homeless in Nepal, nearly 400 died in India and about 15 million were rendered homeless in Bihar and Assam States, and at least 157 people died in Bangladesh and about 6 million were made homeless.
- On June 4–5, the Zeyzoun Dam, near the town of Hama in northwestern Syria, collapsed following weeks of heavy rain. Several villages were flooded, and at least 28 people lost their lives.
- In July, a heat wave in Algeria brought temperatures up to 133°F (56°C), the highest in 50 years, causing at least 50 deaths.
- In July, Typhoon Chata'an killed five people and caused widespread flooding in Japan.
- In mid-July, at least 59 people died during a cold spell in southeastern Peru.
- On July 19, a storm with hailstones the size of eggs killed 16 people and injured about 200 in Henan Province of China.
- On July 21 and 22, up to 3.3 feet (1 m) of snow fell during storms affecting parts of Eastern Cape and KwaZulu/Natal Provinces of South Africa, killing 22 people and causing widespread damage to buildings.
- Torrential rains during August triggered landslides and floods across southern China in which at least 133 people died and more than 100 million were affected.
- On August 7, a mud slide destroyed about 56 homes and killed at least 20 people in the village of Dasht in the Gorno-Badakhshan region of Tajikistan.
- In mid-August, monsoon rains triggered floods that killed nearly 900 people in Nepal, India, and Bangladesh.
- In August, the Elbe, Danube, and Vltava Rivers in central Europe overflowed, causing extensive flooding in Austria, Germany, Romania, Russia, and the Czech Republic. At least 88 people died, and hundreds of thousands were driven from their homes. The cities of Prague, Dresden, Munich, Chemnitz, and Leipzig were badly affected, and flooding was also severe around the German town of Wittenberg.
- On August 31 and September 1, Typhoon Rusa, with winds of up to 124 MPH (200 km/h), killed more than 180 people in South Korea and caused damage costing more than $1 billion.
- On September 12, a landslide that followed heavy rain buried the village of El Porvenir, Guatemala, killing 26 people.

- In mid-September, several days of heavy rain in the Sommières region of France caused floods in which 23 people died.
- Hurricane Lili caused seven deaths and extensive damage in Jamaica and St. Vincent and tore roofs from buildings in the Cayman Islands in late September and early October. More than 120,000 people were evacuated in Cuba. It struck the Louisiana coast on the western side of Vermilion Bay on October 2 with winds of 90 MPH (145 km/h).
- Typhoon Higos struck Japan on October 2, passing across Tokyo and then moving north to Hokkaido. It caused widespread flooding and at least four deaths.
- On October 26 and 27, gales with winds exceeding 90 MPH (145 km/h) crossed the United Kingdom and northwestern Europe, killing seven people in Britain, six in France, at least 10 in Germany, five in Belgium, four in the Netherlands, and one in Denmark. The highest wind speed recorded was 96.6 MPH (155 km/h) at the Mumbles, a town in south Wales.
- A severe storm crossed the coastal waters of West Bengal, India, and Bangladesh on November 13, killing at least 39 people.
- Between November 9 and November 11, a storm front crossed the southeastern and midwestern United States, producing nearly 90 tornadoes that caused destruction from the Gulf of Mexico to the Great Lakes. The death toll was 17 in Tennessee, 12 in Alabama, five in Ohio, and one each in Mississippi and Pennsylvania. More than 200 people were injured.
- On November 24, the Bengueribi River in Morocco overflowed near the town of Berrechid, causing flash floods in which more than 30 people died.
- On the same day, 10 members of the Christian Vapostori sect were killed by lightning while worshiping outdoors near Harare, Zimbabwe, during a storm. Members of the sect do not worship in churches.
- Ice storms struck North and South Carolina on December 4–5, causing power outages that left 1.8 million people without electricity. At least 22 people died.
- On December 8–9, mud slides caused by torrential rain buried many houses in Angra dos Reis, Brazil, killing at least 34 people.
- On December 9, Typhoon Pongsona, category 4, with winds up to 150 MPH (250 km/h), struck Guam and the Mariana Islands.
- A snowstorm in late December covered much of the eastern United State with up to 2 feet (60 cm) of snow and caused at least 18 deaths, most due to traffic accidents.
- Cold weather in late December killed at least 100 people in northern Bangladesh.
- Cyclone Zoe, category 5, with winds up to 220 MPH (350 km/h), struck the Solomon Islands on December 28, causing devastation on the islands of Tikopia and Anuta.

2003

- In January, Cyclone Ami, category 3, struck Fiji with winds up to 125 MPH (200 km/h) and waves up to 98 feet (30 m) high, killing 11 people.
- Severe January weather in Russia, with temperatures down to −35°F (−37° C) in Moscow and −54°F (−48°C) in Murmansk, caused many heating systems to break down. Between October and January 9, the harsh winter claimed at least 240 lives, and 40 ships were trapped in ice in the Gulf of Finland, near St. Petersburg.
- In late January, bitterly cold temperatures affected most of the United States, with strong winds and heavy snow.
- In mid-February, a series of storms brought torrential rain and record falls of snow to Washington, D.C., Baltimore, Philadelphia, New York City, and Boston.
- On February 19, the President's Day storm brought record snowfalls across the eastern United States from New England and New York as far south as Virginia.
- On March 18–20, a blizzard swept through Colorado, dropping up to 7 feet (2 m) of snow in the mountains and bringing 60–70 inches (1.5–1.8 m) of snow to parts of Boulder and Jefferson Counties. More than 200 buildings collapsed in the Denver area.
- On April 21, a spring storm struck Southern California, bringing snow to the high ground—and down to 2,000 feet (610 m) in some areas—and heavy rain to lower ground. The storm caused traffic accidents in which at least four people died.
- Shortly before midnight on April 22, a storm swept through the Dhubri district in the west of Assam State, India. Hundreds of mud and thatch houses collapsed, roofs were torn from government buildings, electricity poles were brought down, and trees were uprooted. At least 30 people were killed and 300 injured. Most victims died when their houses collapsed, but some were electrocuted by wires from fallen poles.
- Monsoon rains arrived in Southern India on June 8, ending the heat wave that had killed more than 1,400 people in the preceding three weeks.
- On June 24, hailstorms and tornadoes struck Nebraska, killing one man. The storms destroyed four homes and seriously damaged at least 100, as well as 25 businesses. A hailstone that fell in Aurora measured 6.5 inches (16.5 cm) in diameter, only slightly smaller than the largest ever recorded in the U.S., at Coffeyville, Kansas, in 1970.
- On July 26, Typhoon Imbudo struck Guangdong Province and the Guangxi region, China, killing at least 20 people.
- Monsoon floods claimed more than 700 lives in India in June and July.
- A tornado damaged or destroyed about 500 homes in Palm Beach County, Florida, on August 8.
- A heat wave gripped western Europe for the first two weeks of August, with temperatures of more than 104°F (40°C), triggering severe wildfires in Spain and Portugal and causing thousands of deaths.

A CHRONOLOGY OF DISCOVERY

ca. 340 B.C.E.

- Aristotle wrote *Meteorologica*, the oldest description of weather phenomena known, and quite possibly the first. It consisted of observations of weather and attempts to explain how they happen and also gave us our word *meteorology* (literally, "discourse on lofty matters"). Aristotle drew on Egyptian, Babylonian, and other sources. He held that weather phenomena occur in the region between the Earth and the Moon and were produced by interactions among the elements composing this region: earth, air, fire, and water.

  Aristotle (384–322 B.C.E.) was a Macedonian who traveled to Athens when he was 17 and studied under Plato. After Plato's death in 347 B.C.E., Aristotle left Athens and traveled widely, spending several years as tutor to Alexander, then a teenager but later to be known as Alexander the Great. Aristotle wrote on many topics but was especially renowned for his scientific work. He emphasized the importance of learning from nature by observation and made many meticulously detailed studies.

140–131 B.C.E.

- In China, Han Ying wrote *Moral discourses illustrating the Han text of the "Book of Songs."* This contained the first known reference to the hexagonal (six sided) structure of snowflakes.

First century B.C.E.

- The octagonal Tower of Winds (or *horologion*) was built in Athens. Designed by Andronicus of Cyrrhus (flourished ca. 100 B.C.E.), the tower was topped by a wind vane representing Triton, a sea god, which pointed toward one or another of eight demigods depicted at the top of its walls. Each of the demigods was associated with particular weather conditions, so the tower indicated the kind of weather people should expect according to the direction of the wind. It was possibly the world's first attempt at weather forecasting. Each side also bore a sundial, so the tower was also a public timepiece.

ca. 55 B.C.E.

- Lucretius proposed that thunder is the sound of great clouds crashing against one another. He was mistaken but may have been the first person to note that thunder occurs only in the presence of large, solid-looking clouds.

Titus Lucretius Carus (ca. 94–55 B.C.E.) was a Roman philosopher and poet. Only one of his works has survived, *De Rerum Natura* ("On the Nature of Things"). He died before completing his final revisions to it. In *De Rerum Natura* Lucretius described in verse form the ideas of the Greek philosopher Epicurus (ca. 342–270 B.C.E.), holding that all matter is composed of arrangements of atoms of varying sizes.

First century C.E.

- Hero of Alexandria wrote a book, *Pneumatica*, in which he demonstrated that air is a substance. He did this by showing that if a vessel is filled with air, water will not enter it unless the air is allowed to escape. It was already known that air can be compressed. Hero argued that this proved air must be made of tiny particles with space between them, so compression made the particles move closer together.

  Hero (or Heron, ca. 60 C.E.) is sometimes described as a Greek engineer and at other times as an Egyptian scientist. He was a talented mathematician and great experimenter, and his writings suggest he taught what we would now call physics. He described many devices, some of which he probably invented. These included coin-operated machines and an "engine" consisting of a hollow sphere containing water with two tubes emerging from it. The tubes were bent and pointed in opposite directions. When the sphere was heated, the water boiled, and steam discharging from the tubes made the device spin rapidly. Hero was also responsible for promoting the idea (brought to the West by the Greek astronomer Hipparchus [flourished 146–127 B.C.E.]) of dividing the circle into 360 degrees.
- The Greek philosopher Theophrastus (371 or 370–288 or 287 B.C.E.) attempted to classify clouds, describing them as "streaks" and "like fleeces of wool."

  Theophrastus was born on the island of Eresus. He studied under Plato in Athens and later under Aristotle, succeeding Aristotle as head of the Lyceum (the academy founded by Aristotle) in 323 B.C.E. He wrote more than 200 books on many subjects, but was best known as the founder of botany.

1555

- Olaus Magnus published, in Rome, a book on natural history containing the first known European depictions of ice crystals and snowflakes.

  Olaus Magnus was the Latinized name of Olaf Mansson (1490–1557), a Swedish priest born at Linköping. In 1523 he traveled to Rome and later lived in Danzig and then Italy with his brother, Archbishop Johannes Magnus (1488–1544). After his brother's death,

Mansson was made archbishop of Sweden. He compiled a detailed map of Scandinavia and wrote a history of its peoples, which became very famous. Translated into English as *History of the Goths, Swedes and Vandals* (1658), it provided the descriptions on which other Europeans continued for many years to base their ideas about Scandinavian people and countryside.

1586

- Simon Stevinus showed that the pressure a liquid exerts on a surface depends on the height of the liquid above the surface and the area of the surface on which it presses, but does not depend on the shape of the vessel containing it.

  Simon Stevin (1548–1620) was a Flemish mathematician born in Bruges. (Stevinus was the Latinized version of his name.) He died in either The Hague or Leiden. While serving as a quartermaster in the Dutch army he devised a system of sluices in the dikes protecting the reclaimed polders (fields lying below sea level and protected by waterproof banks called dykes). He also introduced decimal fractions (that is, representing ½ as 0.5, for example) to mathematics. In the same year that he made his discovery about water, Stevin performed an experiment in which he dropped two different weights at the same time and found they reached the ground together. This experiment is usually attributed to his younger contemporary Galileo (see 1593).

1591

- Thomas Harriot (or Hariot) noted that snowflakes are either six-sided or six-pointed. He did not publish his observation, however but described it in the long correspondence he had with Johannes Kepler (see 1611).

  Thomas Harriot (1560–1621) was an English mathematician born and educated at Oxford. He was scientific adviser to Sir Walter Raleigh on his expedition to Roanoke, Virginia, in 1585–86, about which Harriot wrote *A Briefe and True Report of the New Foundland of Virginia* (published in 1588). Harriot had a special interest in astronomy and was one of several observers who discovered sunspots at about the same time in 1611, but he also made important contributions to the development of algebra.

1593

- Galileo invented an "air thermoscope" to measure temperature (see the illustration on page 11). It was based on the expansion and contraction of a gas in response to changing temperatures and was highly inaccurate, because it failed to allow for the expansion and contraction of air due to changes in pressure. Nevertheless, it was the first attempt at making a thermometer, and it remained in use for about 10 years.

Galileo Galilei (1564–1642), popularly known by his first name only, was one of the greatest scientists who ever lived. He was born in Pisa, Italy, the son of a mathematician, who sent him to study medicine. In those days (and still!) a physician earned a great deal more than a mathematician. While a student, Galileo heard a lecture on geometry and persuaded his father to allow him to study mathematics and science instead of medicine.

Whereas other scientists of his day were prepared to observe natural phenomena, Galileo tried to measure them. He believed that by attaching quantities to phenomena, mathematical relationships would appear that would allow them to be described simply and in ways applicable to a range of similar phenomena. This was his principal scientific innovation and the idea from which his many achievements in astronomy and physics sprang.

Galileo spent the last eight years of his life, from 1633, under house arrest at his small estate at Arcetri, near Florence, following his conviction for heresy by the Inquisition. The story of his trial and the events leading up to it is complicated, but the matter centered on his book *Dialogo dei Massimi Sistemi* ("Dialogue on the Two Chief World Systems"). In this work, two fictional characters debate the astronomical systems of Ptolemy (holding that the Earth is at the center of the universe) and Copernicus (holding that the Sun is at the center of the universe). Galileo made it clear that the Copernican system was superior, and the character opposing it appeared foolish. It was alleged that Galileo had been expressly forbidden to publicly support the Copernican view, the church having declared it to be false. Galileo died at Arcetri.

1611

• Johannes Kepler published *A New Year's Gift, or On the Six-cornered Snowflake*, in which he described snowflakes.

Johannes Kepler (1571–1630) was a German astronomer born at Weil, in Württemberg. He was the son of professional soldier. In 1594 he became professor of mathematics at the University of Graz, Austria, but was forced to leave in 1600 because of religious persecution. He and his wife moved to Prague, where he took up the post of assistant to the Danish astronomer Tycho Brahe (1546–1601). After Brahe's death in 1602, Kepler had access to the observations Brahe had been accumulating for many years. From these, Kepler calculated that planetary orbits are elliptical, with the Sun at one focus, and, further, that if a line is drawn from any planet to the Sun, the area it sweeps out in any given time is always the same, and that the time taken for a planet to complete one orbit is proportional to the cube of its mean distance from the Sun. These are known as Kepler's three laws of planetary motion. Kepler was also an eminent mathematician whose studies prepared the way for the infinitesimal calculus. In 1628 he and his family (his first wife had died and he had remarried) moved to Silesia. He died at Regensburg, Bavaria.

1641

- Ferdinand II, the grand duke of Tuscany, invented a thermometer in the form of a tube containing liquid and sealed at one end. Also see below, 1654 and 1657.

  Ferdinand (1610–70) was the son of Cosimo II and a member of the Medici family. He lacked the political power to prevent the trial of Galileo before the Inquisition but took a keen interest in science generally.

1643

- Torricelli invented the mercury barometer by sealing one end of a glass tube 4 feet (1.2 m) long, filling the tube with mercury, then inverting the tube with its open end immersed in a bath of mercury. He found the mercury fell to a height of about 30 inches (76.2 cm). This is the reading representing average sea-level atmospheric pressure, nowadays described as about 1,000 millibars (mb). Torricelli was investigating a problem put to him by Galileo: Why can a suction pump raise a column of water no higher than about 33 feet (10 m)? Torricelli thought the weight of air pressing down on the exposed surface of the water might exert sufficient pressure to make water rise this high, but no higher, in a tube from which the air had been evacuated. This is the theory his experiment tested, using mercury rather than water. Subsequently he noticed the level of the mercury varied from day to day and interpreted this (correctly) as being due to variations in air pressure.

  Evangelista Torricelli (1608–47) was born at Faenza, Italy, and studied mathematics in Rome. In 1638 he read works by Galileo Galilei (1564–1642) and was inspired to write a treatise developing some of Galileo's ideas. Torricelli's tutor, a former student of Galileo, sent the treatise to Galileo, who read it and invited the young man to visit him. The two met, and Torricelli became an assistant to Galileo, who was then blind, for the last three months of his life. In making his barometer, Torricelli also produced the first artificial vacuum, the space above the mercury in the tube being quite empty except for a small amount of mercury vapor.

1646

- The French physicist Blaise Pascal demonstrated that the pressure exerted by the weight of overlying air decreases with increasing altitude. He suggested that the atmosphere is like an ocean and that climbing to

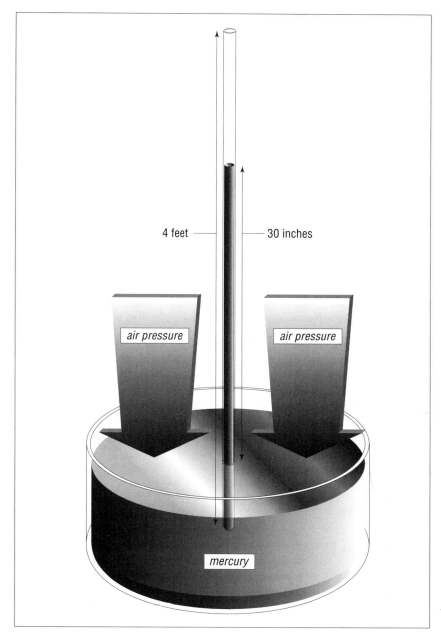

4 feet — 30 inches

air pressure   *air pressure*

mercury

Torricelli's barometer. This drawing shows how the barometer worked. Torricelli was trying to discover why a suction pump can raise water only to a certain height.

greater heights is like ascending toward the surface. (In fact, the atmosphere has no clearly defined surface resembling the surface of the sea.)

Pascal was chronically sick with indigestion and insomnia and unable to climb a mountain himself, so he asked his healthy brother-in-law, Florin Périer, to climb the Puy-de-Dôme, an extinct volcano 4,806 feet

(1,465 m) high, in the Auvergnes region of France, not far from Cler-mont-Ferrand, where Pascal was born. Périer carried one barometer, and a second barometer remained at the foot of the mountain. The mercury level Périer recorded at the summit was 3 inches (76 mm) lower than the reading on the instrument at the foot. This proved that atmospheric pressure decreases with height.

Blaise Pascal (1623–62) was famous as a mathematician and philosopher as well as a physicist. When he was 19 he invented a cal-culating machine that performed additions and subtractions. The com-puter programming language Pascal is named for him in recognition of his invention of this forerunner of the computer. He was one of the founders of the theory of probability, which forms the basis of statistics. In recognition of his work on the effects of pressure on liquids and gases, the international unit of pressure or stress is called the pascal (Pa), equal to a force of one newton per square meter. In the year of the climb up the Puy-de-Dôme, Pascal turned to the Jansenist sect of Roman Catholicism. From that time he became increasingly devout and devoted the remaining years of his life to meditation and writing on religion.

1654

• Ferdinand II, grand duke of Tuscany (see 1641), improved on his ther-mometer, providing the model that would lead in 1714 to the mercury thermometer invented by Gabriel Fahrenheit.

1657

• Ferdinand II, grand duke of Tuscany (see 1641), and his brother Leopold founded the Accademia del Cimento (Academy of Experi-ments) in Florence. This was the forerunner of all other scientific acad-emies. Members of the Accademia took a particular interest in studying the atmosphere.

In the same year, Ferdinand also made one of the earliest accurate hygrometers (for measuring atmospheric humidity). This comprised a vessel supported in a stand above a funnel and calibrated collecting jar. When the vessel was filled with ice, water condensed from the air onto the outside and ran to the bottom, falling through the funnel and into the jar, from which the humidity of the air could be read. The picture of a replica of Ferdinand's hygrometer shows how it worked.

1660

• Robert Boyle published *New Experiments Physico-Mechanical Touching the Spring of Air and Its Effects*. In this he reported that not only can air be compressed, but also that the amount by which it is compressed varies with pressure in a simple way: pv = a constant, where p is pressure and v is volume. This is now known in Britain and North America as Boyle's law, but in France the discovery is attributed to Edmé Mariotte (1620–84) and known as Mariotte's law. The most important conclusion from Boyle's experiment was that since air is compressible it must consist of individual particles separated by empty space, an idea first expressed by Hero of Alexandria (see first century C.E.).

Robert Boyle (1627–91), the Irish chemist and physicist, was the 14th child (and seventh son) of the earl of Cork and was born at Lismore Castle, in Ireland. He was an infant prodigy. By the age of 14 he was studying the work of Galileo. Later he did much to transform alchemy into chemistry, then separated chemistry from medicine and established it as a scientific discipline in its own right. He was a founder member of the Royal Society of London and in 1680 was elected its president, but

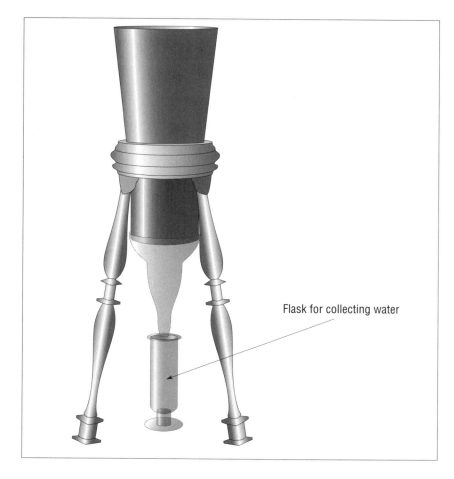

Flask for collecting water

Ferdinand's hygrometer. The vessel was filled with ice. Water condensed onto the outside and trickled down into the measuring jar. This picture is of a reproduction of the original instrument.

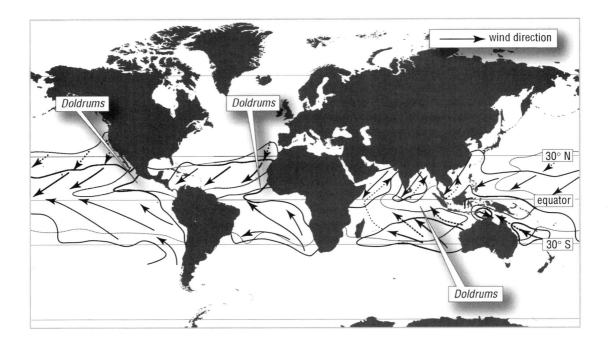

Trade winds and the doldrums. The map shows the direction of the trade winds and the location of the doldrums, where the wind is usually very light.

declined because of his scruples about taking the necessary oath. He was a devout man who wrote essays on religion and financed missionary work in Asia. He died in London.

1665

• Robert Hooke published *Micrographia*, which included illustrations of snowflakes he had observed under the microscope and descriptions of their crystal structure.

Robert Hooke (1635–1703) was an English physicist and in his day was unrivaled as an inventor of instruments. He also improved instruments that already existed. One of these was the barometer, and by demonstrating that the height of the mercury changed before a storm he suggested the possibility of using a barometer to forecast the weather. It was he who first labeled a barometer with the words "change," "rain," "much rain," "stormy," "fair," "set fair," and "very dry." He was fascinated by microscopy and devised a compound microscope (he did not invent it). As well as describing snowflakes, *Micrographia* contained his beautiful drawings of insects, fish scales, feathers, and the structure of cork, which he found contained countless tiny holes. He called these "cells," a word that has remained in use.

Hooke was a close friend of Robert Boyle (see 1660). He was born at Freshwater, Isle of Wright, and died in London.

1686

• Edmund Halley proposed that air is heated more strongly at the equator than elsewhere. The warmed air rises and is replaced at the surface by cooler air flowing toward the equator. Halley was attempting to explain the direction and reliability of the trade winds that blow on either side of the equator, from the northeast in the Northern Hemisphere and from the southeast in the Southern Hemisphere. The map shows the trade wind belt and also the doldrums, which are places where winds are light and variable and sailing ships could be becalmed for long periods. The doldrums are found close to where the trade winds from both hemispheres converge and air rises.

  Edmund Halley (1656–1742) was known mainly as an astronomer. After the "Great Comet" was seen, in 1680, he calculated its orbit (and that of 23 other comets) and predicted it would return in 1758. It did. The comet now bears his name. In 1720 he was appointed Astronomer Royal. His interests were very wide, however, and his explanation of the trade winds formed part of the first-ever map of surface winds over the whole world. He also found a relationship between height and air pressure. Halley was born in London and died at Greenwich, England.

1687

• Guillaume Amontons invented a new type of hygrometer to measure humidity.

  Guillaume Amontons (1663–1705) was born and died in Paris. He became profoundly deaf in his teens and remained so for the rest of his life. Far from regarding this as a disability, however, he believed it allowed him to concentrate more intently on the scientific work that really interested him.

1688

• Guillaume Amontons (see 1687) invented an optical telegraph, which he believed might be of use to deaf persons, and demonstrated it before the king. It worked by writing letters of the alphabet on the sails of windmills. As the windmill turned, the sequence of letters spelled out a coded message that could be seen by an observer with a telescope at another windmill, some distance away, who copied the message onto the sails of that windmill. In this way, Amontons claimed, a message could be sent all the way across France in a matter of three or four hours.

1695

• Guillaume Amontons (see 1687) made a barometer that did not require a reservoir of mercury and that therefore could be used at sea. Readings from a mercury barometer were inaccurate at sea because the movements of the ship made the level of the liquid rise and fall in the reservoir.

In the same year, Amontons improved on Galileo's air thermoscope (see 1593). His thermometer used the expansion and contraction of air in a tube to alter the level of mercury. This instrument was more accurate than Galileo's, and Amontons was able to demonstrate that water always boils at the same temperature.

1714

- Daniel Fahrenheit invented the mercury thermometer. Alcohol and alcohol–water thermometers already existed but were inaccurate and unreliable, although Fahrenheit improved them, and the low boiling point of alcohol meant they could not be used to measure higher temperatures. He also devised for his thermometer the scale that still bears his name. This took as zero the lowest temperature that can be reached with a mixture of ice and salt. He marked 96 divisions above that (first 12 divisions, then each of these subdivided into eight) to reach the blood temperature of a healthy person. On this scale, the freezing point of pure water falls at 32°. He extended it to the boiling point of pure water, adjusting his scale to make this fall at precisely 212°, the effect of the adjustment being to alter the human body temperature to 98.6°. His thermometer and its scale quickly became popular, and the scale remains in use in some countries, although it has been superseded by the Kelvin scale for scientific work. Having 180 divisions between the freezing and boiling temperatures of water, the Fahrenheit scale permits finer whole-number measurements than the Celsius scale, which has only 100 divisions.

  Daniel Gabriel (or Gabriel Daniel) Fahrenheit (1686–1736) was born in Danzig, Germany (now Gdansk, Poland), and moved to Amsterdam in 1701 in order to learn a trade. He became interested in making scientific instruments and in about 1707 left the Netherlands on a tour of Europe to meet scientists and other instrument makers. He returned to Amsterdam in 1717, set up his own instrument-making business, and remained in that city for the rest of his life. He described his method for making thermometers in a paper he submitted to the *Philosophical Transactions of the Royal Society* in 1724, and he was elected to the Royal Society the same year. He died in The Hague.

1735

- George Hadley proposed that the rotation of the Earth causes winds flowing toward the equator to be swung, so they blow from an easterly direction, northeast in the Northern Hemisphere and southeast in the Southern. He believed air warmed at the equator rises and moves at a great height all the way to the poles, where it descends. This circulation, in fact a convection cell, is now known as a Hadley cell, but Hadley's idea

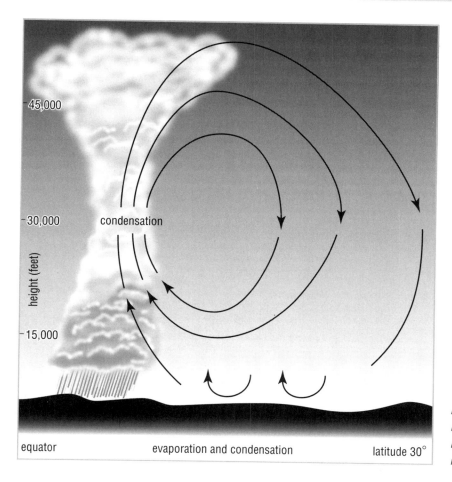

45,000

30,000 condensation

height (feet)

15,000

equator   evaporation and condensation   latitude 30°

Hadley cell. Air rises in the equatorial region and subsides in the subtropics.

of it has been much modified. Instead of the single cell that he proposed, there are now known to be a number of Hadley cells, and rather than extending from the equator to the poles, the Hadley cells form one component of a three-cell model of atmospheric circulation. Air rises over the equator and subsides in the subtropics, as shown in the illustration.

George Hadley (1685–1768) was an English meteorologist, although he trained originally as a lawyer. He was born in London, and his interest in physics led to him being placed in charge of the meteorological observations that were prepared for the Royal Society. He died at Flitton, Bedfordshire. His brother, John, invented the forerunner of the sextant.

1738

• Daniel Bernoulli demonstrated that as the velocity of a flowing liquid or gas increases, its pressure decreases. This is known as "Bernoulli's

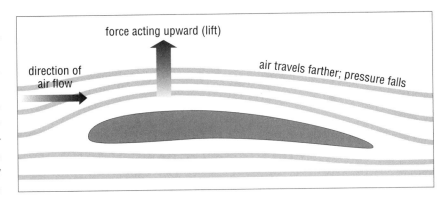

Bernoulli effect. Air flowing over the upper surface of the wing has farther to travel. but no more time to do so. Consequently it accelerates. air pressure over the wing falls. and the difference in pressure above and below the wing produces an upward force called "lift."

principle" and has many applications, the best known of which is the aerofoil design by which the wings of an aircraft, or rotors of a helicopter, generate a strong lifting force. A fluid (gas or liquid) accelerates when it flows through a constriction. The fluid also accelerates when it flows across a convex surface, such as the upper surface of an aerofoil, as shown in the illustration. Acceleration is inevitable, because the fluid crossing the curved surface must travel farther than the fluid unaffected by the obstruction, but all the fluid must arrive together at the downstream end of the obstruction. Pressure decreases in the accelerated fluid. In the case of an aerofoil, pressure is reduced across the upper surface and exerts a force, called "lift," acting upward.

Bernoulli also tried to explain the relationship between the pressure, temperature, and volume of gases. These had already been observed, but no one knew why gases behave as they do.

Daniel Bernoulli (1700–82) was born at Groningen, in the Netherlands, into a Swiss family of mathematicians and physicists. His uncle Jacob (sometimes called Jacques) was almost as great a mathematician as Newton and Leibniz, and his father, Johann (or Jean), was only slightly less accomplished. Daniel had two brothers, two nephews, a cousin, and several other relations, all of whom were distinguished mathematicians or physicists. It was a very remarkable family. Daniel qualified in Switzerland as a doctor of medicine in 1724 and also trained as a mathematician. In 1725 he was appointed professor of mathematics in St. Petersburg, Russia. He returned to Switzerland in 1733 as professor of anatomy and botany at the University of Basel, where he remained until his death.

1742

- Anders Celsius proposed the temperature scale that carries his name, although it is still sometimes referred to as the "centigrade" scale, the name that was officially abandoned internationally in 1948. As Celsius first described it, the scale had the boiling point of water as 0° and the freezing point as 100°, but this was soon reversed. Although the Fahrenheit scale is still used in some English-speaking countries, scientists throughout the world use the Celsius scale or Kelvin scale (in which 1 K = 1°C).

Anders Celsius (1701–44) was a Swedish astronomer. He was born and educated in Uppsala, where his father, Nils, was professor of astronomy at the university. In 1730 he succeeded his father as professor of astronomy. Celsius and his colleagues studied the aurora borealis closely, and Celsius and his assistant Olof Hiorter discovered that auroras are magnetic phenomena. Celsius was one of the first scientists to attempt to measure the magnitude of stars. He persuaded the Swedish government to finance a national observatory; the Celsius Observatory opened in 1741 with Celsius as its first director. He died in Uppsala.

1752

- Benjamin Franklin performed his most famous experiment, in which he used a kite to prove that storm clouds carry electric charge and lightning is an electric spark. Attached to his kite there was a pointed wire to which he had fastened a length of wet silken thread with a metal key tied at the bottom. During a thunderstorm he flew the kite toward the base of the cloud and held his hand close to the key. Sparks flashing from the key to his hand showed that a current had flowed from the cloud and down the silken thread. Then he held a Leyden jar (a device for storing an electric charge) to the key and found that it accumulated a charge. Franklin had proved his point, but he was lucky. The next two people who tried repeating his experiment were killed by it.

His discovery led Franklin to suggest that if pointed metal rods were fixed on the highest points of buildings, with wires from the rods to the ground, the electric charge in storm clouds would be carried away safely and the buildings protected against damage by lightning. By 1782 about 400 lightning conductors had been fitted to buildings in Philadelphia alone. He also calculated the tracks followed by storms crossing North America and was the first to study the warm-water Atlantic current now known as the Gulf Stream.

Benjamin Franklin (1706–90) was born in Boston. In the United States he is best known as one of the founding fathers of the nation, but he also became famous in Europe as a scientist and political philosopher. He invented a wood-burning stove and improved bifocal glasses, but his greatest work was in his studies of electricity. In 1776 Franklin was one of the group of Americans sent to represent the emerging United States of America in France, where he became very famous and highly popular; French intellectuals regarded him as the embodiment of freedom and enlightenment. He held many important positions and received many honors. He died in Philadelphia.

1761

• Joseph Black performed experiments confirming that when ice melts it absorbs heat with no increase in its own temperature. He never published his finding, but from 1761 he included it in his lectures at the University of Glasgow, Scotland, and in 1762 he described it to a Glasgow literary society. In 1764 he and his assistant, William Irvine (1743–87), measured the amount of heat absorbed and released when liquid water evaporates and water vapor condenses. Black concluded that the quantity of heat is not the same thing as the intensity of heat, and that thermometers measure heat intensity. The heat that is absorbed and released when water changes from one phase to another (ice to liquid to vapor) must exist within the substance, where it remains hidden, or "latent." He called it "latent heat." Latent heat plays a very important part in the formation of clouds and the development of thunderstorm clouds (cumulonimbus).

Joseph Black (1728–99) was a Scottish physicist, chemist, and medical doctor. He was born at Bordeaux, France, the son of a wine merchant. He was sent to be educated first in Belfast, then at the University of Glasgow, where he studied medicine and natural sciences. In 1751 he transferred to the University of Edinburgh to complete his medical studies. The thesis he wrote in 1754 for his doctor's degree described how heating magnesium carbonate (known then as "magnesia alba") releases a gas, distinct from air, which he weighed. Expanding on this work, in 1756 he published *Experiments upon Magnesia Alba, Quicklime, and Some Other Alcaline Substances*, proving that when carbonates are heated they lose this gas and become more alkaline, and when they absorb the gas they become less alkaline. He called the gas "fixed air."

The gas had been discovered early in the 17th century by the Belgian chemist and alchemist Jan Baptista van Helmont (1577–1644), who called it "gas sylvestre" (because he obtained it by burning charcoal; the Latin *sylvestris* means "of the woods"). It is known today as carbon dioxide. (Helmont is also believed to have coined the word *gas;* he called vapors by the Greek word *chaos,* but spelled it the way it sounded in Flemish, as "gas.")

In 1756 Black was appointed a lecturer in chemistry at Glasgow and also professor of anatomy, although he exchanged this post for the professorship of medicine and practiced as a physician. In 1766 he became professor of chemistry at the University of Edinburgh, the city where he died.

1767

• Horace Bénédict de Saussure is credited with inventing the solar collector. This was a box with heavily insulated sides and a glass top, containing a thermometer clearly visible from outside. De Saussure used the

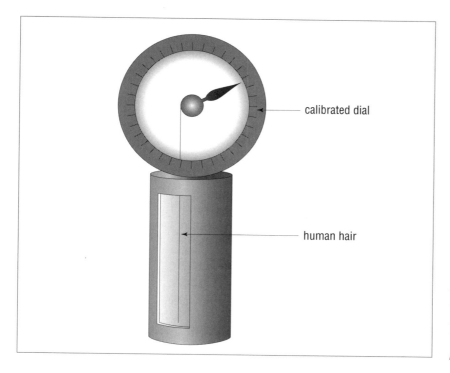

calibrated dial

human hair

Hair hygrometer. This drawing shows how the hygrometer works. The hair is fixed to the bar. As it stretches and contracts, the hair turns the wheel to which the pointer is attached.

A "weather house." It is really a hair hygrometer. One figure emerges when the humidity is low, the other when it is high.

device to investigate why the temperature at the top of a mountain is always lower than the temperature at the foot. He took his box to the summit of a mountain, where the air temperature was 43°F (6°C). Inside the box, however, the temperature rose to 190°F (88°C). De Saussure then repeated the measurements 4,852 feet (1,480 m) further down. There, the air temperature was 77°F (25°C), and the temperature inside the box was almost the same. De Saussure concluded that the sunshine is as warm at high elevations as it is at lower elevations, but that the thin mountain air is unable to trap and hold so much of the warmth as the denser air lower down.

Horace Bénédict de Saussure (1740–99) was a Swiss physicist, born at Conches, near Geneva. From 1762 to 1786 he taught at the University of Geneva, the city in which he was born and died. He was a keen botanist and Alpine explorer and wrote an account of his travels in the Alps titled *Voyages dans les Alpes* ("Journeys in the Alps"), published in 1779. In 1762 he was appointed professor of philosophy (the name then given to what today we call science) at the Geneva Academy. In 1772 he was elected to the Royal Society of London and also founded the Society for the Advancement of the Arts in Geneva. He resigned his professorship in 1787 and moved to the south of France, where he could live at sea level and continue his observations of atmospheric pressure. Financial hardship compelled him to leave France in 1794 and return to the family home at Conches. Thomas Jefferson, hearing of de Saussure's difficulties, considered offering him a position at the University of Charlottesville, but by then the physicist was too ill to move, and he died at Conches.

1783

- Horace Bénédict de Saussure (see 1767) invented the hair hygrometer, still used today. This instrument exploits the fact that a human hair, with all the natural oils removed, increases in length by about 2.5 percent as the relative humidity increases from 0 percent to 100 percent. The hair hygrometer is small (the hair can be wound around a core to save space), with a simple system of gears its reading can be displayed by a needle on a dial, and it can be manufactured cheaply. In its original and simplest form, shown in the illustration, one end of a long hair is attached to a bar, and the other end is wound around a wheel with a pointer attached to it. A calibrated ring surrounds the wheel and pointer. The hair stretches in moist air and contracts in dry air. As it does so, the hair turns the wheel, thus moving the pointer.

  The "weather house," shown in the illustration (previous page), used to be a popular ornament, and many were made by local craftspersons for sale to tourists. The house has two entrances, each with a figure—often of a man and a woman. The figures are mounted at each end of a bar that is pivoted at the center, so that when one figure moves forward, out of the house, the other figure moves backward, into the house. When one figure comes "outdoors" it means the weather will be fine, and when the other comes "outdoors" the weather will be wet. The device is a hair hygrometer. It is the changes in the length of a human hair wound around the pivot that turn the bar and move the figures.

1803

- Luke Howard proposed a scheme for classifying clouds into three main and several secondary types and giving a Latin name to each. In his classification the main types were called stratus (Latin *stratum*, meaning "layer"), cumulus (the Latin word for "heap"), and cirrus (the Latin word for "hair"). A fourth type, called nimbus (the Latin word for "cloud") was a cloud that was producing hail, rain, or snow. These "primitive forms" could become modified. Cumulus, comprising discrete "heaps" of cloud, could spread to become cumulostratus (now called stratocumulus), and cirrus could change into cirrocumulus or cirrostratus. He described his classification in an article called "On the Modification of Clouds" that he read to a meeting of the Askesian Society.

  Howard's classification forms the basis of the classification that is still used today. The present classification lists 10 principal cloud types, called *genera* (singular, *genus*), of which there are 14 species and nine varieties. The illustration shows the genera and the heights at which they are found.

  Luke Howard (1772–1864) was born and died in London. He trained as an apothecary (druggist) and became a very successful chemical manufacturer. He was never a professional scientist, but his cloud classification attracted widespread attention, and he became a celebrity. His fame spread still further following the 1813 publication of *Research about Atmospheric Phaenomenae*, a book containing all his meteorological articles up to that time, collected by his friend Thomas Foster. The German writer Goethe dedicated four poems to Howard.

1806

- Commander Francis Beaufort proposed his scale for wind forces, allotting values from 0 to 12 and specifying the amount of sail warships should carry under winds of each force. In 1838 the British Admiralty adopted the scale officially, and in 1874 it was adopted by the International Meteorological Committee. In 1955 the U.S. Weather Bureau added forces 13 to 17 to describe hurricane-force winds. The Beaufort Scale is still used, especially at sea.

  Sir Francis Beaufort (1774–1857) was born in County Meath, Ireland, the son of the rector of Navan. Francis joined the East India

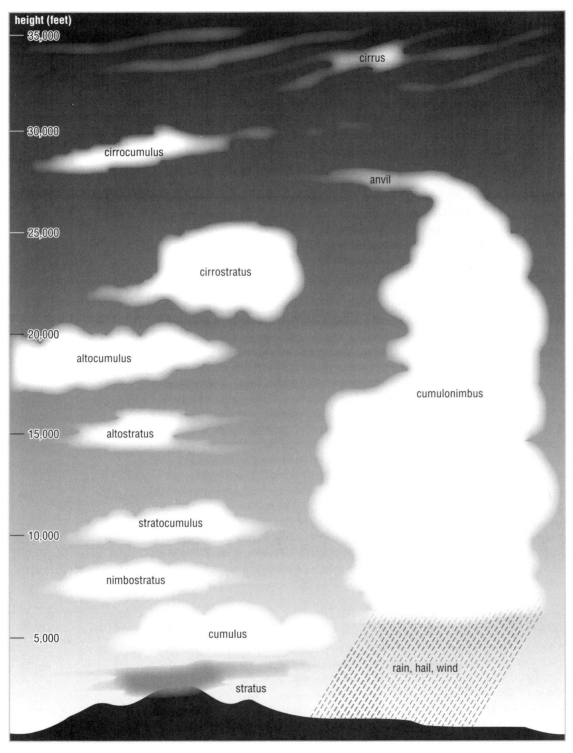

Cloud types. The drawing shows the approximate appearance of each named type and the height at which it forms.

Company in 1789 but left to join the Royal Navy a year later as a cabin boy, aged 16. He was an officer by the age of 22 and received his first command in 1805. By this time he had become a hydrographer—a scientist who studies and charts coastlines, river courses, and the seafloor—and he conducted several surveys before being seriously wounded in 1812, after which he never sailed again. In 1829 he was appointed hydrographer to the navy. He was knighted in 1848 and retired in 1855 with the rank of rear admiral, having served in the Royal Navy for 68 years.

- Luke Howard (see 1803) began publishing his *Meteorological Register*, which appeared regularly for several years in the *Athenaeum Magazine*.

1817

- Luke Howard (see 1803) published a series of his lectures as a book entitled *Seven Lectures in Meteorology*. This was the first textbook on meteorology.

1818

- Luke Howard (see 1803) published *The Climate of London*, in two volumes (the second appearing in 1819). In 1833 he published an expanded second edition in three volumes. This was the first book ever written about urban climates, and it contained what is believed to be the first reference to a *heat island*—an urban area that is warmer than the surrounding countryside.

1820

- John Daniell, an English chemist, physicist, and meteorologist, published an article in the *Quarterly Journal of Science* describing the dew point hygrometer he had invented. A dew point hygrometer, also called a dew cell, measures the dew point temperature directly. The alternative is to use two thermometers, one with a dry bulb and the other with a wet bulb, measure the difference in temperature between their readings (the *dew point depression*), and then read the dew point temperature from a table. Daniell's hygrometer comprised two thin glass bulbs connected by a tube, as shown in the drawing. One bulb contained only air, and the other contained ether and also a thermometer. When the temperature changed inside the bulb containing only air, the change was transmitted to the other bulb, and ether either evaporated or condensed. Latent heat of vaporization either chilled or warmed the glass, and atmospheric water vapor either condensed onto or evaporated from the outside of the bulb. The average temperature at which condensation and vaporization occurred, read from the thermometer, is the dew point temperature.

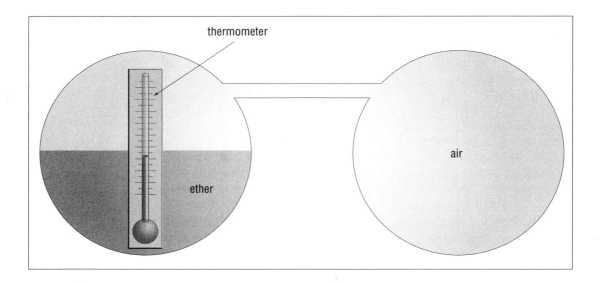

Daniell hygrometer. When the temperature changes in the bulb containing air, the change is transmitted to the ether, which either vaporizes or condenses, releasing latent heat that alters the temperature of the glass. Water vapor then either condenses onto the bulb containing ether or evaporates from it. The average temperature at which this happens is the dew point temperature.

A modern dew point hygrometer contains a thermometer and a mirror that is chilled electrically. A sensor detects the light reflected from the mirror. When water vapor condenses onto the mirror, the change in reflectivity (because the water droplets scatter light) is detected. The cooling circuit is then switched off, and a heating circuit is switched on. As soon as the water droplets evaporate the circuits change again. After several cycles a stable dew point temperature is reached and displayed.

John Frederic Daniell (1790–1845) was born and died in London while attending a meeting of the council of the Royal Society. One of the most eminent scientists of his day, he was also a prolific inventor. As a young man he worked in a sugar refinery and resin factory owned by a relative, and in 1817 he spent some time as manager of the Continental Gas Company, where he developed a new process for making gas from resin. In 1813, aged 23, he was appointed professor of physics at the University of Edinburgh. In 1823 he was elected to the Royal Society, and in 1831 he became the first professor of chemistry at King's College London, which had just been founded. He described his studies of meteorology in *Meteorological Essays*, published in 1823.

1824

- John Daniell (see 1820) published his *Essay on Artificial Climate Considered in Its Applications to Horticulture*, in which he showed that it is important to maintain a moist atmosphere in hothouses growing tropical plants.

1827

• Jean-Baptiste-Joseph Fourier published a paper in which he compared the influence of the chemical composition of the atmosphere on its temperature to the effect of heating a bowl lined with black cork and covered with glass. This may have been the first account of what is now called the "greenhouse effect."

Jean-Baptiste-Joseph Fourier (1768–1830) was a French mathematician most widely known for his development of partial differential equations as a powerful scientific tool. He was born at Auxerre, in central France, the son of a tailor who died when the boy was eight. He wanted to be a soldier and after a mixed early education studied at the École Normale in Paris, later joining its staff and also the staff of the École Polytechnnique. He accompanied Napoleon on his campaign in Egypt in 1798. Napoleon rewarded his mathematical discoveries by making him a baron. Following the fall of Napoleon and the restoration of the Bourbons he received further honors, and in 1822 he became one of the secretaries of the Academy of Sciences. He died in Paris from a disease contracted while he was in Egypt.

1830

• John Daniell (see 1820) erected a water barometer in the hall of the Royal Society of London and used it to make many meteorological observations.

1835

• Gaspard Gustave de Coriolis discovered that anything (not just air and water) moving over the surface of the Earth and not attached to it will be deflected by inertia acting at right angles to its direction of movement. This came to be called the Coriolis force (abbreviated to CorF), but no force is involved in the mechanical sense; today it is usually known as the "Coriolis effect" (but still abbreviated as CorF). It occurs because a body on the surface is traveling eastward at the speed of the Earth's rotation. If that body moves into a different latitude, it retains some of its original eastward motion. The surface beneath it is moving eastward at a different speed, however, because the Earth is a sphere. Consequently, the body will *appear* to be deflected, as shown in the illustration.

It is the Coriolis effect that causes air in the Northern Hemisphere to flow in a clockwise direction (anticyclonically) around areas of high pressure and counterclockwise (cyclonically) around areas of low pressure (these directions are reversed in the Southern Hemisphere). Cyclonic and anticyclonic air motion were discovered independently by Christoph Buys Ballot in 1857 (see 1857). The Coriolis effect also

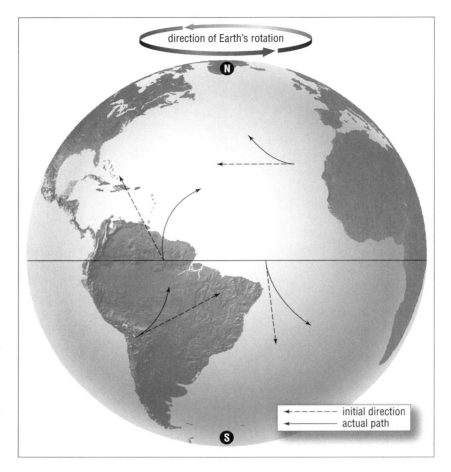

direction of Earth's rotation

N

S

- - - - - - initial direction
———— actual path

Coriolis effect. Moving bodies, including ocean currents and winds, are apparently deflected to the right in the Northern Hemisphere and to the left in the Southern Hemisphere.

deflects ocean currents, causing them to follow curved paths and producing the Ekman effect, discovered in 1905 by the Swedish scientist Vagn Walfrid Ekman (see 1905).

Gaspard Gustave de Coriolis (1792–1843) was born and died in Paris. He was educated at the École Polytechnique, the college that trained government officials, and then at the École des Ponts et Chaussées, studying highway engineering. His health was too poor for him to realize his ambition to become an engineer, and following his father's death he was responsible for the upkeep of the family. In 1816 he became a tutor and later assistant professor of analysis and mathematics at the École Polytechnique. In 1838 he was appointed director of studies. He was professor of mechanics at the École Centrale des Arts et Manufactures from 1829 until 1836, when he became professor of mechanics at the École des Ponts et Chaussées.

1840

• Jean Louis Rodolphe Agassiz (known as Louis Agassiz) published *Études sur les glaciers*, describing the results of studies he made in 1836 and 1837. He had observed that mountain glaciers are not static, but flow. From this and the location of boulders (called "erratics") scattered far from the rock formations to which they belonged, he concluded that in the past glaciers had extended much farther and had pushed the erratics to where they were later found. This led him to conclude that at one time, in the geologically recent past, the whole of Switzerland and much of northern Europe had lain beneath a single ice sheet, much like the one still existing in Greenland, and that there had been a "Great Ice Age." Later he found confirmatory evidence in Scotland and also in many parts of North America, indicating that the Ice Age had affected all of the Northern Hemisphere. Although many scientists had long suspected it, this was the first clear evidence that climates in the relatively recent past had been very different from those of the present and, therefore, that climates can and do change over time.

Agassiz (1807–73) was born at Motier, on the shores of Lake Morat, Switzerland, the son of the local pastor. His mother taught him about natural history, and he developed a love of plants and animals. He was educated at Bienne and Lausanne, then at the Universities of Zurich, Heidelberg, and Munich. He obtained a doctorate of philosophy at Erlangen and a doctorate of medicine at Munich. In 1826 he was asked to complete the classification of fish specimens from Brazil (the scientist who started the work had died), and Agassiz became a leading authority on European fishes, an interest which led him to the study of fossil fishes, on which he became a world authority. In 1832 he went to study in Paris and then in Neuchâtel, Switzerland. With the help of Alexander von Humboldt and Georges Cuvier, two of the most eminent scientists of their day, he was appointed professor of natural history at the University of Neuchâtel, a post he held from 1832 to 1846.

While on vacation in the Alps in 1836, he and his friends built a hut on the ice. After 12 years it had moved more than a mile (1.6 km). He placed a line of stakes directly across the glacier and found they also moved over about two years, forming a ∪ shape. This showed that the ice at the center of the glacier moved faster than the ice at the sides, which was retarded by its contact with the confining rocks.

In 1846 Agassiz was invited to lecture in the United States at Boston's Lowell Institute, in Charleston, and in several other cities. The lectures were highly popular, and Agassiz stayed in America, in 1848 becoming professor of zoology at Harvard. He became an American citizen and remained in the United States for the rest of his life, for most of the time at Harvard University.

Louis Agassiz is said to have been possibly the greatest science teacher ever to have worked in the United States. He was devoted to his students, whom he treated as colleagues, always emphasizing the importance of studying nature at first hand rather than from books. His work on fossil fishes helped support Darwinism, but Agassiz himself was always unsympathetic to the Darwinian view, possibly because he misunderstood it.

Agassiz died at Cambridge, Massachusetts, and is buried at Mt. Auburn. Beside his grave there is a boulder from the Aar glacial moraine in Switzerland. In 1915 Agassiz was elected to the Hall of Fame for Great Americans.

1842

- Matthew Maury was appointed the first director of the U.S. Naval Observatory and Hydrographic Office. He organized the collection of information from merchant ships on winds and currents. From these he discovered the shape of storms. He also charted the course of the Gulf Stream. His work led to an international conference on meteorology held in Brussels in 1853.

  Matthew Fontaine Maury (1806–73) was born in Spotsylvania County, Virginia. He became a naval officer, but an injury sustained in a stagecoach accident rendered him permanently lame and unfit for active service. In 1841 he was made superintendent of the Depot of Charts and Instruments. By the time he left the post in 1861 he had transformed the department into the U.S. Naval Observatory and Hydrographic Office.

  During the Civil War Maury sided with the Confederacy, resigning from the navy on April 20, 1861, following the secession from the Union of his native Virginia. He then joined the Confederate States Navy with the rank of commander. After the war he spent some time in voluntary exile in Mexico and England. In 1868 he became professor of meteorology at the Virginia Military Institute. He died at Lexington, Virginia. There is a Maury Hall at the Naval Academy in Annapolis, Maryland. In 1930 Matthew Maury was elected to the Hall of Fame for Great Americans.

- C. J. Doppler discovered the Doppler effect, which is now applied to the study of weather systems by means of Doppler radar. Doppler found that if a source emitting waves at a constant frequency moves toward an observer, the frequency of its emissions will be shortened, and if the source moves away from an observer, the wavelength will be increased. His idea was tested by the Dutch meteorologist C. H. D. Buys Ballot (see 1857) at Utrecht in 1845, using an open-topped railcar and two groups of musicians. One set of musicians sat on the railcar, all playing the same constant note on trumpets while the car moved past the other group, composed of people chosen because they possessed perfect pitch, standing beside the track. The listeners reported that as the railcar approached, the pitch of the trumpet note rose (implying a reducing wavelength), and after it had passed the pitch fell (implying an increasing wavelength). The Doppler effect applies to all radiation, not only sound. Light becomes bluer if its source is approaching (shortening wavelength) and redder if it is receding (lengthening wavelength). This application is widely used by astronomers measuring the motion of distant galaxies in relation to Earth.

Christian Johann Doppler (1803–53) was born in Salzburg, Austria, and educated there and in Vienna. At first he earned his living as a schoolteacher. When he was 32 he thought of emigrating to America, but was then offered a better teaching position in Prague. This led, in 1841, to his appointment as professor of mathematics at the State Technical Academy in Prague. The paper announcing his discovery in 1842 was called *Über das farbige Licht der Doppelsterne* ("About the colored light of double stars"). In 1850 he was appointed director of the Physical Institute and professor of experimental physics at the University of Vienna. He died in Venice, which in those days was ruled by Austria.

1844

- The first telegraph line in the world was constructed between Baltimore and Washington. Funded reluctantly by the U.S. Congress, it cost $30,000. Samuel Morse claimed to have invented it, and he certainly devised the code—Morse code—used to transmit messages. The first message it carried was "What hath God wrought?" Telegraph networks were soon installed in many countries and made possible the collection of weather observations obtained simultaneously in widely scattered locations. Until then, information could be transmitted no faster than the rider of a galloping horse could carry it.

Samuel Finlay Breese Morse (1791–1872) was born in Charlestown, Massachusetts, the son of a clergyman and geographer. In his early years he was an artist, studying art at Yale University and graduating in 1810. He then persuaded his parents to allow him to study historical painting in England, where he lived from 1811 until 1815. After he returned to the United States, Morse specialized in portraiture. He was one of the founders of the National Academy of Design and its first president, from 1826 to 1845. He also taught art at the University of the City of New York (now New York University). Samuel Morse became well known, but not wealthy. To transmit telegraph messages, he devised the binary code of dots and dashes that bears his name. Following the success of the telegraph system, Morse became involved in long and bitter disputes over his claim to have invented it, but eventually he was awarded the patents. He died in New York. In 1900 Samuel Morse was elected a charter member of the Hall of Fame for Great Americans.

1846

- Joseph Henry was elected the first secretary of the Smithsonian Institution. He used the resources of the institution to obtain weather reports from all over the United States. The system Henry devised provided the basis on which the U.S. Weather Bureau was established.

Joseph Henry (1797–1878) was the most eminent American physicist of his day. He invented a telegraph in 1835, before Morse (see 1844), but failed to patent it, and he helped Morse freely.

He was born in Albany, New York, into a poor family. He left school at 13 and was apprenticed to a watchmaker, but after reading a number of books about science he resumed his education at Albany Academy, paying his way by tutoring and teaching. In 1826 he obtained a post teaching mathematics and science at Albany Academy, and in 1832 he was appointed a professor at the College of New Jersey (now Princeton University). Henry specialized in electromagnetism, and following his discovery of self-induction in 1832, at a meeting in Chicago in 1893 the Congress of Electricians named the henry as the unit of inductance; it is now the SI unit of inductance. Henry died in Washington.

1850

- Matthew Maury (see 1842) charted the floor of the North Atlantic Ocean.

1851

- At the Great Exhibition in London, the world's first weather map was published, showing readings taken simultaneously by instruments at many locations and collated at a central point. It was called a "synoptic" map, from the Greek *syn*, "together," and *opsis*, "seeing." Weather maps covering a wide area are still known as synoptic charts. The illustration shows a typical synoptic chart for the North Atlantic region on a day in April.

1853

- A conference on meteorology and oceanography was held in Brussels, Belgium. The conference had been organized by Matthew Maury (see 1842), who attended as the U.S. representative.

1855

- Urbain-Jean-Joseph Leverrier began supervising the installation of a network to collect meteorological data from astronomical observatories throughout Europe. Once this was completed, Leverrier issued daily weather charts of the North Atlantic based on observations from ships and coastal stations. The observers were scattered widely and unevenly, however, and so compiling the charts involved a good deal of guesswork to fill in the gaps.

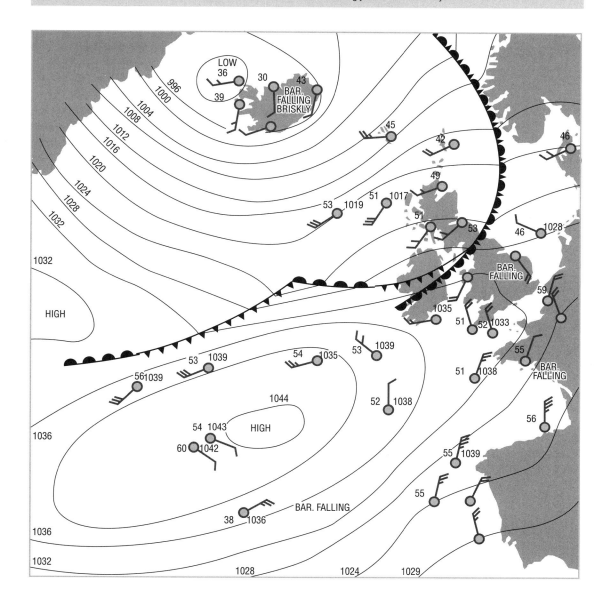

Synoptic chart for the North Atlantic. It shows isobars with pressures marked in millibars; high- and low-pressure centers are labeled; and station circles, indicating the location of weather stations, show the pressure (e.g. 1035); surface air temperature in degrees Fahrenheit; wind direction and wind strength (the "tail" shows the direction and barbs at its end show the strength).

Urbain Jean Joseph Leverrier (1811–77) was born at Saint-Lô, Normandy, France, and died in Paris. He was educated at the Collège de Caen and Collège de Saint-Louis, where he won a prize in mathematics. Later he entered the École Polytechnique in Paris. He started his working life as a chemist but almost accidentally became an astronomer, teaching at the Collège Stanislas and, from 1837, at the École Polytechnique. In

1849 the position of professor of celestial mechanics was created for him at the Sorbonne, and in 1854 he became director of the Paris Observatory.

Leverrier made many important astronomical discoveries and was elected to the Paris Academy of Sciences in 1846. That was the year in which his studies of the motion of the planet Uranus led Leverrier to propose the existence of a previously unknown planet beyond its orbit. Leverrier wrote to his friend and colleague Johann Gottfried Galle (1812–1910) at the Berlin Observatory, asking him to examine a certain place in the sky. On September 23, the first evening of the search, the planet was discovered very close to where Leverrier had predicted. Some French astronomers suggested the new planet be called "Leverrier," but Leverrier named it himself, calling it "Neptune." He was elected to the Royal Society of London in 1837.

1856

- William Ferrel proposed that low-latitude winds blowing toward the equator are deflected not by the rotation of the Earth, but by vorticity—the tendency of moving air to rotate about its own axis. Once this begins, the rotation will be maintained to conserve angular momentum. This led him to propose a mathematical model of the circulation of the atmosphere. He revised his model in 1860 and again in 1889. In 1857 Ferrel also proposed on theoretical grounds what is now known as Buys Ballot's law. This was some months before Buys Ballot discovered it. Ferrel wrote a number of books about meteorology.

William Ferrel (1817–91) was an American climatologist. He was born in Bedford (now Fulton) County, Pennsylvania, and educated at Marshall College (now Marshall and Franklin College) and Bethany College, from where he graduated in 1844. He became a mathematics teacher. His keen interest in tides led to his appointment in 1857 as an assistant in the office of *The American Ephemeris and Nautical Almanac* in Cambridge, Massachusetts. In 1867 he was appointed to a position in the U.S. Coast and Geodetic Survey, a post he held until 1882, when he joined the Army Signal Service with the rank of professor and moved to Kansas City, Missouri. His resignation from the Coast and Geodetic Survey was accepted only on condition that Ferrel complete the work he had started on the design of a machine for predicting tides. This was a mechanical device, worked by levers and pulleys, that showed predicted times and heights of high and low waters. Work constructing the machine began in 1881 and was completed in 1882. It remained in use until computers replaced it in 1991. William Ferrel retired to Maywood, Kansas, where he died.

1857

- Buys Ballot discovered that in the Northern Hemisphere winds circulate counterclockwise around areas of low pressure and clockwise around areas of high pressure, as shown in the diagram. Therefore, if you stand with your back to the wind, the area of atmospheric low pressure will lie to your left and the area of high pressure to your right. In the Southern Hemisphere these directions are reversed. This is known as Buys Ballot's law. Buys Ballot discovered it by observation, but unknown to him it had been calculated theoretically several months earlier by the American meteorologist William Ferrel (see 1856). Buys Ballot acknowledged Ferrel's prior claim, but nevertheless the law continues to bear his name.

  Christoph Hendrick Didericus Buys Ballot (1817–90) was a Dutch meteorologist. He was born at Kloetinge, in Zeeland. In 1847 he was appointed professor of mathematics at the University of Utrecht, and in 1854 he helped to found the Royal Netherlands Meteorological Institute. He was its first director, holding the position from 1854 until his death.

1861

- In England, the Meteorological Department of the Board of Trade issued the first storm warnings for coastal areas on February 6 and for shipping on July 31.
- John Tyndall published a paper in the *Philosophical Magazine and Journal of Science* showing that atmospheric gases absorb heat and, therefore, that the chemical composition of the air affects climate. This was one of the first references to what is now called the "greenhouse effect."

  John Tyndall (1820–93) was an Irish physicist born at Leighlin Bridge, County Carlow, the son of a police officer. He was educated at a school in Carlow. He left school to train as a surveyor with the

Buys Ballot's law. Stand with your back to the wind (in the Northern Hemisphere), and the center of low pressure is to your left and the center of high pressure to your right. In the Southern Hemisphere, the opposite is true.

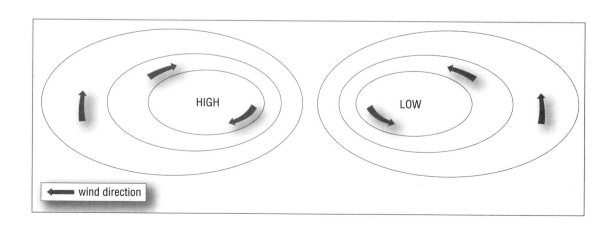

HIGH   LOW

← wind direction

Ordnance Survey, the government agency responsible for mapping the country. He left the Ordnance Survey in 1843 and worked as a surveyor for a private company. In 1847 he obtained a post teaching mathematics at Queenwood College, Hampshire, where he met and became friendly with Edward Frankland (1825–99), the science teacher. Under Frankland's influence he read widely and attended scientific lectures whenever he could, and in 1848 both men enrolled at the University of Marburg, Germany, where Tyndall studied physics, calculus, and chemistry. His chemistry teacher was Robert Bunsen (1811–99), who helped and encouraged him. Tyndall obtained a doctorate in 1850 and in 1851 returned to Queenwood College. He was elected to the Royal Society of London in 1852, and following a highly successful course of lectures he gave at the Royal Institution in 1853, in 1854 he was appointed professor of natural philosophy there, later becoming director of the institution.

His most important work concerned the conduction of heat and the scattering of light by small particles. He found that this scattering makes it possible to read in shadow, which would be impossible on the Moon, where light is not scattered, and it allowed him to explain the blue color of the sky. Tyndall was a great popularizer of science, writing books and lecturing in language that nonscientists could understand. In 1872 and 1873 he made a lecture tour of the United States, donating the proceeds to a trust for the support of American science. He also studied glaciers and was a keen mountaineer. He was one of the first people to climb the Matterhorn, was the first to climb the Weisshorn, and climbed Mont Blanc several times. He was often unwell, however, and he retired from the Royal Institution in 1887. He and his wife went to live in Hindhead, Surrey, where he died.

1863

- The first network of meteorological stations linked by telegraph to a central point opened in France.
- Francis Galton, in his book *Meteorographica*, introduced the word *anticyclone* and devised a method for mapping weather systems that is the basis of the one still used today. To do this, he sent a questionnaire to weather stations in various parts of Europe asking for the results of measurements made on a specified date and plotted these on a map. Galton then produced weather charts for publication in *The Times* of London. He helped find a way to print the charts using movable type and modified a drawing instrument so that it would score grooves in a soft material that could be used to make casts for printing blocks. Galton also proposed to measure the speed and direction of the upper wind by means of the smoke emitted by a shell exploding at a specified location and height. This was tried experimentally under the auspices of the Meteorological Office, and it worked well. The shells exploded at the

predetermined height of 9,000 feet (2,745 m), and tracking the smoke was simple.

Sir Francis Galton (1822–1911) was an English geographer, anthropologist, and statistician who had wide interests and a passion for scientific investigation. He was born at Sparkbrook, Birmingham, England, into a Quaker family and educated at Birmingham General Hospital, King's College London, Trinity College at Cambridge University, and St. George's Hospital, London. In 1844, the year he graduated from Cambridge, his father died and left him a fortune large enough to finance his work. He traveled through the Balkans and Near East, then explored parts of southwest Africa. He advanced the science of meteorology but is best known for his anthropological studies, inspired by the publication in 1859 of *On the Origin of Species* by his cousin, Charles Darwin. Galton sought to discover the extent to which human characteristics are inherited or produced by the conditions under which children are brought up. To help make sense of the data he collected, in 1888 Galton invented a way to calculate the correlation coefficient, an important statistical technique. Galton invented eugenics, the idea that superior humans can be produced by selective breeding, and was the person mainly responsible for introducing fingerprinting for the identification of criminals. He was knighted in 1909 and died at Haslemere, Surrey.

1869

• From September 1, the *Weather Bulletin* was published on a regular daily basis from the Cincinnati Observatory at the instigation of the observatory director, Cleveland Abbe. This was the first daily weather bulletin in the world. The service proved very popular and led to the establishment of a national bureau headed by an army general and, from 1871, with Abbe as scientific assistant.

Cleveland Abbe (1838–1916) became known as the "father of the Weather Bureau." He was born and educated in New York City, then studied astronomy at the University of Michigan and as a private student with Benjamin Apthorp Gould (1824–96) at Cambridge, Massachusetts. He taught at the University of Michigan for several years, then spent the years 1864–66 completing his astronomical studies at Pulkovo Observatory, in Russia. On his return to the United States he was appointed director of the Cincinnati Observatory, where he received telegraphic reports of storms across the country. He plotted the location and timing of these on maps and used them as the basis of his daily reports. When the U.S. Weather Bureau was transferred from the Army Signal Corps to the Department of Agriculture in 1891, Abbe was made meteorologist in charge. He held this position for the rest of his life, combining it with conducting research and teaching meteorology at Johns Hopkins University. He died at Chevy Chase, Maryland.

1870

- On February 9, President Ulysses S. Grant signed a joint resolution of Congress authorizing the secretary of war to establish a weather service within the army. The Army Signal Corps operated the service until 1891.

1871

- As scientific assistant at the U.S. Weather Bureau, Cleveland Abbe (see 1869) began issuing three-day weather forecasts on February 19. On November 8, the bureau issued the first "cautionary storm signal"; it was for the Great Lakes region.

1874

- The International Meteorological Congress was founded.

1875

- *The Times* of London published the first weather map to appear in a newspaper. It had been drawn by Francis Galton (see 1863).

1878

- In England, the Meteorological Office published its first *Weekly Weather Report* on February 11.

1883

- Léon-Philippe Teisserenc de Bort discovered that the climate of middle latitudes on either side of the North Atlantic Ocean is strongly influenced by the balance of atmospheric pressure between a region of low pressure permanently centered over Iceland (the "Iceland low") and a region of high pressure centered over the Azores (the "Azores high"). Changes in this balance are now known as the "North Atlantic Oscillation."

  Léon-Philippe Teisserenc de Bort (1855–1913) was born in Paris, the son of an engineer. In 1880 he started work at the meteorological department of the Central Bureau of Meteorology in Paris and in 1892 became chief meteorologist of the bureau. He resigned in 1896 to found a private meteorological observatory at Trappes, near Versailles, which is where he conducted his experiments. These were primarily studies of the upper atmosphere conducted by using balloons to obtain measurements. He was a pioneer in the use of balloons for atmospheric research. He died at Cannes.

1884

• S. P. (Samuel Pierpont) Langley published a paper on the climatic effect of the absorption of heat by atmospheric gases, an early reference to what is now known as the greenhouse effect. Langley had also measured the spectrum of light reflected by the Moon at different seasons and with the Moon at different heights above the horizon. This allowed Arrhenius (see 1896) to calculate how much heat carbon dioxide and water vapor absorb.

   Samuel Pierpont Langley (1834–1906) was an American astronomer born at Roxbury, Massachusetts. He studied at Boston Latin School and Boston High School, from where he graduated in 1851, but he largely educated himself. Langley worked as a civil engineer and architect, mainly in Chicago and St. Louis, from 1857 to 1864, meanwhile studying astronomy. When he returned to Boston in 1865 he was offered a post as an assistant at Harvard University Observatory. He left in 1866 to teach mathematics at the U.S. Naval Academy, in Annapolis, Maryland. In 1867 he was appointed director of the Allegheny Observatory, in Pennsylvania, and professor of physics and astronomy at the Western University of Pennsylvania. In 1887 he became secretary and later director of the Smithsonian Institution. He retained this post until his death.

   In 1881 he invented a bolometer—an instrument for measuring very small quantities of heat very accurately—and used it to measure the amount of solar radiation. He was also enthusiastic about aviation and made a number of studies of the way that air flows across solid bodies moving at constant speed. The results allowed him to show that thin wings of a particular shape could support the weight of an airplane. In 1896 he built a model aircraft powered by steam that flew for about three-quarters of a mile (1.2 km). The government gave him a total of $50,000 to build a full-size model, but the materials he used were not strong enough to survive the stresses, and the three trials he made between 1897 and 1903 all failed. This led the *New York Times* to attack him in an editorial for wasting public money; the editorial also predicted that humans would not fly for 1,000 years. Nine days later, the Wright brothers did precisely that. Langley died at Aiken, South Carolina.

1891

• On July 1, operation of the weather bureau was transferred from the Army Signal Corps to the Department of Agriculture, and it became the U.S. Weather Bureau, a civilian service. Cleveland Abbe (see 1863) was appointed meteorologist in charge.

1893

• Edward Maunder discovered that the coldest part of the Little Ice Age, between 1645 and 1715, coincided with a period of very low sunspot activity, not a single sunspot having been reported for 32 years. This period is now known as the "Maunder Minimum," and earlier Maunder Minima have also been found to coincide with periods when the climate cooled appreciably, though not to the extent of a full ice age.

Edward Walter Maunder (1851–1928) was a British astronomer, although he possessed no formal qualification as an astronomer. He was born in London, the son of a Methodist minister, and educated at King's College London. He went to work in a bank, but in 1873 he passed the entrance examination for the civil service and obtained a position at the Royal Observatory, Greenwich, as a photographic and spectroscopic assistant. His job was to photograph sunspots and note their sizes and positions. While occupied with this task, his attention was drawn to the earlier discovery by the German astronomer Gustav Spörer of a period, 1400–1510, when very few sunspots were recorded. Maunder began searching through old records at the observatory and discovered the 1645–1715 sunspot minimum.

Maunder was made a fellow of the Royal Astronomical Society in 1873. He died at Greenwich.

1895

• Charles F. Marvin (1858–1943), chief of the U.S. Weather Bureau, first used kites to obtain measurements of conditions above the surface. Marvin was a major proponent of this method and took a keen interest in the development of any instrument that might assist in atmospheric monitoring.

Dr. Marvin was appointed a junior professor in the Office of the Chief Signal Officer of the U.S. Army in 1884, when the weather service was operated by the Army Signal Corps. When the service became the U.S. Weather Bureau in 1891, Marvin joined it as a professor of meteorology, holding this position until 1913, when President Wilson, acting on the recommendation of the National Academy of Sciences, made him chief of the bureau. He remained in his post until his retirement in 1934.

1896

• In April, Svante August Arrhenius published an article in the *Philosophical Magazine and Journal of Science* in which he linked changes in the atmospheric concentration of carbon dioxide with climate. This is now called the "greenhouse effect." To do this he performed somewhere between 10,000 and 100,000 calculations (with no help from a calculator or computer!) and predicted that a doubling of the CO_2 concentration would cause the average global temperature to rise by 9–11°F (5–6°C). The present estimate by the Intergovernmental Panel on Climate Change (IPCC) is 2.5–10.4°F (1.4–5.8°C). Arrhenius thought that changes in CO_2 were due mainly to changes in the frequency, magnitude, and type of volcanic eruptions and that these might cause ice ages to start and end. He estimated it would take 3,000 years to double atmospheric CO_2 by burning fossil fuels. Arrhenius thought such a global warming would be beneficial, increasing crop yields and raising standards of living.

Arrhenius was not the first scientist to suspect a link between climate and the chemical composition of the atmosphere (see 1827, 1861, and 1884), but he was the first to calculate the change that would result from an increase in atmospheric CO_2.

Svante August Arrhenius (1859–1927) was a Swedish physical chemist. He was born at Wijk, near Uppsala, and by the age of three had taught himself to read. He studied at the University of Uppsala, then moved to the University of Stockholm to work for a higher degree. His most famous work was on the conduction of an electric current through certain solutions called electrolytes. For this he was awarded the 1903 Nobel Prize in chemistry. His interests were very wide, and in *Worlds in the Making*, a book he published in 1908, he suggested that life on Earth developed from living spores that arrived from space (a theory known as "panspermia"). In 1895, he was appointed a professor at the University of Stockholm, and in 1905, he became director of the Nobel Institute for Physical Chemistry, a post he held until shortly before his death. He died in Stockholm.

- The International Meteorological Congress published its standard classification of cloud types in the *International Cloud Atlas*, which has been revised and updated several times. This work is now published by the World Meteorological Organization (WMO) of the United Nations.

1898

- The U.S. Weather Bureau established 16 kite stations (a 17th was added later) in the central and eastern United States and permanent observatories at Pikes Peak, Colorado, and Mt. Weather, Virginia. These stations provided a national picture of weather phenomena for the next 20 years.

1902

- L. P. Teisserenc de Bort (see 1883) discovered the stratosphere using balloons carrying instruments that revealed that the atmosphere has two layers. In the lower layer, temperature decreases with height. He called this the "troposphere" (from the Greek *tropos*, meaning "turning"). Above about 7 miles (11 km), Teisserenc de Bort found that temperature remained constant with height. He called this layer the "stratosphere" (from the Latin *sternere*, meaning to "strew" or "spread in layers"), and he called the boundary between these layers the "tropopause." He suggested that gases in the stratosphere might form layers, with oxygen at the bottom, nitrogen (which is lighter) above it, helium above that, and hydrogen (the lightest gas of all) at the top. In fact, gases are not arranged in layers in the stratosphere, and although the air is very thin, its chemical composition is similar to that of tropospheric air. The diagram shows the structure of the atmosphere as this is understood today. About 99.9 percent of the mass of the atmosphere lies below the stratopause.

1904

• Vilhelm Bjerknes published *Weather Forecasting as a Problem in Mechanics and Physics*, one of the first scientific studies of weather forecasting.

Vilhelm Frimann Koren Bjerknes (1862–1951) was a Norwegian physicist and meteorologist. He was born and died in Oslo. As a student, he helped his father, Carl Anton Bjerknes, who was professor of mathematics at Christiania University (now the University of Oslo). Vilhelm spent 1890 and 1891 in Germany working as an assistant to and collaborator with the German physicist Heinrich Hertz and also spent two years lecturing at the School of Engineering in Stockholm. In 1895 he was appointed professor of applied mechanics and mathematical physics at the University of Stockholm.

Vilhelm Bjerknes devised a method for forecasting weather mathematically. He described this in a scientific paper published in 1904. The Carnegie Foundation was providing financial support that allowed Bjerknes to establish schools (research institutes) in Leipzig, Germany, and Bergen, Norway, where he employed many "Carnegie assistants." Bjerknes returned to Norway in 1907 to become a professor at Kristiania University (the spelling had changed). In 1912 he was appointed professor of geophysics at the University of Leipzig and founded the Leipzig Geophysical Institute. He returned to Norway in 1917 to found the Bergen Geophysical Institute, now part of the University of Bergen. During World War I Bjerknes established a series of weather stations throughout Norway. Information from these allowed Bjerknes and his colleagues, who included his son, Jakob, and Tor Harold Percival Bergeron (1891–1977), to develop their theory of air masses bounded by fronts.

1905

• V. W. (Vagn Walfrid) Ekman discovered the reason why floating sea ice drifts at an angle of 45° to the right of the wind direction. The Norwegian explorer Fridtjof Nansen (1861–1930) had observed this in the 1890s. Ekman investigated the phenomenon for his doctoral thesis and discovered that it is due to the combined effects of the wind direction and strength, the Coriolis effect, and friction between different layers of

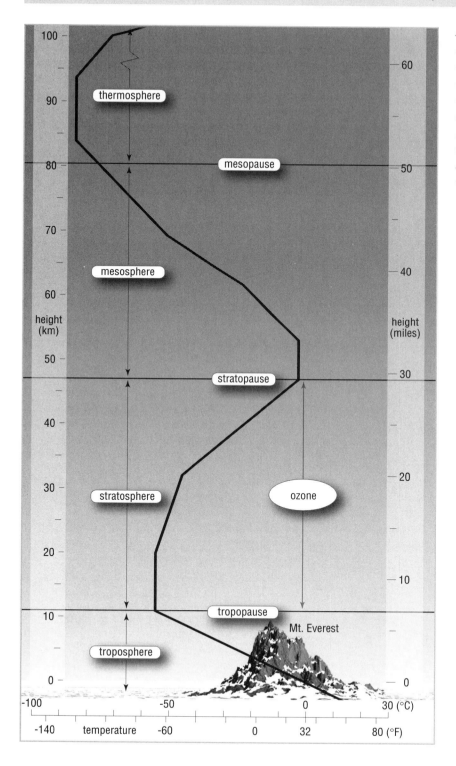

Atmospheric structure. The atmosphere consists of a series of layers, one outside the other, identified mainly by the way temperature changes with height within them.

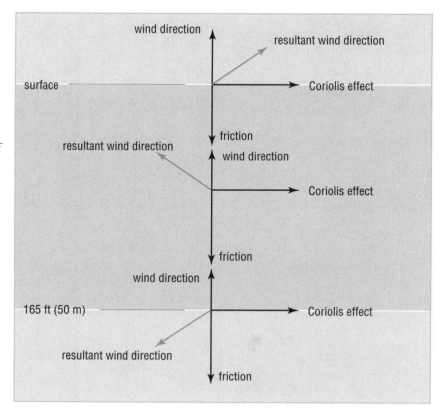

The Ekman spiral. With increasing depth, the balance of forces swings the direction of an ocean current to the left (in the Northern Hemisphere) until, at the Ekman depth, it flows in the opposite direction to that at the surface. Wind direction also changes in this way through the planetary boundary layer, where it is affected by friction with the surface.

water. Wind-driven sea currents also move at an angle of 45° to the right of the wind direction in the Northern Hemisphere (and to the left in the Southern Hemisphere). Ekman also discovered that friction increases with increasing depth, and consequently currents are slowed and deflected further and there is a depth at which the current flows in the opposite direction to the surface current. This "Ekman depth" varies but averages about 165 feet (50 m) over much of the ocean. These forces are illustrated in the figure. Between the surface and this depth, the current direction describes a spiral known as the Ekman spiral. It was later discovered that wind direction also forms an Ekman spiral with increasing altitude.

Vagn Walfrid Ekman (1874–1954) was a Swedish oceanographer and physicist. He was born in Stockholm and educated at the University of Uppsala, where he received his doctorate in 1902 for his discovery of the Ekman spiral. He described this work in "On the Influence of the Earth's Rotation on Ocean-Currents," an article published in *Arkiv för Matematik, Astronomi och Fysik* in 1905. In 1902 Ekman moved to Norway to take up a post as an assistant at the International Laboratory for Oceanographic Research in Oslo. He returned to Sweden in 1908, and in 1910 he was appointed professor of mathematical physics at Lund University. He remained in this post until he retired in 1954.

1913

- Marie-Paul-Auguste-Charles Fabry, a French physicist, discovered the ozone layer of the stratosphere. This is a region of the atmosphere at a height of 66,000–98,000 (ft (20–30 km) where there is a higher concentration of ozone than is found elsewhere. The ozone (O_3) forms in a two-step reaction driven by energy from ultraviolet (UV) radiation. First, UV radiation splits oxygen molecules into their constituent atoms ($O_2 + UV \rightarrow O + O$); then, in the presence of an atom of any other substance, M (but usually nitrogen), oxygen atoms bond to oxygen molecules ($O + O_2 + M \rightarrow O_3 + M$). Ozone is also broken down by UV radiation at a different wavelength, but this reaction predominates at higher altitudes. This, combined with some mixing of the air, results in a surplus of ozone accumulating in the ozone layer.

  Fabry made the discovery by means of the Fabry-Pérot interferometer and Fabry-Pérot etalon, two instruments he invented in collaboration with Albert Pérot (1863–1925). The instruments break light into its constituent wavelengths with a high resolution, and Fabry found that some atmospheric gas was filtering UV radiation. He found that the gas was ozone.

  Fabry (1867–1945) was one of the most distinguished physicists of his generation. He was born in Marseilles and educated there prior to enrolling at the École Polytechnique in Paris in 1885. He graduated in 1889, then moved to the University of Paris, where he was awarded a doctorate in physics in 1892. He taught physics in several schools before joining the staff of the University of Marseilles in 1894. In 1904, he was appointed professor of industrial physics. He moved to Paris in 1914 to work on a government research project, and in 1921 he became professor of physics at the Sorbonne, later combining this post with that of professor of physics at the École Polytechnique and director of the International Committee on Weights and Measures. He retired in 1917 and died in Paris.

1917

- Vilhelm Bjerknes (see 1904) founded the Bergen Geophysical Institute as part of the Bergen Museum (it is now part of the University of Bergen). It was there that Bjerknes and his colleagues—known as the "Bergen School"—developed their theory of air masses separated by fronts. The illustrations show how fronts are represented on modern weather maps and how they might appear in cross section.

Cross-section through a warm front. A front is named for the air behind it. As a warm front passes, cold air is replaced by warmer air. Colder air follows behind a cold front. A warm front slopes at an angle of 0.5– 1.0°, a cold front at about 2°.

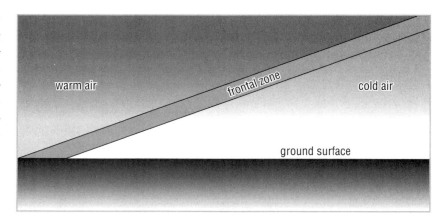

Frontal symbols. Weather fronts are represented by standard symbols: triangles (sometimes colored blue) for cold fronts and semicircles (sometimes colored red) for warm fronts. These usually indicate the place where fronts are at ground level.

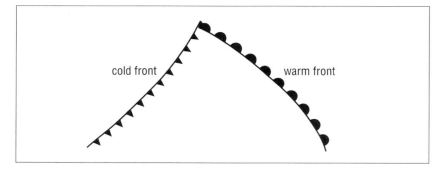

1918

- W. P. (Wladimir Peter) Köppen published a system for classifying climates according to the vegetation typical of them. He divided climates into six groups, broadly based on temperature and the seasonality of precipitation. A winter temperature of 64°F (18°C) is critical for certain tropical plants, for example, a summer temperature of 50°F (10°C) is necessary for trees, and a temperature of 27°F (–3°C) indicates snow at some time every winter. His climate groups were labeled tropical rainy; arid; warm, temperate, rainy; rainy; tundra; and permanent frost and icecaps. He later modified his system, completing the modifications in 1936. The Köppen classification is still widely used.

  Köppen (1846–1940) was born of German parents in St. Petersburg, Russia. He went to school in the Crimea, where he first became interested in the relationship between plants and climate. He then studied at the Universities of Heidelberg and Leipzig. From 1872 to 1873 he worked in the Russian meteorological service. In 1875 he moved to Hamburg, Germany, where he headed a new division of the Deutsche Seewarte formed to issue weather forecasts for the land and sea areas of

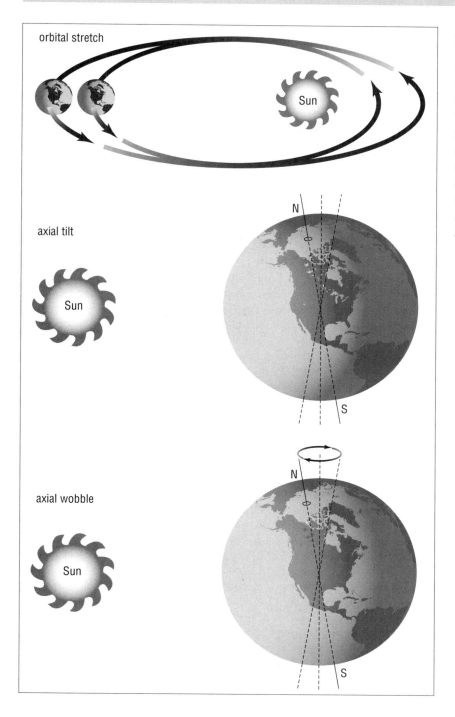

orbital stretch

axial tilt

axial wobble

Milankovitch cycles. There are three cycles that affect the onset and ending of ice ages: The Earth's orbit stretches, so it becomes more elongated, the tilt of the Earth's rotational axis changes, and the rotational axis wobbles.

northern Germany. He was able to devote himself entirely to research from 1879. He died in Graz, Austria.

1920

• Milutin Milankovitch proposed that when three variations in the movement of the Earth in relation to the Sun coincide, they may trigger the commencement and ending of ice ages. His theory is now widely accepted by climatologists.

Earth follows an elliptical path in its solar orbit. Over a cycle of about 100,000 years, the ellipse lengthens, then shortens again. This changes the distance between the Earth and the Sun, thus altering the amount of solar radiation received at the surface. Over a cycle of about 40,000 years, the Earth's axis of rotation moves in a small circle, like a wobbling gyroscope, altering the angle between the axis and the radiation coming from the Sun. This changes the distribution of solar radiation over the Earth's surface. Over a cycle of about 21,000 years, the date at which the Earth is closest to the Sun (perihelion) in its orbit moves through a complete year; at present perihelion is reached in January, and 10,000 years from now it will be reached in July. This alters the intensity of solar radiation received at the surface in winter and summer. The drawing illustrates these cycles.

Milankovitch calculated the timing of these astronomical cycles over several hundred thousand years, then matched them to see when they had coincided, so that solar radiation at the Earth's surface reached maxima and minima. He found that the coincidences corresponded to the onset and ending of ice ages. Climatologists were doubtful of this, because the extent of the change in radiation seemed too small to account for such large climatic events. Studies of sediment cores taken from the ocean floor in 1976 supported the Milankovitch theory, however, and it is now generally accepted.

Milutin Milankovitch (1879–1958) was a Serbian mathematician and climatologist. He was born in the village of Dalj, on the Croatian side of the border between Croatia and Serbia, near the Croatian town of Osijek (Croatia was then part of Austria-Hungary, and Serbia was an independent nation). He studied at the Vienna Institute of Technology, and in 1904 he was awarded a doctorate in technical science. Milankovitch worked for a time as the chief engineer for a construction company, but in 1909 he accepted an offer to teach applied mathematics at the University of Belgrade. He remained in this post for the rest of his life, except during World War I, when he was a prisoner of war, captured while serving in the Serbian army. His captivity was very civilized. The Austro-Hungarian authorities allowed him to continue his researches in the library of the Hungarian Academy of Science in Budapest. Milankovitch died in 1958.

1921

• Vilhelm Bjerknes (see 1904) published *On the Dynamics of the Circular Vortex with Applications to the Atmosphere and to the Atmospheric Vortex and Wave Motion*, in which he established that the lower atmosphere is composed of air masses. These are distinguished from one another by temperature, pressure, and humidity. Air masses form over large areas and are classified as continental (c) or maritime (m). They are further defined as arctic (A), polar (P), tropical (T), and equatorial (E). These types are combined to produce continental arctic (cA), continental polar (cP), continental tropical (cT), maritime tropical (mT), maritime polar (mP), maritime arctic (mA), and maritime equatorial (mE). There is no such thing as continental equatorial air, because oceans cover almost all of the equatorial region. The map shows the air masses that affect North America and the weather conditions each type brings.

Air masses affecting North America. The map shows the source of each air mass, the direction it travels, and the weather it brings.

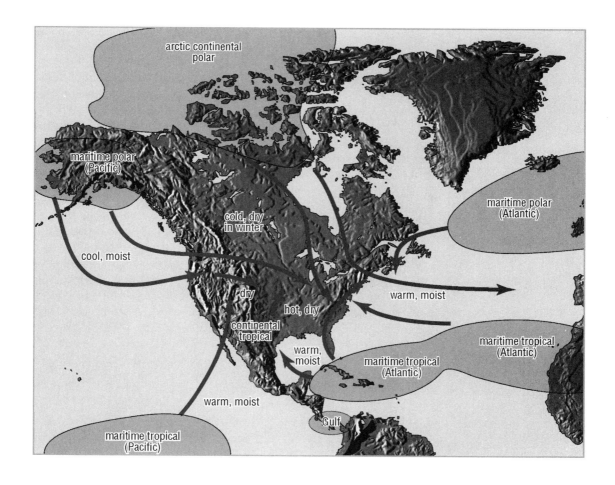

• Sakuhei Fujiwara suggested the possibility that two tropical cyclones might orbit about their common center of mass. This was called the "Fujiwara effect" and can occur if the storms are less than 900 miles (1,448 km) apart. If one of the storms is much larger than the other storm, the greater will usually absorb the lesser. If they are of approximately equal size they may merge. The combined storm will then intensify. Fujiwara observed the effect by observing vortices in water. If two vortices approach each other and both are turning in the same direction, they will circle around each other for a short time before they merge. If they are turning in opposite directions (one clockwise and the other counterclockwise), the two vortices will repel each other.

Dr. Sakuhei Fujiwara (sometimes spelled Fujiwhara) was head of the Central Meteorological Bureau in Tokyo shortly after World War I.

1922

• L. F. (Lewis Fry) Richardson published *Weather Prediction by Numerical Process*, in which he described a numerical method for forecasting the weather. His method was based on the idea that a rise or fall in surface atmospheric pressure reflects a convergence or divergence of air throughout the column of air that extends from the surface all the way to the tropopause. By applying the laws of physics to the observed situation, he believed it possible to calculate how the atmosphere would change for hours or days ahead. His system failed, partly for want of accurate measurements of conditions in the upper atmosphere and partly because the convergence and divergence of air varies at different heights and these differences are much more important than overall convergence and divergence throughout the column. The method was also very laborious, necessitating many separate calculations, which in those days had to be made without the help of calculators and computers, although Richardson invented a

Calculator invented by Lewis Fry Richardson for use in numerical forecasting. The calculator, resembling a cylindrical slide rule, allows the operator to perform mathematical operations rapidly. Nevertheless, it was too slow for the vast number of calculations needed to forecast the weather before that weather arrived.

cylindrical, hand-held calculator to help. This resembled a slide rule and is shown in the illustration.

A variant of his "numerical forecasting" was introduced in the 1950s, however, and is still used. The first routine forecasts calculated in this way were made in 1955 in the United States and 1965 in Britain. Modern numerical forecasting uses data obtained from measurements made at many different heights and calculates changes and their effects on one another at each level, and also allows for many more influences on the weather than was possible earlier. So many calculations are required that numerical forecasting became practicable only with the introduction of fast supercomputers. Without them, it took so long to prepare the forecast that the predicted weather had passed before the forecast could be issued.

Lewis Fry Richardson (1881–1953) was a British mathematician and meteorologist born at Newcastle-upon-Tyne, in northeastern England, into a Quaker family and educated in York and at Cambridge University. He received his doctorate in 1927, when he was 47 years of age, from the University of London—one year after he had been elected to a fellowship of the Royal Society. Richardson worked for the National Physical Laboratory from 1903 to 1904. He joined the Meteorological Office in 1913 but resigned in 1920 when the Meteorological Office was absorbed into the Air Ministry. As a member of the Society of Friends, for whom pacifism is a basic tenet, he could not work for a military establishment. He became head of the physics department at Westminster Training College, and in 1929 he was appointed principal of Paisley Technical College (now the University of Paisley), where he remained until his retirement in 1940.

Many of the ways Richardson found of applying mathematics to complex problems were imaginative and years ahead of their time. He even used mathematics to try to discover the causes of war. He died at Kilmun, Argyll, Scotland.

1923

- Sir Gilbert Thomas Walker (1868–1958) proposed that close to the equator there is a high-level movement of air flowing from west to east, counterbalancing the trade winds blowing near the surface. This upper-air flow is now called the Walker circulation. Walker also published a description of periodic changes in the distribution of tropical air pressure that are associated with it. He called these the Southern Oscillation. By the 1970s they were recognized as contributing to the appearance of El Niño, a current in the tropical South Pacific linked to major climatic events. Today both are considered as a single phenomenon, called an El Niño—Southern Oscillation (ENSO) event. The diagram shows how changes in the pressure distribution—the Southern Oscillation—drive El Niño.

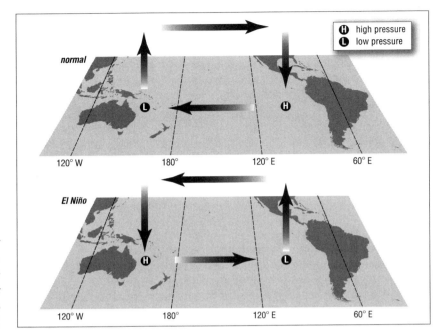

*El Niño—
Southern Oscillation.
A reversal of pressure
distribution that
allows warm water to
flow eastward.*

Sir Gilbert Thomas Walker was a British meteorologist and professor of meteorology at Imperial College, London. He was appointed director of the Indian meteorological service in 1904. There had been severe famines in 1877 and 1899 due to the failure of the Indian monsoon, and Walker was asked to investigate the possibility of predicting monsoon failures, a topic in which he took a particular interest. It was his study of the monsoons that led him to his discovery of the Walker circulation and the Southern Oscillation.

1924

• G. M. B. (Gordon Miller Bourne) Dobson invented the Dobson spectrophotometer, an instrument that measures the intensity of ultraviolet (UV) radiation at different wavelengths. Ozone absorbs UV at certain known wavelengths, therefore spectrophotometer measurements can be used to infer the concentration of atmospheric ozone. Ozone concentrations are reported in "Dobson units." These refer to the thickness of the layer that would result if all other atmospheric gases were removed and the ozone subjected to sea-level pressure. One Dobson unit (DU) is equal to a thickness of 0.0004 inch (0.01 mm).

Gordon Miller Bourne Dobson (1889–1976) was a British physicist and meteorologist. He was director of the experimental department at the Royal Aircraft Establishment in Farnborough during World War I, and in 1920 he became a lecturer in meteorology at the University of Oxford. During World War II, Dobson studied atmospheric humidity in order to forecast the altitude at which aircraft condensation trails would form. In the course of this research he invented the first frost-point hygrometer. Dobson was elected a fellow of the Royal Society in 1927, and in 1945 Oxford University conferred the title of professor on him. He retired in 1956 but continued to study ozone. He died in Oxford.

1931

- Wilson Alwyn Bentley published *Snow Crystals*, a book containing more than 2,000 of the more than 5,000 photomicrographs (photographs taken through a microscope) he had taken of snowflakes over a number of years. His photographs were of such high quality that they aroused scientific interest in the subject and contributed to the development of an international system for classifying types of snowflakes.

  Wilson Alwyn Bentley (1865–1931) was an American farmer and meteorologist who lived in Jericho, Vermont, where snow falls every winter. He was educated at home by his mother, a former schoolteacher. She used a microscope as a teaching aid, and Wilson was fascinated by the world it revealed to him. He was especially entranced by the beauty of snowflakes, dewdrops, frost crystals, and hailstones. He drew what he saw, but this proved unsatisfactory. Eventually he was able to buy a bellows camera and microscope objective, allowing him to take micrographs. All of his micrographs were taken using this original equipment. He never changed it.

  In summer, when there was no snow, he studied raindrops and devised a method for measuring their size. He would expose a dish containing a layer of sifted flour about 1 inch (2.5 cm) deep. When raindrops fell into the flour, they formed balls of dough he could measure. This method is still used. From their sizes, Bentley deduced how the raindrops had formed. He made more than 300 measurements of raindrops between 1898 and 1904.

  In 1898 Bentley wrote his first magazine article, for *Popular Scientific Monthly*. Many more popular articles followed, but *Snow Crystals* was his only book.

  In 1924 Bentley received the first research grant ever awarded by the American Meteorological Society. He maintained meticulous meteorological records throughout most of his life. He died on his farm.

- C. W. (Charles Warren) Thornthwaite published a system for classifying climates. He divided climates into groups according to the types of natural vegetation typical of them. This is determined by what Thornthwaite called "precipitation effectiveness," calculated by dividing the total monthly precipitation (P) by the total monthly evaporation (E). The 12 monthly values are then added to produce a P/E index, from which five "humidity provinces" are defined. A P/E index of more than

127 (called "wet") indicates rain forest; 64–127 (humid) is forest; 32–63 (subhumid) is grassland; 16–31 (semiarid) is steppe; and less than 16 (arid) is desert. In 1948, Thornthwaite revised his system to incorporate a moisture index, which relates the water needed by plants to the available precipitation by calculation of an index of potential evapotranspiration (PE). He also included an index of thermal efficiency, calculated from monthly temperatures, with 0 indicating a frost climate and 127 a tropical climate.

Charles Warren Thornthwaite (1889–1963) was one of the most eminent climatologists of his generation, with an international reputation. He was born in Bay County, Michigan, and educated at Central Michigan High School (now University), from which he graduated in 1922 as a science teacher, and he received his doctorate in 1929 from the University of California, Berkeley. He taught on the faculties of the Universities of Oklahoma (1927–34), Maryland (1940–46), and Johns Hopkins University (1946–55). He was head of the Division of Climatic and Physiographic Research of the U.S. Soil Conservation Service (1935–42), and from 1946 until his death he was director of the Laboratory of Climatology at Seabrook, New Jersey, and professor of climatology at Drexel Institute of Technology, Philadelphia. He was president of the Section of Meteorology of the American Geophysical Union from 1941 to 1944, and in 1951 he was elected president of the Commission for Climatology of the World Meteorological Organization. He held this post until his death.

1936

- Ukichiro Nakaya became the first person to grow artificial snow crystals in a laboratory at the University of Hokkaido, Japan.

  Ukichiro Nakaya (1900–62) was trained as a nuclear physicist. In 1932 he was appointed a professor at the University of Hokkaido. The university had no facilities for conducting nuclear research, and so, inspired by the work of Wilson A. Bentley (see 1931), Nakaya turned his attention to snowflakes, which were abundant. Growing crystals allowed him to describe the way snowflakes form under different conditions. He identified and cataloged all the major snowflake types.

1940

- Carl-Gustav Arvid Rossby discovered large undulations in the westerly winds of the middle and upper troposphere. These are now known as Rossby waves. They have wavelengths of 2,500–3,750 miles (4,000–6,000 km) and are also known to occur in the oceans. Rossby showed that the upper winds have a powerful effect on the weather. When they blow strongly, active frontal systems develop beneath them, producing stormy conditions. When they are weak, cold air is able to move south.

Carl-Gustav Arvid Rossby (1898–1957) was one of the most eminent meteorologists of the 20th century. He made major contributions to our understanding of the behavior of air masses and air movements. After 1954 he initiated and led worldwide studies in atmospheric chemistry.

He was born and educated in Stockholm, Sweden. After graduating with a degree in theoretical mechanics from the University of Stockholm in 1918, he worked at the Bergen Geophysical Institute, collaborating with Vilhelm Bjerknes (see 1902). Bjerknes took a post at the University of Leipzig in 1921, and Rossby went with him. In 1922 Rossby returned to Stockholm to join the Swedish Meteorological Hydrologic Service. He went on several oceanographic expeditions, while at the same time studying mathematics, graduating in 1925 from the University of Stockholm with a licentiate—a degree one rank below a doctorate. He visited the United States in 1926 with a scholarship from the Scandinavian-American Foundation and joined the staff of the U.S. Weather Bureau in Washington, D.C. He moved to California in 1927, and in 1928 he was appointed professor of meteorology at the Massachusetts Institute of Technology (MIT). In 1939 he became assistant chief of research and education at the Weather Bureau but left in 1940 to become chairman of the Institute of Meteorology at the University of Chicago. He returned to Sweden in 1947 in order to establish the Institute of Meteorology at the University of Stockholm. He died in Stockholm.

- On June 30, the U.S. Weather Bureau was transferred from the Department of Agriculture to the Department of Commerce.

1946

- Vincent Joseph Schaefer discovered that pellets of dry ice (solid carbon dioxide) at about −9.5°F (−23°C) injected into moist air caused water vapor to be deposited directly as ice crystals. Like many discoveries, this one was made by accident. Schaefer and his colleague Bernard Vonnegut were working at the General Electric Research Laboratory in Schenectady, New York, as research assistants to Nobel laureate Irving Langmuir (1881–1957). They were investigating the crystallization of ice from moist air, a topic of some importance because of problems due to the icing of the wings of airplanes. (This reduced the lift produced by the wings and was the cause of many crashes.) Schaefer and Vonnegut used a refrigerated box in which they attempted to make crystals form on various types of dust particle. There was a spell of very hot weather in July 1946, and keeping the temperature in the box low enough for the experiments became difficult. Schaefer tried chilling the air in the box by dropping dry ice pellets into it, and within moments a miniature snowstorm filled the box.

Realizing the importance of his discovery, on November 13, 1946, Schaefer tried a bigger experiment. He was flown above a layer of cloud over Pittsfield, Massachusetts, dropped 6 pounds (2.7 kg) of dry ice pellets into the cloud, and triggered a snowstorm. This success led to many attempts at modifying or controlling the weather and was the start of the science of experimental meteorology.

Vincent Joseph Schaefer (1906–93) was born and died in Schenectady. He dropped out of school at 16, went to work in the machine shop of the General Electric Corporation (GE) but later returned to his studies. He graduated in 1928 from the Davey Institute of Tree Surgery and for a time worked as a tree surgeon. Throughout his life he had a great love of the open air (and skiing), but although he enjoyed working with trees, financial pressures forced him to return to GE. Langmuir made him an assistant in 1933 and they worked together throughout World War II, inventing several devices that proved useful. Schaefer left GE in 1954 and from then until 1958 was research director at the Munitalp Foundation, after which he devoted his time to research and education. He joined the faculty of the State University of New York in 1959, became a founder of the Atmospheric Sciences Research Center in 1960, and was its director from 1966 to 1976.

Bernard Vonnegut (1914–97) was born at Indianapolis, Indiana, and educated at the Massachusetts Institute of Technology (MIT), graduating in 1936. He obtained his doctorate from MIT in 1937 for research into aircraft icing. He worked for the Hartford Empire Company from 1939 to 1941, and from 1941 to 1945 he was a research associate at MIT. He moved to GE in 1945. Following the cloud-seeding experiments using dry ice, Vonnegut sought other materials that were easier to handle and might produce a similar effect. He proposed using silver iodide crystals. Experiments with these proved successful, and silver iodide is now the substance most often used. It can be stored at room temperature, and, unlike dry ice, there is no need to release it from an aircraft flying above a target cloud. Silver iodide can be released from the ground to be carried upward by air currents. Vonnegut moved to the Arthur D. Little Corporation in 1952, and in 1967 he was appointed distinguished research professor at the State University of New York. He held this position until his death at Albany, New York.

1949

- Radar was first used to obtain meteorological data as part of the U.S. Thunderstorm Project.

1951

- An international system was adopted by the International Commission on Snow and Ice for the classification of types of snow crystals. It divides

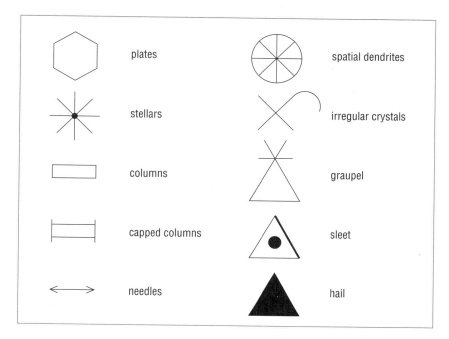

plates		spatial dendrites	
stellars		irregular crystals	
columns		graupel	
capped columns		sleet	
needles		hail	

Snow crystals. There are seven basic crystal types and three types of icy precipitation, each represented by a symbol.

snow crystals into seven principal types, each of which can be divided into subtypes, and an additional three types of frozen precipitation: graupel, sleet (ice pellets), and hailstones. The classification allows crystals to be grouped in seven major ways to form 41 types of snowflakes, according to a scheme devised by Ukichiro Nakaya (see 1936). In 1966 the Nakaya scheme was expanded to describe 80 distinct snowflake types. The illustration shows the standard symbols that are used to describe snow crystals.

1954

- Ukichiro Nakaya, of the University of Hokkaido, Japan (see 1936), published *Snow Crystals*, the classic work on the form and structure of snowflakes.

1959

- The U.S. Weather Bureau began publishing a temperature-humidity index (THI) as an indication of how comfortable or uncomfortable people will feel a hot day to be and whether or not the conditions represent a risk to health. The index is a number representing the apparent temperature, which is calculated from the actual air temperature and the relative humidity (RH). These values can then be arranged as a chart, shown in the illustration.

To use the chart, measure the temperature and relative humidity. Find the temperature in the left-hand column and the RH in the row along the top. Where the row from the temperature meets the column from the RH, the value is the THI. A value of less than 80 presents no risk to most people. Caution should be exercised at 80–90 and extreme caution at 90–106. Values of 106–130 are dangerous, and any value above 131 is extremely dangerous.

1960

• *Tiros 1* (Television and Infrared Observation Satellite), the first weather satellite, was launched by the United States on April 1.

1961

• Edward Norton Lorenz discovered that weather systems behave chaotically. While developing a computer model of weather systems, Lorenz ran the model, but for a second run decided to save time by omitting the last few decimal places in some of the initial values. This was equivalent to a difference of 1/1000. Nevertheless, during its second run the model described the development of a completely different weather pattern.

Edward Norton Lorenz was born in 1917 in West Hartford, Connecticut. He was educated at Dartmouth College, Harvard University, and the Massachusetts Institute of Technology (MIT). During World War II Lorenz served in the U.S. Army Air Corps as a weather forecaster. He obtained a post at MIT in 1946, where he received a doctorate of science in 1948. From 1962 to 1981 he was professor of meteorology at MIT and has been emeritus professor of meteorology since 1981.

Temperature-humidity index. Measure the air temperature and relative humidity, and then check these against each other to read the apparent temperature.

temp.	relative humidity (%)									
°F (°C)	10	20	30	40	50	60	70	80	90	100
80 (27)	75	77	78	79	81	82	85	86	88	91
85 (29)	80	82	84	86	88	90	93	97	102	108
90 (32)	85	87	90	93	96	100	106	113	122	
95 (35)	90	93	96	101	107	114	124	136		
100 (38)	95	99	104	110	120	132	144			
105 (40)	100	105	113	123	135	149				
110 (43)	105	112	123	137	150					
115 (46)	111	120	135	151						

1964

- The satellite *Nimbus 1* was launched on August 24. This was the first weather satellite to produce high-quality photographs taken at night.

1965

- On July 13, the U.S. Weather Bureau became part of the Environmental Science Administration.

1966

- The *Applications Technology Satellite-1* (*ATS-1*), the first meteorological satellite to be placed in geostationary orbit, was launched by the United States over the Pacific on December 6.
- The U.S. Army drilled an ice core 4,600 feet (1,403 m) long from the Greenland ice cap. The Danish geophysicist Willi Dansgaard and his colleagues used this to construct a history of climate over the past 100,000 years by means of measuring the ratio of two isotopes of oxygen ($^{16}O:^{18}O$) in the ice.

  Willi Dansgaard was born in 1922 in Copenhagen and was educated at the University of Copenhagen, receiving his doctorate in 1961. He is now professor emeritus of geophysics at Copenhagen University and a member of the Royal Danish Academy of Science and Letters, the Royal Swedish Academy of Sciences, and the Danish Geophysical Society.

1967

- The U.S. Weather Bureau was renamed the National Weather Service.

1971

- T. Theodore Fujita, his wife and collaborator Sumiko Fujita, and Allen Pearson published a standard six-point scale for reporting tornado intensity. The Fujita Tornado Intensity Scale relates wind speed to the damage caused.

  Tetsuya Theodore Fujita (1920–98; he adopted the name Theodore in 1968) was born in Kitakyushu City, Japan. He was a student specializing in tropical cyclones when the atomic bomb was dropped on Hiroshima on August 6, 1945. The bomb generated firestorms with associated tornadoes. Fujita became keenly interested in tornadoes. He moved to the United States in 1950 to take a post at the University of Chicago, where he continued to pursue this research topic and where he later became professor of meteorology. Fujita found that a single storm could trigger a number of tornadoes; he called these "tornado families." He also identified and described the *downburst* and *microburst*, two important meteorological phenomena.

Allen D. Pearson was appointed director of the Severe Local Storms Warning Center (SELS) in 1965, based in Kansas City, Missouri. In 1966 the Weather Bureau Office was renamed the National Severe Storms Forecast Center (NSSFC). It moved from Kansas City to Norman, Oklahoma in 1997. Dr. Pearson was transferred to Central Region Headquarters of the Environmental Services Administration in 1980.

1973

• Doppler radar was used for the first time to study processes inside a tornado funnel.

1974

• Frank Sherwood Rowland and Mario José Molina proposed that chlorofluorocarbon (CFC) compounds used as aerosol propellants, working fluids in refrigerators, freezers, and air conditioners, and in making foam plastics may survive in the atmosphere long enough for significant amounts to penetrate the stratosphere. There they might engage in a chain of chemical reactions leading to the depletion of ozone. For this work they shared with Paul Crutzen the 1995 Nobel Prize for chemistry.

Frank Sherwood Rowland was born in 1927 in Delaware, Ohio. He was educated at schools in Delaware, and in 1943 he enrolled at Ohio Wesleyan University. In 1945 he enlisted in the navy, resuming his studies after his discharge. He graduated in 1948 and moved to the University of Chicago, where he received his doctorate in 1952 and went to Princeton University as an instructor in the chemistry department. He was an assistant professor at the University of Kansas (1956–64), and in 1964 he was appointed professor of chemistry at the University of California, Irvine, where he is now Donald Bren Research Professor of Chemistry and Earth System Science. From 1953 to 1994 Rowland also conducted research at the Brookhaven National Laboratory.

Mario José Molina was born in 1943 in Mexico City. He was educated in Switzerland and at the Universidad Nacional Autónoma de Mexico in Mexico City, graduating in chemical engineering. He taught and conducted research there and at the University of California at Irvine and worked at the Jet Propulsion Laboratory of the California Institute of Technology in Pasadena from 1982 to 1989. He moved to the department of earth, atmospheric and planetary sciences and department of chemistry at the Massachusetts Institute of Technology (MIT) in 1989. In 1997 he was named MIT Institute Professor.

Paul Crutzen was born in 1933 in Amsterdam, the Netherlands. His schooling was interrupted by World War II and later by ill health, but from 1951 to 1954 he studied civil engineering. From 1954 to 1958 he worked for the Bridge Construction Bureau of the City of Amsterdam, but in 1958 he obtained a job as a computer programmer in the department of meteorology of the University of Stockholm. He received his doctorate in 1968 and a doctorate of science (a higher degree than a Ph.D) in 1973, both from the University of Stockholm. Crutzen left Stockholm in 1969 to work first at the University of Oxford and from 1974 to 1980 at the National Center for Atmospheric Research at Boulder, Colorado. In 1980 he was appointed director of the atmospheric chemistry division of the Max Planck Institute for Chemistry at Mainz, Germany, and was executive director from 1983 to 1985. He held a part-time professorship at the University of Chicago (1987–91) and since 1992 has been a part-time professor at the Scripps Institution of Oceanography of the University of California.

1975

- The first Geostationary Operational Environmental Satellite (*GOES-1*) was launched by the United States on October 16.

1977

- *Meteosat 1*, the first European meteorological satellite to be placed in geostationary orbit, was launched by the United States on November 23. It remained functional until 1985.

1979

- On December 29, Edward Lorenz (see 1961) presented a paper to the annual meeting of the American Association for the Advancement of Science, being held in Washington, D.C. His paper was called "Predictability: Does the Flap of a Butterfly's Wings in Brazil Set Off a Tornado in Texas?" This was the first reference to the "butterfly effect," a metaphor referring to a system that is extremely sensitive to minute variations in its initial conditions. The consequence is that two sets of conditions that appear identical because the differences between them are too small to be observable may develop along widely divergent paths.

1981

- *Meteosat-2*, replacing the original Meteosat, was launched in June.

1985

- J. C. Farman, B. G. Gardiner, and J. D. Shanklin, three scientists working for the British Antarctic Survey, reported the depletion of the ozone layer over Antarctica. Theirs was the first report of the "ozone hole."

1988

- The Intergovernmental Panel on Climate Change (IPCC) was founded by the United Nations Environment Programme (UNEP) and the World Meteorological Organization (WMO).

1989

- The European Space Agency launched the French-built *Meteosat-4*.

1992

- The Topex-Poseidon satellite was launched. It carried instruments to measure very accurately the height of sea level. It achieved this with two measurements. One used a radar signal to measure the distance between the satellite and the ocean surface, the second measures the gravity field of the Earth and calculated from this what the distance from the satellite to the ocean surface would be if the ocean were still. By subtracting one measurement from the other, oceanographers could calculate the height of waves and track the movement of ocean currents. It also allowed scientists to observe changes in the Equatorial Current that precede the onset of an El Niño–Southern Oscillation (ENSO) event. This brought closer the time when ENSO events could be predicted.

1993

- Using powerful supercomputers and advanced climate models, the National Weather Service was able to forecast a major storm five days in advance. This was the first time a storm had been forecast so far ahead.

1995

- F. Sherwood Rowland, Mario Molina, and Paul Crutzen shared the Nobel Prize for chemistry (see 1974).
- On June 3 Joshua Wurman and Jerry M. Straka, scientists at the School of Meteorology at the University of Oklahoma, used new equipment to observe the internal structure of a tornado near Dimmitt, Texas, in more detail than had been possible previously. They used a pencil-beam Doppler radar mounted on a small truck. It transmitted a beam only 1.2° wide from a range of 1.2–3.7 miles (1.9–6 km; the range changed as the tornado moved) and revealed the structure of the tornado, the wall of debris surrounding the core, wind speeds, and the speed (more than 56 MPH, or 90 km/h) of the central downdraft.

WEATHER DATA

BEAUFORT WIND SCALE

Speed MPH (km/h)	Name	Description
0.1 (1.6) or less	Calm	Air feels still. Smoke rises vertically.
1–3 (1.6–4.8)	Light air	Wind vanes and flags do not move, but rising smoke drifts.
4–7 (6.4–11.2)	Light breeze	Drifting smoke indicates the wind direction.
8–12 (12.8–19.3)	Gentle breeze	Leaves rustle, small twigs move, and flags made from lightweight material stir gently.
13–18 (20.9–28.9)	Moderate breeze	Loose leaves and pieces of paper blow about.
19–24 (30.5–38.6)	Fresh breeze	Small trees that are in full leaf sway in the wind.
25–31 (40.2–49.8)	Strong breeze	It becomes difficult to use an open umbrella.
32–38 (51.4–61.1)	Moderate gale	The wind exerts strong pressure on people walking into it.
39–46 (62.7–74)	Fresh gale	Small twigs torn from trees.
47–54 (75.6–86.8)	Strong gale	Chimneys are blown down. Slates and tiles are torn from roofs.
55–63 (88.4–101.3)	Whole gale	Trees are broken or uprooted.
64–75 (102.9–120.6)	Storm	Trees are uprooted and blown some distance. Cars are overturned.
more than 75 (120.6)	Hurricane	Devastation is widespread. Buildings are destroyed and many trees are uprooted.

SAFFIR/SIMPSON HURRICANE SCALE

Category	Pressure at Center mb in. of mercury cm of mercury	Wind Speed MPH km/h	Storm Surge ft. m	Damage
1	980 28.94 73.5	74–95 119–153	4–5 1.2–1.5	Trees and shrubs lose leaves and twigs; mobile homes destroyed.
2	965–979 28.5–28.91 72.39–73.43	96–110 154.4–177	6–8 1.8–2.4	Small trees blown down; exposed mobile homes severely damaged; chimneys and tiles blown from roofs.
3	945–964 27.91–28.47 70.9–72.31	111–130 178.5–209	9–12 2.7–3.6	Leaves stripped from trees; large trees blown down; mobile homes demolished; small buildings damaged structurally.
4	920–944 27.17–27.88 69.01–70.82	131–155 210.8–249.4	13–18 3.9–5.4	Extensive damage to windows, roofs, and doors; mobile homes destroyed completely; flooding to 6 miles (10 km) inland; severe damage to lower parts of buildings near exposed coasts.
5	920 or lower below 17.17 below 69	more than 155 more than 250	more than 18 more than 5.4	Catastrophic; all buildings severely damaged, small buildings destroyed; major damage to lower parts of buildings less than 15 feet (4.6 m) above sea level to 0.3 mile (0.5 km) inland.

FUJITA TORNADO INTENSITY SCALE

Rating	Wind Speed		Damage
	MPH	km/h	
Weak			
F–0	40–72	64–116	Slight
F–1	73–112	117–180	Moderate
Strong			
F–2	113–157	182–253	Considerable
F–3	158–206	254–331	Severe
Violent			
F–4	207–260	333–418	Devastating
F–5	261–318	420–512	Incredible

CLOUD CLASSIFICATION

Cloud Level	Height of Base					
	Polar Regions		Temperate Latitudes		Tropics	
	thousands of ft.	thousands of m	thousands of ft.	thousands of m	thousands of ft.	thousands of m
High Cloud:	10–26	3–8	16–43	5–13	16–59	5–18

Types: CIRRUS, CIRROSTRATUS, CIRROCUMULUS

Middle Cloud:	6.5–13	2–4	6.5–23	2–7	6.5–26	2–8

Types: ALTOCUMULUS, ALTOSTRATUS, NIMBOSTRATUS

Low Cloud:	0–6.5	0–2	0–6.5	0–2	0–6.5	0–2

Types: STRATUS, STRATOCUMULUS, CUMULUS, CUMULONIMBUS

CLOUD GENERA

Low-level cloud

Stratus (St) An extensive sheet of featureless cloud that will produce drizzle or fine snow if it is thick enough.

Stratocumulus (Sc) Similar to St, but broken into separate, fluffy-looking masses. If thick enough, it also produces drizzle or fine snow.

Cumulus (Cu) Separate, white, fluffy clouds, usually with flat bases. There may be many of them, all with bases at about the same height.

Cumulonimbus (Cb) Very large cumulus, often towering to a great height. Because they are so thick, Cb clouds are often dark at the base. If the tops are high enough, they will consist of ice crystals and may be swept into an anvil shape.

Medium-level cloud

Altocumulus (Ac) Patches or rolls of cloud joined to make a sheet. Ac is sometimes called "wool-pack cloud."

Altostratus (As) Pale, watery, featureless cloud that forms a sheet through which the Sun may be visible as a white smudge.

Nimbostratus (Ns) A large sheet of featureless cloud, often with rain or snow, that is thick enough to obscure the Sun, Moon, and stars completely. It makes days dull and nights very dark.

High-level cloud

Cirrus (Ci) Patches of white, fibrous cloud, sometimes swept into strands with curling tails ("mares' tails").

Cirrocumulus (Cc) Patches of thin cloud, sometimes forming ripples, fibrous in places, and with no shading that would define their shape.

Cirrostratus (Cs) Thin, almost transparent cloud forming an extensive sheet and just thick enough to produce a halo around the Sun or Moon.

COMPOSITION OF THE PRESENT ATMOSPHERE

Gas	Chemical Formula	Abundance
Major constituents		
nitrogen	N_2	78.08%
oxygen	O_2	20.95%
argon	Ar	0.93%
water vapor	H_2O	variable
Minor constituents		
carbon dioxide	CO_2	365 ppmv
neon	Ne	18 ppmv
helium	He	5 ppmv
methane	CH_4	2 ppmv
krypton	Kr	1 ppmv
hydrogen	H_2	0.5 ppmv
nitrous oxide	N_2O	0.3 ppmv
carbon monoxide	CO	0.05–0.2 ppmv
xenon	Xe	0.08 ppmv
ozone	O_3	variable
Trace constituents		
ammonia	NH_3	4 ppbv
nitrogen dioxide	NO_2	1 ppbv
sulfur dioxide	SO_2	1 ppbv
hydrogen sulfide	H_2S	0.05 ppbv

AIR DENSITY AND HEIGHT

Height		Density	
km	miles	kg m^{-3}	lb ft^{-3}
30	18.6	0.02	0.0012
25	15.5	0.04	0.0025
20	12.4	0.09	0.0056
19	11.8	0.10	0.0062
18	11.2	0.12	0.0075
17	10.6	0.14	0.0087
16	9.9	0.17	0.0106
15	9.3	0.20	0.0125
14	8.7	0.23	0.0143
13	8.1	0.27	0.0169
12	7.5	0.31	0.0193
11	6.8	0.37	0.0231
10	6.2	0.41	0.0256
9	5.6	0.47	0.0293
8	5.0	0.53	0.0331
7	4.3	0.59	0.0368
6	3.7	0.66	0.0412
5	3.1	0.74	0.0462
4	2.5	0.82	0.0512
3	1.9	0.91	0.0568
2	1.2	1.01	0.0630
1	0.6	1.11	0.0693
0	0	1.23	0.0768

ALBEDO

Surface	Value
Fresh snow	0.75–0.95
Old snow	0.40–0.70
Cumuliform cloud	0.70–0.90
Stratiform cloud	0.59–0.84
Cirrostratus	0.44–0.50
Sea ice	0.30–0.40
Dry sand	0.35–0.45
Wet sand	0.20–0.30
Desert	0.25–0.30
Meadow	0.10–0.20
Field crops	0.15–0.25
Deciduous forest	0.10–0.20
Coniferous forest	0.05–0.15
Concrete	0.17–0.27
Black road	0.05–0.10

MEAN SNOW LINE

Latitude	Northern Hemisphere		Southern Hemisphere	
	ft.	m	ft.	m
0–10	15,500	4,727	17,400	5,310
10–20	15,500	4,727	18,400	5,610
20–30	17,400	5,310	16,800	5,125
30–40	14,100	4,300	9,900	3,020
40–50	9,900	3,020	4,900	1,495
50–60	6,600	2,010	2,600	793
60–70	3,300	1,007	0	0
70–80	1,650	503	0	0

CONVERTING SNOWFALL TO RAINFALL EQUIVALENT

Snow to Water Ratios

Temperature		Ratio
°F	°C	
35	1.7	7:1
29–34	–1.7–1.1	10:1
20–28	–6.7– –2.2	15:1
10–19	–12.2– –7.2	20:1
0–9	–17.8– –12.8	30:1
less than 0	less than –17.8	40:1

UV INDEX

UV Category	UVI Value	Time to Burn	Precautions
		minutes	
Minimal	0–2	30–60	Wear a hat
Low	3–4	15–20	Wear a hat; use sunscreen SPF 15+
Moderate	5–6	10–12	Wear a hat; use sunscreen SPF 15+; keep in shade
High	7–9	7–8.5	Wear a hat; use sunscreen SPF 15+; keep in shade; stay indoors between 10 A.M. and 4 P.M.
Very high	10–15	4–6	Stay indoors as much as possible; outdoors, wear a hat and use sunscreen SPF 15+

AVALANCHE CLASSES

*There are five classes. Each class is 10 times
stronger than the one preceding it.*

Class	Damage	Path Width
1	Could knock someone over, but not bury them.	10 m (33 ft.)
2	Could bury, injure, or kill someone.	100 m (330 ft.)
3	Could bury and wreck a car, damage a truck, demolish a small building, break trees.	1,000 m (3,330 ft.)
4	Could wreck a railroad car or big truck, demolish several buildings, or destroy up to 4 ha (10 acres) of forest.	2,000 m (6,560 ft.)
5	Largest known; could destroy a village or up to 40 ha (100 acres) of forest.	3,000 m (9,800 ft.)

GLOBAL WARMING POTENTIALS
FOR PRINCIPAL GREENHOUSE GASES

Gas	Global Warming Potential
Carbon dioxide	1
Methane	21
Nitrous oxide	310
CFC-11	3,400
CFC-12	7,100
Perfluorocarbons	7,400
Hydrofluorocarbons	140–11,700
Sulfur hexafluoride	23,900

Glossary

ablation   The disappearance of ice and snow from the surface because it has melted or sublimed (changed directly from solid to gas).

absolute humidity   The mass of water present in a unit volume of air, usually expressed as grams of water vapor per cubic meter of air.

absolute temperature   Temperature measured on the kelvin scale and reported in kelvins (K), without a degree sign (that is, as 300K, not 300° K). 1K = 1°C = 1.8°F.

absolute vorticity   Relative vorticity plus the local effect of the rotation of the Earth about its own axis. *See* RELATIVE VORTICITY; VORTICITY.

absolute zero   Zero on the kelvin scale (0K). It is the temperature at which the kinetic energy of atoms and molecules is at a minimum. According to the third law of thermodynamics, 0K cannot be attained, although temperatures within a few millionths of a degree of 0K have been reached experimentally. 0K = –273.15°C = –459.67°F.

accessory cloud   A small cloud that is attached to a much larger cloud. The most common accessory clouds are pileus, tuba, and velum.

acid precipitation   Rain, snow, mist, fog, or dew that has a pH lower than 5.0 (that is, it is more acid than ordinary rain). *See* DRY DEPOSITION.

adiabat   The rate at which a parcel of air cools as it ascends and warms as it descends.

adiabatic   A change in the temperature and pressure of a mass of air that occurs without any exchange of energy with the surrounding air. When a "parcel" of air rises it expands and cools adiabatically; when it descends it contracts and warms adiabatically. *See* DIABATIC TEMPERATURE CHANGE.

advection   The horizontal transfer of heat that occurs when warm air moves across a cold surface or cold air moves across a warm surface and heat is exchanged between the air and the surface.

advection fog   Fog that forms when warm, moist air moves over a cold land or water surface. The air is cooled by contact with the surface, causing some of its water vapor to condense. *See* RADIATION FOG.

aerial plankton   Bacteria, spores, and other biological material and organisms that are carried aloft by air currents and transported, often for long distances.

aerosol   Solid or liquid particles that are suspended in the air, such as soil particles, dust, salt crystals, smoke, and aerial plankton.

airborne expendable bathythermograph system buoys (AXBT buoys) Buoys carrying instruments to measure atmospheric and sea-surface conditions that are dropped into the ocean by aircraft. The buoys transmit data by radio.

air frost   The condition in which the air temperature is below freezing.

airlight Light that is scattered toward an observer by aerosols and air molecules lying between the observer and more distant objects, rendering these less clearly visible. Airlight decreases at sunset, allowing the stars to become visible, and increases at dawn, causing the stars to become invisible.

air mass Air that covers a very large area, such as an ocean or continent, and throughout which the temperature, pressure, and humidity are approximately constant at every height.

albedo The reflectivity of a surface to solar radiation. A light-colored surface, such as snow, reflects a high percentage of the light and radiant heat falling on it and has a high albedo; a dark-colored surface absorbs a high percentage of the light and radiant heat falling on it and has a low albedo. Albedo is expressed as the percentage of radiation reflected from the surface, either as a percentage (such as 80 percent) or as a decimal fraction (such as 0.8).

Alberta low An area of low atmospheric pressure that sometimes develops over the eastern slopes of the Rocky Mountains in Alberta, Canada. Air passing over the mountains acquires a cyclonic (counterclockwise) circulation. As the low moves eastward it brings storms and heavy precipitation.

Aleutian low An area of low atmospheric pressure that is centered over the Aleutian Islands, at about 50° N. The low generates many storms that travel eastward and tend to merge. The low is present for most of the winter and is almost stationary.

amphidromic point Where the tide flows into a confined area and circulates around it (counterclockwise in the Northern Hemisphere and clockwise in the Southern Hemisphere), the point around which the wave moves. At the amphidromic point there is no rise and fall of water with the tides.

anabatic wind A wind that blows up the side of a hill or other gradient.

anemometer An instrument for measuring wind speed. Some measure the pressure against a plate exposed at right angles to the wind, but the commonest design consists of small cups

Anemometers. The drawings show two widely used types. the rotating-cups and swinging-plate anemometer.

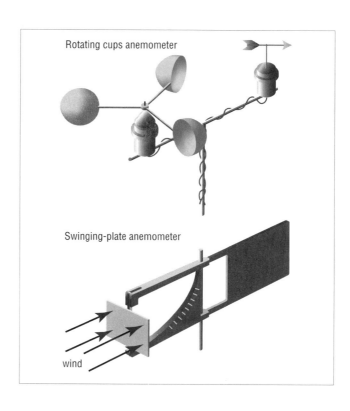

Rotating cups anemometer

Swinging-plate anemometer

wind

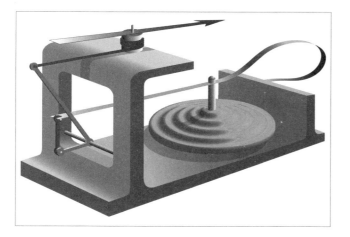

Aneroid barometer. The metal box expands and contracts with changes in air pressure. A spring and levers transfer these movements to a pointer on a dial.

mounted at the ends of horizontal arms and free to spin about a vertical axis. (*See* illustration.) The pressure on the plate or rotational speed of the spinning cups is converted into wind speed and shown on a dial.

aneroid barometer   A barometer that comprises a small, corrugated metal box that expands and contracts with changes in air pressure. Its movements are either measured electrically and translated into values for air pressure displayed digitally, or by means of levers and a spring connected to a needle on a dial. (*See* illustration.)

angular momentum   The combination of forces acting on any body spinning about its own axis. These include the mass of the body, its rate of spin (angular velocity), and the radius of rotation measured from the rotational axis to the furthest point on the body. (*See* diagram.) In the absence of friction and outside forces acting on the body, angular momentum remains constant (is conserved), so that if one of its components changes, one or more of the others changes to compensate.

Angular momentum. Angular momentum is determined by the mass of the rotating body, its radius of rotation, and its angular velocity (speed of rotation).

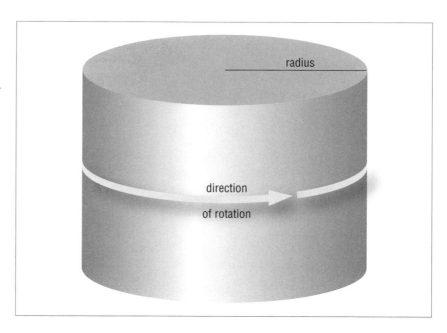

angular velocity   The number of degrees through which a rotating body turns in one second.

anticyclone   A region in which the air pressure is higher than it is in the surrounding air.

anticyclonic   Adjective describing the situation in which a fluid (usually air) flows around an area of relatively high pressure, such that pressure increases toward the center. Anticyclonic flow is clockwise in the Northern Hemisphere and counterclockwise in the Southern Hemisphere.

aqueduct   A channel built to carry water, often over low-lying around.

aquiclude (aquifuge)   A rock that is almost impermeable, so that although it may be saturated, water is unable to flow through it.

aquifer   Porous rock, gravel, sand, or other granular material below the ground surface that is saturated with water and through which water flows very slowly. *See* CONFINED AQUIFER; PERCHED AQUIFER; UNCONFINED AQUIFER.

aquifuge   *See* AQUICLUDE.

arctic sea smoke   Fog that forms when water evaporating into a boundary layer of relatively warm air rises through that layer and into much colder air flowing from the surface of an ice sheet or glacier. Arctic sea smoke is often very dense, but confined to a layer no more than about 35 feet (10 m) deep.

Atlantic conveyor   *See* GREAT CONVEYOR.

Atlantic multidecadal oscillation   A climate change over the North Atlantic Ocean that occurs over a 50–70-year cycle and produces temperature changes of several tenths of a degree Celsius to either side of the mean.

atmometer   An instrument that measures the rate of evaporation.

atmosphere   *See* STANDARD ATMOSPHERE.

avalanche wind   A wind consisting of air that is pushed ahead of an avalanche. A major avalanche can generate a wind of up to 185 MPH (300 km/h).

axial tilt   The angle between the Earth's rotational axis and a line perpendicular to the plane of the ecliptic (*see* diagram). This angle varies from 22.1° to 24.5° over a period of about 41,000 years; at present it is 23.45°. The axial tilt determines the latitude of the Tropics (23.45°)

Axial tilt. The Earth's rotational axis is tilted with respect to a line perpendicular to the plane of the ecliptic. At present the tilt is 23.45°.

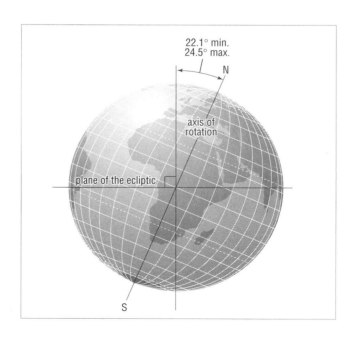

and also the height of the Sun above the horizon at the summer solstice at the poles (23.45°).

Azores high   A region of high atmospheric pressure that is centered approximately over the Azores, 800 miles (1,290 km) west of Portugal. It sometimes extends as far as Bermuda, when it is known in North America as the Bermuda high.

backing   A counterclockwise change in wind direction, for instance from west to southwest. *Compare* VEERING.

balloon sounding   A measurement of atmospheric conditions made by instruments carried below a weather balloon.

bar   A unit of pressure; 1 bar = 10^5 newtons m^{-2} = 10^6 dynes cm^{-2}. Weather reports and forecasts often quote pressure in millibars (1 bar = 1,000 mb), but the scientific unit of pressure is the pascal (1 mb = 100 Pa).

Beaufort scale   A scale for estimating wind speed by its effect on everyday objects, such as falling leaves, smoke, and trees. The scale was devised in 1806 by Francis Beaufort (eventually Rear Admiral Sir Francis Beaufort), originally to guide sailors as to the amount of sail their ships should carry in various wind conditions. The scale allots a force to each wind strength from 0 to 12; five more values were added in 1955 by meteorologists at the U.S. Weather Bureau to describe hurricane-force winds.

Bermuda high   *See* AZORES HIGH.

Bernoulli effect   The fall in pressure in a fluid passing through a constriction. It was discovered in 1738 by the Swiss mathematician Daniel Bernoulli and explains why aerofoil surfaces generate lift, why hurricane winds can lift roofs from buildings, and why the pressure at the center of a vortex must be lower than the pressure outside.

biological oxygen demand (BOD)   A measure of water pollution by organic material such as sewage or decaying vegetation. A sample of water is taken and the amount of oxygen dissolved in it measured. The sample is then stored in darkness at constant temperature for several days and the content of dissolved oxygen measured again. The reduction in this amount is due to oxygen consumed by the bacterial oxidation of organic matter and can be used as a pollution measure. *See* CHEMICAL OXYGEN DEMAND.

black blizzard   A dust storm comprising mainly dark-colored particles.

blackbody   An object (body) that absorbs all of the radiant energy falling on it, then radiates all of the energy it has absorbed at a wavelength proportional to its temperature.

blackbody radiation   Radiation from a blackbody.

black frost   A frost that blackens plants but produces no ice crystals on surfaces. It occurs when the air is extremely dry, so the temperature can fall far below freezing without causing saturation. Moisture freezes inside plant tissues, but no frost forms on exposed surfaces.

black ice   Ice that forms a layer over exposed surfaces when rain that is close to freezing falls onto surfaces that are below freezing. The raindrops spread on impact and freeze almost instantly, forming a thin layer onto which further raindrops spread and freeze.

blizzard   Wind-driven snow combined with a very low air temperature. The National Weather Service defines a blizzard as a wind of at least 35 MPH (56 km/h), with a temperature of 20°F (–7°C) or lower, and snow falling heavily enough to produce a layer not less than 10 inches (250 mm) thick or snow blown up from the surface, the snow reducing horizontal visibility to less than 1/4 mile (400 m).

blocking   The effect of a stationary mass of high-pressure air, bringing settled fine weather to the region over which it lies and forcing other weather systems to move around it.

BOD   *See* BIOLOGICAL OXYGEN DEMAND.

bolometer   An instrument that measures radiant energy.

boundary layer   A layer of air lying adjacent to a surface and within which air conditions are strongly influenced by the proximity of the surface.

burst of monsoon   The abrupt onset of the summer (wet) monsoon.

Buys Ballot's law   The observation, made in 1857 by the Dutch meteorologist Christoph Buys Ballot, that in the Northern Hemisphere winds flow clockwise around areas of high pressure and counterclockwise around areas of low pressure (these directions are reversed in the Southern Hemisphere). Expressed another way, if you stand with your back to the wind, in the Northern Hemisphere the area of low pressure is to your left. A few months before Buys Ballot published his observation, the American meteorologist William Ferrel calculated from the laws of physics that this would be the case.

Campbell-Stokes sunshine recorder   An instrument that measures the daily number of hours of sunshine. It comprises a spherical lens that focuses sunlight onto a card that partly encircles the lens and that is graduated with a time scale.

CAT   *See* CLEAR AIR TURBULENCE.

catchment   In Britain, the area from which water drains into a river or groundwater system. *See* DIVIDE; WATERSHED.

CCN   *See* CLOUD CONDENSATION NUCLEI.

ceiling   The height of the cloud base or of anything else that obscures the sky.

ceilometer   A device for measuring the height of the ceiling. It comprises a projector and a detector. The projector has two lamps, each of which emits a focused beam through a shutter. The focusing mirrors and lamps rotate, so the projector transmits light pulses at a predetermined frequency onto the ceiling. The detector, set some distance away, responds electronically to light pulses at that frequency reflected from the ceiling. The height of the ceiling is calculated by trigonometry from the angles of the transmitted and reflected beams and the known distance between the projector and detector. (*See* illustration.)

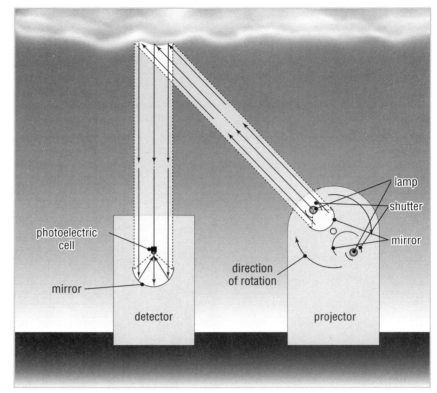

Ceilometer. The projector transmits light pulses that are reflected from the base of the cloud (the ceiling). The detector receives the reflections. It is then possible to calculate the ceiling height by trigonometry.

lamp

shutter

mirror

photoelectric cell

mirror

direction of rotation

detector

projector

chemical oxygen demand (COD) A measure of the pollution of water by organic matter in which dichromate is added to a water sample. The sample is heated, and after two hours it is examined spectrographically to determine the change in color produced by the oxidation of the organic compounds. The test is simpler and quicker than that for biological oxygen demand (BOD), and since the ratio of COD:BOD is fairly constant for a particular type of contaminant, BOD can be inferred from COD *See* BIOLOGICAL OXYGEN DEMAND.

clear air turbulence (CAT) Vertical air currents in unstable, unsaturated air. Because the air is unsaturated, no cloud forms. Wind shear close to the jet stream is the commonest cause of CAT.

climate diagram A graph that shows the average monthly temperature and rainfall for a specified place. Additional information is often added. (*See* illustration.)

cloud condensation nuclei (CCN) Small particles onto which vapor will condense readily when the relative humidity approaches 100 percent.

cold cloud A cloud whose temperature is below freezing throughout and which therefore consists entirely of ice crystals and snowflakes. *Compare* MIXED CLOUD; WARM CLOUD.

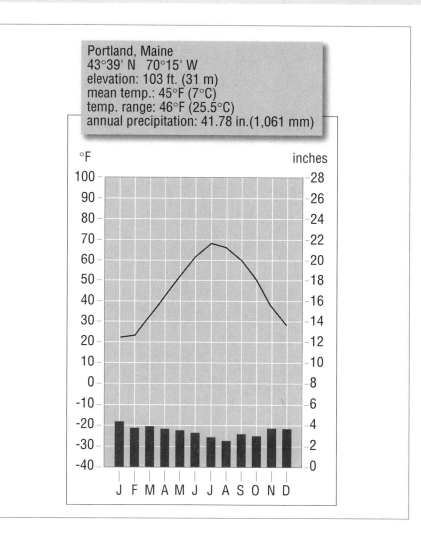

Portland, Maine
43°39' N 70°15' W
elevation: 103 ft. (31 m)
mean temp.: 45°F (7°C)
temp. range: 46°F (25.5°C)
annual precipitation: 41.78 in.(1,061 mm)

Climate diagram. This shows the average temperature and rainfall month by month for a specified place, with the location, elevation, and annual averages shown at the top.

cold wave A large and rapid drop in temperature. Over most of the United States, a cold wave is defined as a drop in temperature of at least 20°F (11°C) over a period not exceeding 24 hours that reduces the temperature to 0°F (–18°C) or lower. In California, the Gulf Coast states, and Florida, the temperature drop must be of 16°F (9°C) or more to a temperature of 32°F (0°C) or lower.

conditional instability The condition of air that is cooler and therefore denser than air above and so remains at a constant height (it is stable), but that becomes unstable if it is forced to rise high enough for its water vapor to start condensing. Condensation releases latent heat, warming the air and making it less dense than the air above it.

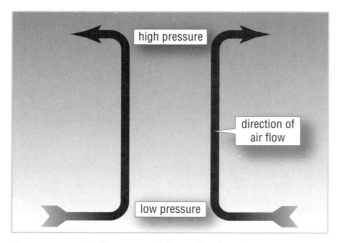

Convergence. Air flows inward from all sides, then rises, producing low pressure near the surface and high pressure above, where the rising air diverges.

confined aquifer   An aquifer that lies beneath a layer of impermeable material. *Compare* UNCONFINED AQUIFER; *See* PERCHED AQUIFER.

contingent drought   Drought that results from a prolonged lack of rain in regions where rainfall is highly variable everywhere, but usually high enough to prevent drought.

convergence   The condition when air approaches an area from different directions. The converging air rises. This produces an area of low surface pressure. Where the rising air meets an inversion level it produces an area of high pressure, from which it diverges. (*See* diagram.)

CorF   *See* CORIOLIS EFFECT.

Coriolis effect (Coriolis force; CorF)   The apparent eastward deflection of a fluid that flows away from the equator and westward deflection of one flowing toward the equator. No force is involved, the deflection being wholly due to the rotation of the Earth, the Earth's surface traveling at a different speed from the fluid crossing it. This explains the flow of air around areas of high and low pressure (*see* BUYS BALLOT'S LAW) and the approximately circular flow of ocean currents. The effect was discovered in 1835 by the French physicist Gaspard de Coriolis.

Coriolis force   *See* CORIOLIS EFFECT.

cyclone   A region in which the air pressure is lower than it is in the surrounding air. Midlatitude cyclones are often called "depressions" or "lows." A tropical cyclone that develops in the northern Bay of Bengal is also called a cyclone. *See* TROPICAL CYCLONE.

cyclonic   Adjective describing the situation in which a fluid (usually air) flows around an area of relatively low pressure, such that pressure decreases toward the center. Cyclonic flow is counterclockwise in the Northern Hemisphere and clockwise in the Southern Hemisphere.

cyclostrophic wind   A low-level wind that follows a tightly curved path. It can produce a DUST DEVIL.

dangerous semicircle   The side of a tropical cyclone (hurricane or typhoon) that is farthest from the equator. Winds on this side blow in the same direction as the storm as a whole is traveling. Consequently, the storm speed adds to the wind speed, and the winds tend to drive vessels into the path of the storm. *Compare* NAVIGABLE SEMICIRCLE.

deposition   The change of water vapor directly into ice crystals without passing through the liquid phase. *See* DRY DEPOSITION; SUBLIMATION.

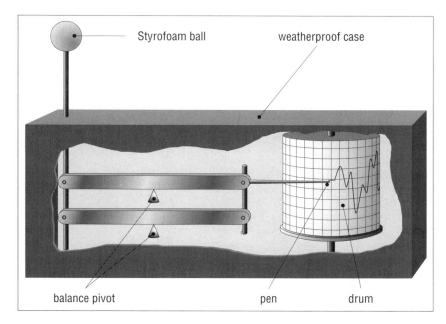

Styrofoam ball   weatherproof case

balance pivot   pen   drum

*Dew gauge. As
dew condenses
onto or evaporates
from the styrofoam
ball, the pen on a
chart fixed to a
rotating drum
records changes
in its weight.*

depression   *See* CYCLONE.

dew cell   *See* DEW POINT HYGROMETER.

dew gauge (surface wetness gauge)   An instrument that measures the amount of dew. It comprises a styrofoam ball of standard size fixed to the end of a vertical arm. The arm is connected to a system of balances. As dew condenses onto the ball, its weight increases. This change is transmitted to a pen that makes a continuous record on a chart fastened to a rotating drum. (*See* illustration.)

dew point hygrometer (dew cell)   A hygrometer that measures the dew point temperature directly.

dew point   The temperature to which air must be cooled for water vapor to start condensing from it. This temperature varies according to the absolute humidity of the air.

dew point front   *See* DRY LINE.

diabatic temperature change   A change in air temperature due to contact between the air and its surroundings.

diffusion   1. Mixing that occurs when one gas or liquid is added to another, but the mixture is not stirred, shaken, or agitated in any way. The random movement of particles results in the even distribution of the ingredients. 2. The scattering of light that is reflected from a rough surface or that passes through a translucent material, such as frosted glass.

direct cell   Part of the general circulation of the atmosphere that is driven by convection. Hadley cells and polar cells are direct cells.

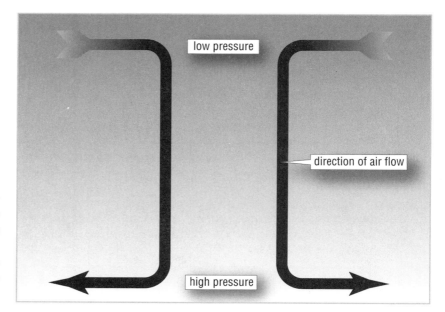

Divergence. Subsiding air produces high pressure at the surface, from where it flows outward in all directions. Above, air converges as it is drawn into the downward flow, producing low pressure.

divergence   The condition when air flows out in different directions from an area of high surface pressure. This draws air down from above, producing a region of convergence and low pressure at a higher level. (*See* diagram.)

divide   The boundary between two drainage basins, such that water drains in one direction to one side of the divide and in a different direction on the other side. In Britain, a divide is sometimes known as a watershed.

Dobson unit (DU)   The unit that is used to report the concentration of a gas that is present in the atmosphere. It refers to the thickness in millimeters of the layer that gas would form if it were separated from all other atmospheric gases and subjected to standard sea-level pressure. Dobson units are most often used to describe the amount of ozone in the ozone layer, where 1 DU = 0.01 mm (0.0004 inch) and the amount of ozone in the ozone layer is typically 220–460 DU, corresponding to a layer 2.2–4.6 mm (0.09–0.18 inch) thick. The unit was devised by the British meteorologist G. M. B. Dobson.

doldrums   Areas over the tropical oceans where winds are usually light and variable.

Doppler effect   The change in frequency of waves perceived by an observer if the source of those waves is moving toward or away from the observer. As the source approaches, the wave frequency increases, and as it recedes, the frequency decreases. The effect was discovered in 1842 by the Austrian physicist Christian Doppler.

drizzle   Fairly constant precipitation comprising water droplets smaller than 0.02 inch (0.5 mm) diameter.

dropsonde An instrument package that descends by parachute from an aircraft, gathering measurements as it descends and transmitting them by radio.

dry deposition The delivery of airborne solid particles to a surface in dry air.

dry ice Solid carbon dioxide. At standard sea-level pressure it sublimes at −109.3°F (−78.5°C, 194.7K).

dry line (dew point front) A boundary that often forms in spring and summer over the Great Plains between hot, dry air to the west and warm, moist air to the east. Advancing dry air lifts the moist air ahead of it, often producing huge cumulonimbus clouds and storms that are frequently tornadic.

dust devil A rapidly rotating wind that occurs in dry desert air. Often many dust devils occur close together. They extend to heights of more than 5,000 feet (1,525 m) and are strong enough to raise dust and sand and may damage buildings.

easterly jet A jet stream that blows in summer, from east to west at a height of about 9 miles (15 km) from the South China Sea to the southeastern Sahara.

easterly wave A weak trough of low pressure that occurs in the Tropics and shows as a wave on a weather map (*see* illustration). As it travels across the ocean it may weaken and disappear or strengthen, eventually into a TROPICAL CYCLONE.

Ekman effect The result of the effects of surface wind, friction, and the Coriolis effect on the direction of flow of a layer of air or water moving in relation to the layers above and below it. Wind-driven surface currents in the Northern Hemisphere flow at about 45° to the right of the wind direction. This angle increases with depth until currents

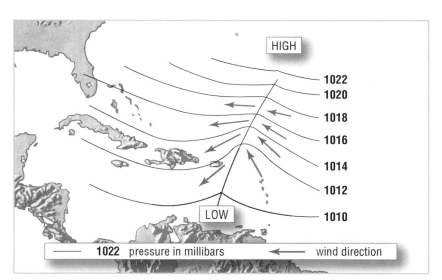

Easterly wave. The wave distorts the isobars, altering the direction of the trade winds as the weather system approaches the Caribbean Islands.

below the surface may flow in the opposite direction to those at the surface, the direction forming a spiral with increasing depth. The effect was explained in 1905 by the Swedish oceanographer Vagn Walfrid Ekman.

El Niño   *See* ENSO.

emissivity   The amount of radiation a body emits, expressed as a proportion of the amount that a blackbody at the same temperature would emit at the same wavelength.

Evaporimeter. As water evaporates from the filter paper in the funnel. the water level falls in the graduated reservoir. Readings taken at regular intervals indicate the rate of evaporation.

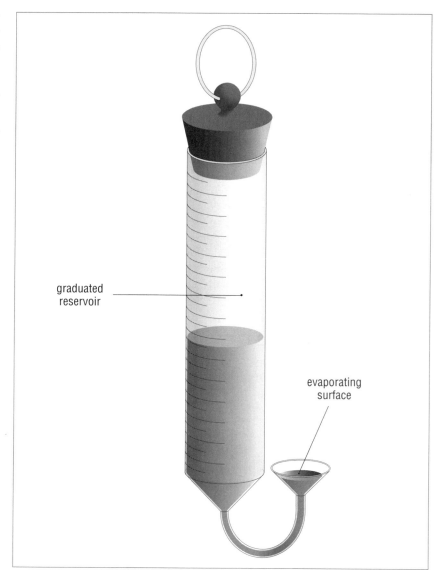

graduated reservoir

evaporating surface

ENSO   Abbreviation for the combined El Niño–Southern Oscillation, a change in the distribution of atmospheric pressure over the Tropics that weakens or reverses the South Pacific trade winds and causes a warm current (El Niño) to flow toward the west coast of South America.

equation of state   The equation relating the temperature, pressure, and density of air. Meteorologists use it to calculate one of these when the other two are known. $p = dRT$, where p is pressure, d is density, T is temperature in kelvin (0K = $-273.15°C$; 1 K = 1°C), and R is the universal gas constant (8.314 joules per kelvin per mole).

equatorial trough   The region of low surface atmospheric pressure around the equator where trade winds from the Northern and Southern Hemispheres meet.

equatorial wave   A disturbance in the equatorial trough over the Pacific Ocean that may develop when the trough is far enough from the equator for the Coriolis effect to produce cyclonic motion.

evaporimeter   An instrument for measuring the rate of evaporation. There are several designs. The simplest (*see* illustration) comprises a sealed, graduated reservoir with a U-tube at the bottom leading to an open surface of known area covered with a filter paper. There is a ring in the stopper by which the instrument can be hung. As water evaporates from the filter paper the level in the reservoir falls.

extratropical hurricane   A severe storm with winds of hurricane force that occurs in a high latitude, far from the Tropics. It has many of the characteristics of a tropical cyclone, but forms by a different mechanism.

eyewall   The circle of towering cumulonimbus clouds that surrounds the calm center of a tropical cyclone or extratropical hurricane.

Ferrel cell   An indirect cell that forms part of the general circulation of the atmosphere. It is driven by the direct Hadley cells on the side nearest the equator and the polar cells on the side nearest the poles. Its existence was discovered by the American meteorologist William Ferrel.

fetch   The distance over which wind blows across the sea, generating waves.

fiducial point   A fixed position from which other positions are measured. The term is often used for the standard temperature at which a particular barometer gives a correct reading at latitude 45°. If the barometer is used at any other temperature or in any other latitude its reading must be corrected.

firn   Snow that falls during one winter, fails to melt during the summer, and is still lying at the onset of the following winter.

flood peak formula   Any one of a number of mathematical formulae that use measurements of rainfall duration and intensity, drainage patterns, and other relevant factors to predict the maximum height floodwaters will reach.

freezing fog   Fog that forms when the air temperature is close to freezing and surfaces are below freezing. The fog droplets freeze on contact with the surfaces.

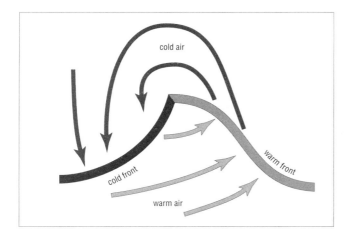

Frontal wave. A wave appears in a front separating warm from cold air. so that now the cold air flows around the wave crest. with a cyclonic motion that will produce a frontal depression. What was formerly a single front is now two fronts. as the cold air pushes in behind the partly enclosed wedge of warm air.

freezing nuclei   *See* SUPERCOOLED WATER.

freezing rain   Rain consisting of supercooled droplets that freeze on contact with cold surfaces. *See* SUPERCOOLED WATER.

front   A boundary between two air masses with different characteristics. Fronts move across the surface of land and sea. If the air behind the front is cooler than that ahead of it, the front is said to be a cold front; if the air behind the front is warmer, it is a warm front.

frontal depression   *See* FRONTAL WAVE.

frontal inversion   A temperature inversion that occurs at a front, where warm air lies above cool air.

frontal wave (frontal depression)   A wave that develops in a front. As the system develops, air moves cyclonically around the wave, surrounding a center of low pressure (a depression), and the frontal system travels with a warm front ahead of a wedge-shaped body of warm air, followed by a cold front. (*See* illustration.)

frost point   The temperature to which air must be cooled for its water vapor to start forming ice crystals on exposed surfaces. This occurs when the dewpoint temperature is below the freezing temperature.

frost smoke   Fog consisting of ice crystals that forms when the temperature is well below freezing.

F scale   *See* FUJITA TORNADO INTENSITY SCALE.

Fujita Tornado Intensity Scale (F scale)   A system that classifies tornadoes on a six-point scale (F-0 to F-5) according to the speed of their winds and the damage they are likely to cause. The scale was devised in 1971 by T. Theodore Fujita, his wife Sumiko Fujita, and Allen Pearson.

Fujiwara effect   The orbiting of two tropical cyclones about a common center, which occurs when the cyclones approach within less than 900 miles (1,450 km) of each other. The phenomenon was first described in 1921 by the Japanese meteorologist Sakuhei Fujiwara.

funnel cloud   A funnel-shaped cloud that forms beneath another cloud and extends toward the ground. When it touches the ground it becomes a tornado.

gas laws   The physical laws that describe the relationship between the density, pressure, and temperature of a gas such as air. *See* EQUATION OF STATE.

general circulation   The atmospheric movements that transport heat away from the equator, producing winds, clouds, and precipitation.

geostrophic wind   A wind that blows almost parallel to isobars, its direction being determined wholly by the pressure-gradient force and Coriolis effect. This wind occurs far enough above the surface to be unaffected by friction with the ground or by obstacles such as trees or buildings on the ground. (*See* illustration.)

glacioisostasy The slow rise of the land surface following the melting of a thick ice sheet.

global warming potential The amount of climatic forcing a specified greenhouse gas exerts, compared with the forcing exerted by carbon dioxide, which is given a value of 1.

graupel Soft hail, resembling small snow pellets.

Great Conveyor (Atlantic Conveyor) The system of ocean currents that carry cold, dense water along the ocean floor from the edge of the Atlantic sea ice all the way to Antarctica (*see* NORTH ATLANTIC

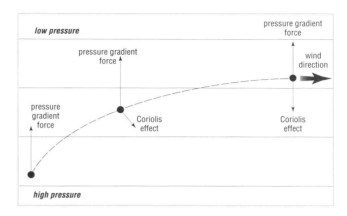

Geostrophic wind. The balance between the pressure gradient force and the Coriolis effect results in a wind that flows parallel to the isobars.

The Great Conveyor. This system of ocean currents carries cold water from the poles to the equator and warm water from the equator to the poles. It has a major effect on world climates.

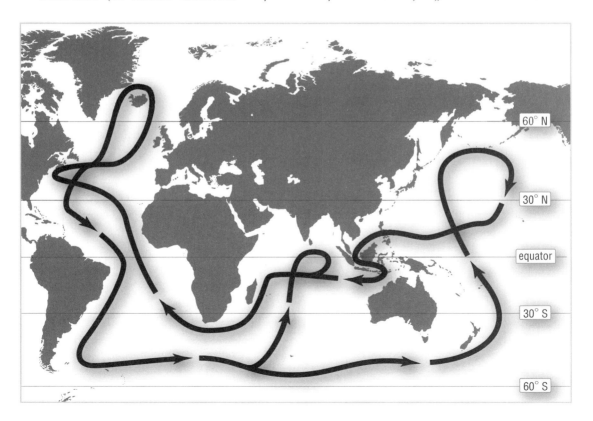

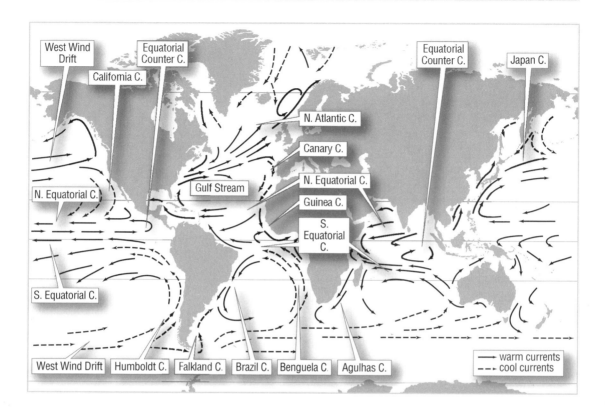

West Wind Drift

Equatorial Counter C.

California C.

Equatorial Counter C.

Japan C.

N. Atlantic C.

Canary C.

N. Equatorial C.

Gulf Stream

N. Equatorial C.

Guinea C.

S. Equatorial C.

S. Equatorial C.

West Wind Drift | Humboldt C. | Falkland C. | Brazil C. | Benguela C. | Agulhas C.

→ warm currents
--→ cool currents

Gyres. The surface currents in all the oceans flow approximately in circles.

DEEP WATER), and replace it with warmer surface water flowing north. (*See* illustration.) This is the most important oceanic mechanism for transferring heat from the equator to high latitudes and has a strong influence on climates.

greenhouse effect   The warming of the lower atmosphere due to the absorption by certain gas molecules of long-wave radiation from the surface. The absorbed heat is then reradiated, warming other gas molecules.

greenhouse period   A time when there were no ice sheets or glaciers anywhere on Earth.

ground frost   The condition in which the air temperature is above freezing, but the temperature at the ground surface is below freezing.

groundwater   Water that has drained downward from the ground surface and saturates a layer of porous rock or particles above a layer of impermeable material.

gust front   A region immediately ahead of an advancing storm, where air is being drawn into the upcurrents inside the storm cloud, generating strong wind gusts.

gyre   One of the major systems of currents, found in all oceans, that flows in an approximately circular direction, clockwise in the Northern

Hemisphere and counterclockwise in the Southern Hemisphere. (*See* illustration.) Gyres are centered at about 30° north and south of the equator and to the west of the ocean center.

Hadley cell   The rising of air in the tropics and sinking of air in the subtropics, forming a convective cell described in 1735 by the English meteorologist George Hadley.

haze   A condition of reduced horizontal visibility due to the absorption and scattering of sunlight by aerosols. Visibility remains greater than 1.2 miles (2 km).

heat capacity   The amount of heat required to raise the temperature of a unit mass of a substance by one kelvin (1K = 1°C). Scientists measure the amount of heat in joules and the mass in grams.

heat lightning   Silent flashes of sheet lightning that are produced by a storm more than about 6 miles (10 km) away. The storm itself is too distant to be visible, and all of the sound waves are absorbed by the air or refracted upward before reaching the observer.

high level inversion   A temperature inversion at an altitude of 1,000 feet (300 m) or more that develops when air subsiding in an anticyclone is chilled by contact with a cold ground surface.

hill fog (upslope fog)   Fog that forms when moist air is forced to rise up a hillside and cool adiabatically to below its dewpoint temperature.

hoarfrost   A thin, white layer of ice crystals that is seen early in the morning on exposed surfaces. It forms on clear nights, when grass, other plants, spiderwebs, and similar objects radiate away the heat they absorbed during the day and their temperature falls below freezing. Air immediately adjacent to the surfaces is chilled to below its frost point, and its water vapor is deposited as ice.

horse latitudes   The latitudes lying beneath the permanent areas of high pressure in the Tropics, at about 30° in both hemispheres, where winds are light and variable and sailing ships are often becalmed. When horses were carried as cargo, some would die when supplies of drinking water ran low, and their bodies were thrown overboard.

hot lightning   Lightning that starts wildfires, because the current carried by the lightning stroke is sustained for long enough to raise the temperature of dry material high enough to ignite it.

humidity   The amount of water vapor (not liquid water or ice crystals) present in the air. *See* ABSOLUTE HUMIDITY; MIXING RATIO; RELATIVE HUMIDITY; SPECIFIC HUMIDITY.

humidity mixing ratio   *See* MIXING RATIO.

hurricane   A tropical cyclone that forms in the North Atlantic or Caribbean.

hygrometer   An instrument for measuring atmospheric humidity.

hygroscopic nucleus   A cloud condensation nucleus made from a substance that absorbs moisture, swelling as it does so, and eventually dissolves.

Iceland low   A region of low atmospheric pressure that is centered approximately over Iceland.

indirect cell Part of the general circulation of the atmosphere that is driven by the adjacent direct cells rather than by convection. FERREL CELLS are indirect cells.

infrared radiation Electromagnetic radiation with a wavelength of 0.7 µm–1 mm (0.00003–0.04 inch).

insolation The amount of solar radiation that falls on a unit area of the Earth's surface. The word is a contraction of *in*coming *sol*ar radi*ation*. *See* SOLAR CONSTANT.

instability The condition of air that is rising by convection and continues to rise because at every height it is warmer and therefore less dense than the surrounding air.

intertropical convergence The region near the equator where the trade winds from the Northern and Southern Hemispheres meet and converge.

invisible drought A period following a drought when the ground is extremely dry and water tables low, so that apparently abundant rainfall fails to recharge aquifers and fill reservoirs and restrictions on water use introduced during the drought emergency must remain in force.

isobar A line on a weather map joining points where the atmospheric pressure is the same.

isobaric surface A surface where the atmospheric pressure is the same throughout. The elevation of such a surface will vary, producing shapes resembling hills and valleys.

isohel A line on a weather map joining points that experience the same number of hours of sunshine.

isohyet A line on a weather map joining points where the amount of rainfall is the same.

isoneph A line on a weather map joining points where the amount of cloud cover is the same.

isotherm A line on a weather map joining points where the temperature is the same.

jet stream A narrow belt of strong wind blowing in a generally west-to-east direction at speeds of 100–200 MPH (160–320 km/h) or sometimes more, at a height of 6–9 miles (10–15 km). Jet streams form where tropical and polar air meet (the polar front jet stream) and at the high-latitude boundary between sinking tropical and subtropical air (the subtropical jet stream), in each case the jet stream lying inside the warmer air. *See* EASTERLY JET.

Joseph effect The tendency of a particular type of weather to persist and perpetuate itself. The name is taken from the dream Pharoah described to Joseph (Genesis 41:29–30), in which seven years of plenty were followed by seven years of famine.

katabatic wind A wind that blows down the side of a hill or other gradient.

kinetic energy The energy a body possesses by virtue of being in motion, defined in terms of the amount of work the body could do if it were brought to rest. If the body is moving in a straight line, its kinetic energy is equal to $1/2\ mv^2$, where m is its mass and v its velocity. If the body is rotating, its kinetic energy is equal to $1/2\ I\Omega^2$, where I is its moment of inertia and Ω is its angular velocity. *Compare* POTENTIAL ENERGY.

knot (kt) A unit of speed equal to one nautical mile per hour. 1 kt = 1.15 MPH = 1.852 km/h.

langley (ly) A unit of solar radiation equal to one calorie per square centimeter per minute. It is named for the American astronomer Samuel Pierpont Langley.

La Niña The opposite condition to El Niño, in which the pressure difference over the equatorial Pacific intensifies, the trade winds strengthen, and there is drought in western South America and heavy rain in Indonesia.

lapse rate The rate at which air temperature changes with altitude.

latent heat The heat that must be absorbed to break molecular bonds and convert a substance from a solid to a liquid and a liquid to a gas (for instance, ice to water and water to water vapor). The same amount of heat is released when the molecular bonds reform as a gas condenses to a liquid and a liquid solidifies. Latent heat is absorbed and released without altering the temperature of the substance itself, but is taken from or released into the surrounding medium.

line squall *See* SQUALL LINE.

Little Ice Age The period from about 1550 to about 1860 during which temperatures all over the world were lower than they had been prior to 1550 or after 1860 and glaciers expanded everywhere. In England, average temperatures in the 1690s were about 2.7°F (1.5°C) lower than in the middle of the 20th century.

low *See* CYCLONE.

lysimeter An instrument used to measure the rate of evapotranspiration.

macroclimate The climate of a large area, such as a continent or the entire Earth.

mamma One of a number of projections below the base of a cloud, most commonly a big cumulonimbus that may produce tornadoes.

Maunder minimum The period between 1645 and 1715 during which the number of sunspots recorded was much lower than usual; several 10-year periods elapsed when no sunspots at all were seen. This period coincided with the coldest part of the Little Ice Age. Other prolonged episodes of cold climate have since been linked to sunspot minima and episodes of warm climate to sunspot maxima. The original minimum was described in 1894 by the British astronomer Edward Maunder.

mb *See* MILLIBAR.

Medieval Warm Period A time when the global climate was warmer than during the centuries preceding and succeeding it. Temperatures in Greenland began to rise around the year 600, and around 800 elsewhere, and reached a peak between 1100 and 1300.

meridional flow   Movement of air or water in a northerly or southerly direction (that is, approximately parallel to lines of longitude, or meridians). *Compare* ZONAL FLOW.

mesocyclone   A region of rapidly rotating air, up to 6 miles (10 km) in diameter, inside a large storm cloud. Rotation starts in the middle of the cloud and extends downward, sometimes all the way to the ground, where it becomes a tornado.

microclimate   The climate of a very small area, such as a forest clearing or the region between the ground and the top of the plants in grassland or a field crop, that is clearly different from the climate in the surrounding area.

microwaves   Electromagnetic radiation with a wavelength of 0.04–4 inches (1 mm to 10 cm).

Milankovitch theory   An explanation for ice ages and the interglacials separating them, proposed in 1920 by the Serbian climatologist Milutin Milankovitch. He suggested that three cycles affecting the amount of solar radiation the Earth receives at different latitudes periodically coincide. When the effect is to reduce solar radiation to a minimum, the onset of an ice age is triggered, and when the effect is to maximize the solar radiation received, the world climate grows warmer.

millibar (mb)   One-thousandth of a bar. A widely used unit for reporting atmospheric pressure in newspaper and TV weather reports and forecasts; the preferred scientific unit is the pascal (Pa). 1 bar = 1 atmosphere = 1000 dynes per sq cm = 100,000 pascals = 750 mm of mercury = 30 inches of mercury; 1 mb = 100 Pa.

mist   Precipitation comprising water droplets 0.0002–0.002 inch (0.005–0.05 mm) across that reduce horizontal visibility, but not to less than 1,094 yards (1 km).

mixed cloud   A cloud in which the temperature of the upper part is below freezing and that of the lower part is above freezing. The cloud contains both ice crystals and water droplets. *Compare* COLD CLOUD; WARM CLOUD.

mixing ratio   In a mixture of two gases, the ratio of the mass of one to that of the other. The ratio of the mass of water vapor to the mass of dry air containing it is called the humidity mixing ratio.

moment of inertia (*I*)   The equivalent of mass for a rotating body, equal to the sum of all the products of multiplying each element of mass by the square of its distance from the axis.

NADW   *See* NORTH ATLANTIC DEEP WATER.

navigable semicircle   The side of a tropical cyclone (hurricane or typhoon) that is closest to the equator. On this side the wind blows in the opposite direction to the one in which the storm as a whole is traveling. Consequently, wind speeds are reduced by the speed of the storm itself, and they tend to drive vessels behind the storm and into safer waters. *Compare* DANGEROUS SEMICIRCLE.

near infrared radiation Infrared radiation with a wavelength of 1–3 μm, the shortest in the infrared waveband.

nitrogen oxides (NOx) Nitrogen oxide (NO) and nitrogen dioxide (NO_2), gases released mainly by burning fossil fuels and plant material that react with other substances to produce ozone and photochemical smog.

North Atlantic Deep Water (NADW) Cold, dense water that forms near the edge of the sea ice in the North Atlantic, sinks to the ocean floor, and flows south all the way to Antarctica. *See* GREAT CONVEYOR.

North Atlantic Oscillation (NAO) A periodic change in the difference in surface air pressure between the AZORES HIGH and ICELAND LOW. Winds around these centers drive weather systems crossing the Atlantic, and so changes in the difference between them have a large effect on climates over much of the Northern Hemisphere.

oxygen isotope ratios The ratio of the two common isotopes of oxygen, ^{16}O and ^{18}O, in material obtained from cores drilled from ice sheets or seabed sediments and that can be dated. The ratio reveals information about past climates. An increase in ^{18}O in calcium carbonate indicates cooling, and an increase in ^{18}O in ice indicates warming.

ozone layer A layer of the stratosphere, at a height of 10–20 miles (16–32 km), where ozone (O_3) accumulates, reaching a concentration of up to 10 parts per million.

perched aquifer Flowing groundwater that lies above an aquiclude.

permanent drought Drought that is due to a generally arid climate, where rainfall is sparse and unreliable.

PGF *See* PRESSURE GRADIENT FORCE.

plane of the ecliptic The plane of the Earth's orbit around the Sun (*see* diagram).

Plane of the ecliptic. The path the Earth follows in its orbit about the Sun marks the circumference of an imaginary disk: the plane of the ecliptic.

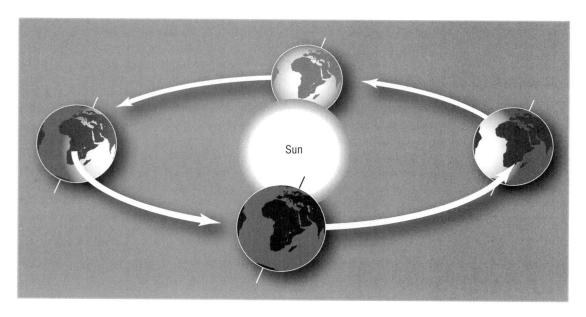

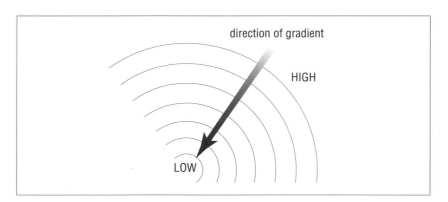

Pressure gradient. The change in pressure across the distance between regions of high and low air pressure forms a gradient, like the slope of a hillside.

polar front   The boundary in middle latitudes between polar and tropical air. Depressions form along it. The front moves toward the equator in winter and toward the pole in summer.

polar low   An area of low atmospheric pressure that forms where very cold air flowing off an ice sheet meets much warmer air over the ocean, producing cumulus clouds and heavy snowstorms.

potential energy   The energy a body possesses by virtue of its position. For example, a book on a shelf possesses potential energy that will be converted to KINETIC ENERGY if it should fall.

precipitation   Water that falls from the air to the ground, regardless of its form. The term includes drizzle, rain, snow, graupel, hail, dew, frost, mist, and fog.

pressure gradient   The rate at which the atmospheric pressure changes over a horizontal distance. This is indicated on a weather map by the distance between ISOBARS. The closer together the isobars are, the steeper the pressure gradient is (*see* illustration).

pressure gradient force (PGF)   The force acting on air in the direction of a center of low atmospheric pressure, that is, at right angles to the isobars surrounding the center. (*See* diagram.) Its strength is proportional to the rate at which the pressure changes with horizontal distance (the PRESSURE GRADIENT).

primary pollutant   A pollutant that is present in the form in which it was emitted from its source; it has undergone no reactions with other pollutants.

psychrometer   An instrument for measuring humidity using a wet-bulb and dry-bulb thermometer. (*See* illustration.) *See also* WHIRLING PSYCHROMETER.

radiation fog   Fog that forms in still air when the ground surface has cooled overnight by radiating away the heat it absorbed by day. Contact with the chilled ground cools the surface layer of air to below its dew point temperature, causing water vapor to condense. *See* ADVECTION FOG.

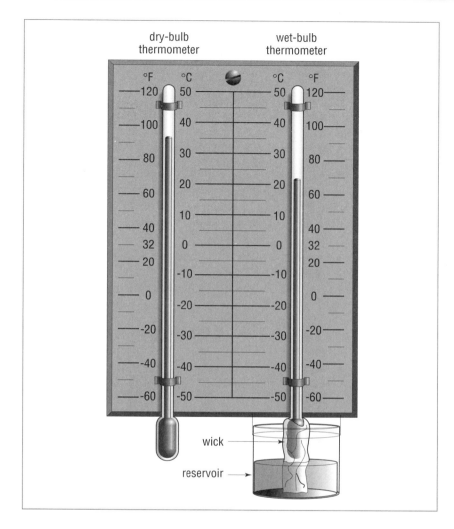

Psychrometer. One thermometer has a dry bulb, the other a bulb covered in wet muslin from which water is constantly evaporating, chilling the bulb by removing latent heat. The relative humidity and dew point temperature can be calculated from the difference in the two thermometer readings.

radiosonde   A package of instruments for taking measurements of atmospheric temperature, pressure, and humidity that is carried aloft by a balloon and transmits its readings by radio.

rawinsonde   A radiosonde that also carries a radar reflector allowing it to be tracked from the ground to provide data on wind speed and direction at the heights it reaches.

relative humidity   The amount of water vapor present in the air, expressed as the percentage of the amount that would saturate the air at that temperature and pressure. *See also* ABSOLUTE HUMIDITY; MIXING RATIO.

relative vorticity   The amount of rotation of a fluid about an axis (usually a vertical axis) in relation to the surface of the Earth. *See* ABSOLUTE VORTICITY.

ridge   An area of high atmospheric pressure with an elongated shape; on an isobaric map it would stand above the surface like a ridge on a landscape.

rime frost   A layer of white ice with an irregular surface that covers exposed surfaces. It forms when supercooled droplets in fog or drizzle freeze on contact with surfaces at or below freezing. *See also* SUPERCOOLED WATER.

riprap   Large boulders or concrete blocks that are laid against a seawall, dam, or other surface exposed to the sea in order to absorb the energy of waves and so protect the structure from erosion.

Rossby waves   Undulations, 2,485–3,728 miles (4,000–6,000 km) from crest to crest, that develop in moving air in the middle and upper troposphere. Similar waves occur in the oceans. They were discovered and explained in 1940 by the Swedish-American meteorologist Carl-Gustav Rossby.

Saffir-Simpson scale   A five-point scale for reporting the severity of tropical cyclones (hurricanes) devised by meteorologists at the National Oceanic and Atmospheric Administration.

scattering   The deflection of electromagnetic waves (such as sunlight) by gas molecules, particles, and irregular surfaces.

seasonal drought   Drought characteristic of regions with dry and rainy seasons that occurs when the dry season is drier or longer than usual.

secondary pollutant   A pollutant that is produced by reactions among other (primary) pollutants.

shear   A force acting parallel to a plane, rather than at right angles to it.

sleet   Ice pellets, no bigger than 0.04 inch (1 mm) in diameter, that do not melt before reaching the ground. In Britain, *sleet* is a mixture of snow and rain.

Snowball Earth   The Earth covered almost completely by snow and ice. Some scientists believe this condition occurred four times between 750 million and 580 million years ago.

snow blitz   The rapid onset of an ice age that might occur if in some extensive areas the winter snow failed to melt during the summer. The surviving snow would reflect solar heat and light, keeping the ground cool, and the following winter more snow would accumulate and the area of year-round snow would increase.

solar constant   The amount of energy the Earth receives from the Sun per unit area at the outermost edge of the atmosphere, calculated at a point perpendicular to the Sun's rays. The value is not known precisely but is estimated to be 1,367 watts per square meter (1.98 langleys).

specific humidity   The ratio of the mass of water vapor to a unit mass of that air, including the water vapor it contains.

Spörer minimum   The period 1400–1510, identified by the German astronomer Gustav Spörer, when very few sunspots were observed.

The period coincided with very low temperatures and was known as the Little Ice Age.

squall line (line squall)   A series of storms arranged in a line ahead of a cold front.

stability   The condition of air that will return to its former level if it is forced to rise, because it is cooler and therefore denser than the air above it.

standard atmosphere   The average atmospheric pressure at sea level, assuming the temperature is 59°F (15°C, 188.16K), acceleration due to gravity is 9.80655 m s^{-2}, and the atmosphere consists of a perfect gas. The standard atmosphere is 101.325 kPa (kilopascals) = 1013.25 millibars = 1.01325×10^5 newtons m^{-2} = 29.9213 inches (760 mm) of mercury = 14.691 lb in^{-2}.

stratopause   The upper boundary of the stratosphere at a height of about 30 miles (50 km), separating the stratosphere from the mesosphere above. At the stratopause, the average temperature is about 32°F (0°C); above it temperature decreases with height.

stratosphere   The layer of the atmosphere at heights between about 6 and 30 miles (10–50 km) that is bounded by the tropopause below and stratopause above and that contains the ozone layer. In the lower stratosphere temperature remains constant with height, at about –76°F (–60°C), but in the upper stratosphere the absorption of ultraviolet radiation by oxygen and ozone increases the temperature to about 32°F (0°C) at the stratopause.

sublimation   The direct change of a substance from solid to gas, without passing through a liquid phase. *See* DEPOSITION.

suction vortex   A miniature tornado that forms in the turbulent air around the edge of a large tornado. Suction vortices follow circular paths around the main tornado, usually for less than one complete revolution before dying, but generate winds up to 100 MPH (160 km/h) faster than those of the main tornado.

supercell   A convection cell that develops inside a large cumulonimbus storm cloud when the upcurrents in the cell are at an angle to the vertical. Precipitation falling from near the top of the cloud drags cold air with it, creating cold downcurrents that fall into the upcurrents of an ordinary convection cell and eventually suppress them. This does not happen in a supercell, because the upcurrents and downcurrents are separate. Within a supercell, air may be rising at up to 100 MPH (160 km/h), and the cell may break through the tropopause, rising to a height of more than 10 miles (16 km). Supercells last much longer than ordinary convective storm cells, and they can trigger tornadoes.

supercooled water   Water that is chilled to below freezing without forming ice. Ice crystals form on the surfaces of small particles called freezing nuclei, and in the absence of such nuclei water can be cooled to –40°F (–40°C) before it freezes spontaneously. MIXED CLOUD contains many supercooled droplets.

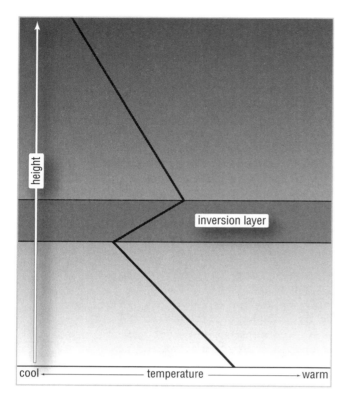

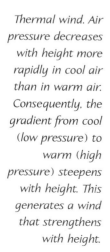

Temperature inversion. A layer of warm air lies above cooler air, producing a region where the air temperature increases with height. Air rising by convection is trapped beneath the inversion layer.

supertyphoon   A tropical cyclone in the Pacific that covers an area up to 3 million square miles (8 million km^2).

surface wetness gauge   *See* DEW GAUGE.

synoptic chart   A chart that shows weather conditions at a particular time over a large area.

temperature inversion   A layer of the lower atmosphere in which temperature remains constant or increases with height. Air rising from below by convection cannot penetrate the inversion, because it comprises air at the same or lower density than the rising air, so air

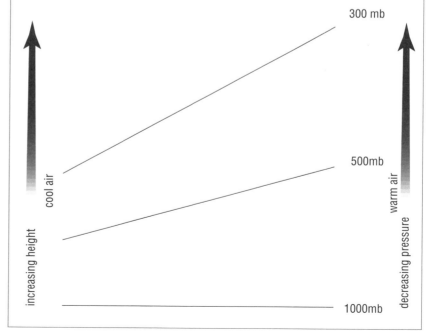

Thermal wind. Air pressure decreases with height more rapidly in cool air than in warm air. Consequently, the gradient from cool (low pressure) to warm (high pressure) steepens with height. This generates a wind that strengthens with height.

becomes trapped beneath the inversion, together with any smoke or other pollutants it carries. (*See* illustration.)

thermal wind   A wind that is produced by a sharp temperature difference between two adjacent air masses. It is due to the fact that cool air is denser than warm air, and therefore air pressure decreases with height more rapidly in cool than in warm air. In the Northern Hemisphere a thermal wind blows with the cold air to its left and in the Southern Hemisphere to the right at a speed proportional to the rate of temperature change (the temperature gradient). (*See* illustration.)

three cell model   A simplified description of the general circulation of the atmosphere that comprises two sets of direct cells—the Hadley and polar cells—and one set of indirect cells—the Ferrel cells (*see* illustration).

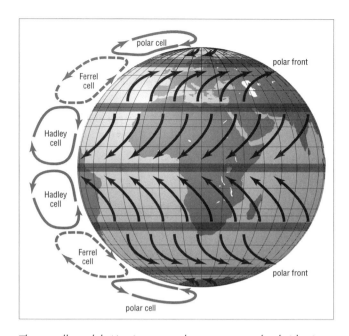

Three cell model. Air rises over the equator and subsides in the subtropics (Hadley cell). Air subsides over the poles and rises in middle latitudes (polar cell). These direct cells drive the Ferrel cell, with air rising in middle latitudes and subsiding in the subtropics.

trade winds   The prevailing winds that blow to either side of the equator, from the northeast in the Northern Hemisphere and from the southeast in the Southern Hemisphere.

tropical cyclone   A region of low pressure in the Tropics that generates fierce storms, winds with sustained speeds greater than 75 MPH (121 km/h), and heavy rain. *See* CYCLONE; HURRICANE; TYPHOON.

Tropics   Two lines of latitude, the Tropic of Cancer at 23.5° N and the Tropic of Capricorn at 23.5° S, and the region lying between them. These latitudes, equal to the Earth's axial tilt, mark the limits of the area within which the Sun is directly overhead at noon on one day in the year.

tropopause   The boundary between the lower (troposphere) and upper (stratosphere) layers of the atmosphere, marking the level at which temperature ceases to decrease with height. Its altitude varies according to the temperature of the sea surface and with the seasons, but averages 6–7 miles (10–11 km) over the poles (sometimes lower) and about 10 miles (16 km) over the equator.

troposphere   The lowest layer of the atmosphere, extending from the surface to the tropopause, within which temperature decreases with height.

trough   An area of low atmospheric pressure with an elongated shape; on an isobaric map it appear as a depression in the surface.

typhoon   A tropical cyclone that develops over the Pacific Ocean.

ultraviolet radiation (UV)   Electromagnetic radiation with a wavelength of about 4–400 nanometers (nm). UV radiation is divided into near UV (400–300 nm), far UV (300–200 nm), and extreme or vacuum UV (less than 200 nm). It is also divided into UV-A (315–380 nm), UV-B or soft UV (280–315 nm), and UV–C or hard UV (less than 280 nm).

unconfined aquifer   An aquifer that is not bounded on its upper side by a layer of impermeable material. Water can drain freely into it from above.

upslope fog   *See* HILL FOG.

UV   *See* ULTRAVIOLET RADIATION.

veering   A change in wind direction in a clockwise direction, for instance from west to northwest. *Compare* BACKING.

virga   Precipitation falling from a cloud that evaporates before it reaches the ground. It appears as a thin, gray veil beneath the cloud.

vorticity   A measure of the rotation of a fluid; in meteorology the term usually refers to relative vorticity about a vertical axis. *See* ABSOLUTE VORTICITY; RELATIVE VORTICITY.

Walker circulation   The west-to-east airflow in the upper troposphere over the tropical Pacific Ocean that acts as a counterflow to the low-level east-to-west airflow caused by the Hadley cell circulation and trade winds. It was discovered in 1923 by Sir Gilbert Walker. (*See* illustration.)

wall cloud   A region of rotating cloud below the main base of a large storm cloud. It often releases little or no rain, but tornadoes may be forming in the cloud behind it.

Walker circulation. Where the northeasterly and southeasterly trade winds meet. air rises. Near the tropopause the air flows from west to east. then descends to rejoin the trade winds.

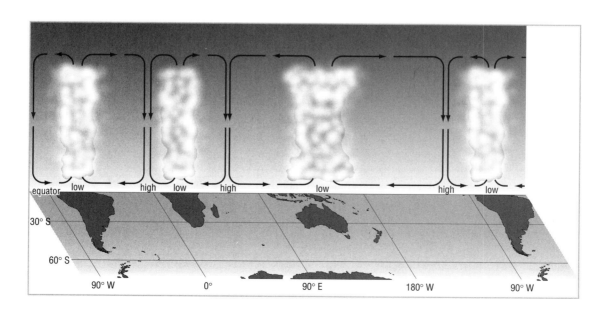

warm cloud   A cloud whose temperature is above freezing throughout and therefore consists wholly of water droplets. *Compare* COLD CLOUD; MIXED CLOUD.

watershed   The area within which surface water drains into a particular groundwater and river system. A divide separates one watershed from another. In Britain, a watershed is often called a catchment, and a divide is often called a watershed.

waterspout   An intense vortex of air that forms over water. It closely resembles a tornado and in some cases is a tornado that formed over land and subsequently crossed water. Waterspouts that form over water do not require a mesocyclone for their development and are smaller and weaker than true tornadoes. Most occur over shallow water in the tropics.

Whirling psychrometer. The instrument can be swung by hand. This ensures an even flow of air across both thermometer bulbs.

water table   The upper boundary of groundwater, below which the soil is fully saturated.

wet bulb–dry bulb thermometer   An instrument used to measure the evaporation of water, from which the relative humidity and dew point temperature of the air can be calculated or, more usually, read from tables. The instrument comprises two thermometers. The dry bulb thermometer reads the air temperature. The bulb of the wet bulb thermometer is wrapped in muslin, part of which is immersed in distilled water. The temperature indicated on the thermometer is depressed, because latent heat to evaporate water from the muslin is drawn from the bulb itself. The difference between the dry bulb and wet bulb temperatures is called the wet bulb depression and varies with the rate of evaporation, which in turn is determined by the humidity of the air. Relative humidity and dew point temperature are calculated from the wet bulb depression.

whirling psychrometer   A psychrometer that is whirled through the air manually to ensure an even flow of air across both thermometer bulbs. (*See* illustration.)

zonal flow   A movement of air or water in a generally east-to-west or west-to-east direction, approximately parallel to lines of latitude. *Compare* MERIDIONAL FLOW.

Bibliography and further reading

"Air Pollution." Fact Sheet No. 187. Geneva: World Health Organization, September 2000. www.who.int/inf-fs/en/fact187.html.

"The Air Quality Index." Available on-line. URL: www.apcd.org/aq/aqi.html. Revised September 6, 2002.

Allaby, Michael. *Dangerous Weather: Blizzards.* New York: Facts On File, 2004.

———. *A Change in the Weather.* New York: Facts On File, 2004.

———. *Droughts.* New York: Facts On File, 2003.

———. *Floods.* New York: Facts On File, 2003.

———. *Fog, Smog, and Poisoned Rain.* New York: Facts On File, 2003.

———. *Hurricanes.* New York: Facts On File, 2003.

———. *Tornadoes.* New York: Facts On File, 2004.

———. *The Facts On File Weather and Climate Handbook.* New York: Facts On File, 2002.

———. *Encyclopedia of Weather and Climate.* 2 vols. New York: Facts On File, 2001.

———. *Basics of Environmental Science.* New York: Routledge, 2nd ed., 2000.

———. *Deserts.* New York: Facts On File, 2000.

———. *Temperate Forests.* New York: Facts On File, 1999.

———. *Elements: Earth.* New York: Facts On File, 1993.

———. *Elements: Fire.* New York: Facts On File, 1993.

———. *Elements: Water.* New York: Facts On File, 1992.

American Lung Association. "Major Air Pollutants." *State of the Air 2002.* Available on-line. URL: www.lungusa.org/air/envmajairpro.html. October 22, 2002.

American Wind Energy Association. Available on-line. URL: www.awea.org. Updated September 13, 2002.

Arnold, J. B., G. Wall, N. Moore, C. S. Baldwin, and I. J. Shelton. "Soil Erosion—Causes and Effects." Ministry of Agriculture and Food, Government of Ontario. Available on-line. URL: www.gov.on.ca/OMAFRA/english/engineer/facts/87-040.htm. Last reviewed 1996; accessed November 6, 2002.

Ayscue, Jon K. "Hurricane Damage to Residential Structures: Risk and Mitigation: Natural Hazards Research Working Paper #4." Natural Hazards Research and Applications Information Center, Institute of Behavioral Science, University of Colorado. Available on-line. URL: www.colorado.edu/hazards/wp/wp94/wp94.html. November 1996.

Baird, Stuart. "Wind Energy." Energy Fact Sheet. Energy Educators of Ontario. Available on-line. URL: www.iclei.org/efacts/wind.htm. Accessed October 22, 2002.

———. "Ocean Energy Systems." Energy Fact Sheet. Energy Educators of Ontario. Available on-line. URL: www.iclei.org/efacts/ocean.htm. Accessed October 22, 2002.

Bapat, Arun. "Dams and Earthquakes." *Frontline*, vol. 16, no. 27, 1999–2000. Available on-line. URL: www.flonnet.com/fl1627/16270870.htm. Accessed November 6, 2002.

Barry, Roger G., and Richard J. Chorley. *Atmosphere, Weather & Climate*. 7th ed. New York: Routledge, 1998.

"The Beaufort Scale." Available on-line. URL: www.met-office.gov/uk/education/historic/beaufort.html. Accessed November 2, 2002.

"Beaufort Wind Scale." Available on-line. URL: www.psych.usyd.edu.au/vbb/woronora/maritime/beaufort.html. Accessed November 2, 2002.

Bell, Ian, and Martin Visbeck. "North Atlantic Oscillation." Columbia University. Available on-line. URL: www.ldeo.columbia.edu/NAO/main.html. Accessed November 27, 2002.

"Bernoulli's Principle." Available on-line. URL: www.mste.uiuc.edu/davea/aviation/bernoulliPrinciple.html. Accessed November 2, 2002.

Bijlsma, Floris, Herman Harperink, and Bernard Hulshof. "About Lightning." Dutch Storm Chase Team. Available on-line. URL: www.stormchasing.nl/lightning.html. Accessed November 4, 2002.

Bluestein, Howard B. *Tornado Alley: Monster Storms of the Great Plains*. New York: Oxford University Press, 1999.

Brewer, Richard. *The Science of Ecology*. 2d ed. Ft. Worth: Saunders College Publishing, 1994.

British Antarctic Survey. Natural Environment Research Council. Home Page. Available on-line. URL: www.antarctica.ac.uk/Living_and_Working/Stations. Accessed November 13, 2002.

Bryant, Edward. *Climate Process & Change*. Cambridge, U.K.: Cambridge University Press, 1997.

Burroughs, William James. *Climate Change: A Multidisciplinary Approach*. Cambridge, U.K.: Cambridge University Press, 2001.

Campbell, Neil A. *Biology*. 3d ed. Redwood City, Calif.: Benjamin/Cummings, 1993.

Cane, H. "Hurricane Alley." Available on-line. URL: www.hurricanealley.net. Accessed November 2, 2002.

Cane, Mark A. "ENSO and Its Prediction: How Well Can We Forecast It?" Available on-line. URL: www.brad.ac.uk/research/ijas/ijasno2/cane.html. Accessed October 23, 2002.

Capella, Chris. "Dance of the Storms: The Fujiwhara Effect." Available on-line. URL: www.usatoday.com/weather/wfujiwha/htm. Accessed January 6, 1999.

"Climate Effects of Volcanic Eruptions." Available on-line. URL: www.geology.sdsu.edu/how_volcanoes_work/climate_effects.html. Accessed October 21, 2002.

CNN Interactive. "Deadly Smog 50 Years Ago in Donora Spurred Clean Air Movement." Available on-line. URL: www.dep.state.pa.us/dep/Rachel_Carson/clean_air.htm. October 27, 1998.

Colbeck, I., and A. R. MacKenzie. "Chemistry and Pollution of the Stratosphere." In Harrison, Roy M., ed. *Pollution: Causes, Effects and Control*. 2d ed. London: Royal Society of Chemistry, 1990.

Corfidi, Steve. "A Brief History of the Storm Prediction Center." NOAA. Available on-line. URL: www.spc.noaa.gov/history/early.html. Accessed January 30, 2003.

Danish Wind Industry Association. "Wind Energy: Frequently Asked Questions." Available on-line. URL: www.windpower.org/faqs.htm. April 17, 2002.

"Desalination—Producing Potable Water." Available on-line. URL: http://resources.ca.gov/ocean/97Agenda/Chap5Desal.htm. Accessed October 25, 2002.

Doddridge, Bruce. "Urban Photochemical Smog." Available on-line. URL: www.meto.umd.edu/~bruce/m1239701.html. February 6, 1997.

"Dry Farming." Available on-line. URL: www.rootsweb.com/~coyuma/data/souvenir/farm.htm. Accessed October 24, 2002.

"The Dust Bowl." Available on-line. URL: www.usd.edu/anth/epa/dust.html. Accessed October 24, 2002.

Dutch, Steven. "Glaciers." Available on-line. URL: www.uwgb.edu/dutchs/202ovhds/glacial.htm. Updated November 2, 1999.

Eberlee, John. "Investigating an Environmental Disaster: Lessons from the Indonesian Fires and Haze." *Reports: Science from the Developing World.* International Development Research Centre, October 9, 1998. Available on-line. URL: www.idrc.ca/reports/read_article_english.cfm?article_num=283.

Ecological Society of America. "Acid Rain Revisited: What Has Happened Since the 1990 Clear Air Act Amendments?" Available on-line. URL: www.esa.org/education/edupdfs/acidrainrevisited.pdf. Accessed March 10, 2003.

Emiliani, Cesare. *Planet Earth: Cosmology, Geology, and the Evolution of Life and Environment.* Cambridge: Cambridge University Press, corrected and updated 1995.

———. *The Scientific Companion: Exploring the Physical World with Facts, Figures, and Formulas.* 2d ed. New York: John Wiley, 1995.

Eumetsat. Available on-line. URL: www.eumetsat.de. Accessed January 14, 2003.

"Factors Influencing Air Pollution." Available on-line. URL: www.marama.org/atlas/factors.html. Updated November 17, 1998.

"Facts about Antarctica." Available on-line. URL: ast.leeds.ac.uk/haverah/spaseman/faq.shtml. Accessed October 23, 2002.

Faoro, Margaret. "HEVs (Hybrid Electric Vehicles)." University of California, Irvine, February 2002. Available on-line. URL: http://darwin.bio.uci.edu/~sustain/global/sensem/Faoro202.htm.

Fink, Micah. "Extratropical Storms." Available on-line. URL: www.pbs.org/wnet/savageplanet/02storms/01extratropical/indexmid.html.

"Flue Gas Desulfurization (FGD) for SO_2 Control." Available on-line. URL: www.iea-coal.org.uk/CCTdatabase/fgd.htm. Accessed October 22, 2002.

Foth, H. D. *Fundamentals of Soil Science.* 8th ed. New York: John Wiley, 1991.

"Fuel Cells 2000: The On-line Fuel Cell Information Center." Available on-line. URL: www.fuelcells.org. Updated October 21, 2002.

Fuelcellstore.com. "Hydrogen Storage." Available on-line. URL: www.fuelcellstore.com/information/hydrogen_storage.html. Accessed October 22, 2002.

"General Circulation of the Atmosphere." Available on-line. URL: http://cimss.ssec.wisc.edu/wxwise/class/gencirc.html. October 2002.

Geoscience Australia. "Tsunamis." Available on-line. URL: www.agso.gov.au/factsheets/urban/20010821_7.jsp. Updated September 15, 2002.

GISP2 Science Management Office. "Welcome to GISP2: Greenland Ice Sheet Project 2." Climate Change Research Center, Institute for the Study of Earth, Oceans and Space, University of New Hampshire. Available on-line. URL: www.gisp2.sr.unh.edu/GISP2. Updated March 1, 2002.

Goodman, Jason. "Statistics of North Atlantic Oscillation Decadal Variability." Massachusetts Institute of Technology. Available on-line. URL: www.mit.edu/people/goodmanj/NAOI/NAOI.html. February 23, 1998.

Gordon, John Mark Niles, and LeRoy Schroder. "USGS Tracks Acid Rain." USGS Fact Sheet FS-183-95. Available on-line. URL: btdqs.usgs.gov/precip/arfs.htm. Accessed October 21, 2002.

"Greenland Guide Index." Available on-line. URL: www.greenland-guide.gl/default.htm. Accessed October 29, 2002.

Hamblyn, Richard. *The Invention of Clouds.* New York: Farrar, Straus & Giroux, 2001.

Harrison, Roy M., ed. *Pollution: Causes, Effects and Control.* 3d ed. London: Royal Society of Chemistry, 1996.

Hartwick College. "Ice Ages and Glaciation." Available on-line. URL: http://info.hartwick.edu/geology/work/VFT-so-far/glaciers/glacier1.html. Accessed November 19, 2002.

Hayes, William A., and Fenster, C. R. "Understanding Wind Erosion and Its Control." Cooperative Extension, Institute of Agriculture and Natural Resources, University of Nebraska. Available on-line. URL: www.ianr.unl.edu/pubs/soil/g474.htm. August 1996.

"Hazards: Storm Surge." Available on-line. URL: hurricanes/noaa.gov/prepare/surge.htm. Accessed November 5, 2002.

Heck, Walter W. "Assessment of Crop Losses from Air Pollutants in the United States." In MacKenzie, James J., and Mohamed T. El-Ashry, eds. *Air Pollution's Toll on Forests & Crops.* New Haven, Conn.: Yale University Press, 1989.

Heidorn, Keith C. "Luke Howard." Available on-line. URL: www.islandnet.com/~see/weather/history/howard.htm. May 1, 1999.

Helfferich, Carla. "Beaufort's Scale: Article #911." Alaska Science Forum, University of Alaska, Fairbanks. Available on-line. URL: www.gi.alaska.edu/ScienceForum/ASF9/911.html. February 2, 1989.

———. "Consequences of Kuwait's Fires: Article #1051." Alaska Science Forum, University of Alaska, Fairbanks. October 10, 1991. Available on-line. URL: www.gi.alaska.edu/ScienceForum/ASF10/1051.html.

Henderson-Sellers, Ann, and Peter J. Robinson. *Contemporary Climatology.* New York: John Wiley, 1986.

Herring, David, and Robert Kannenberg. "The Mystery of the Missing Carbon." NASA, Earth Observatory, 2002. Available on-line. URL: http://earthobservatory.nasa.gov/Study/BOREASCarbon.   Accessed November 2, 2002.

Hillger, Don. "Geostationary Weather Satellites." Colorado State University. Available on-line. URL: www.cira.colostate.edu/ramm/hillger/geo-wx.htm. Updated December 27, 2002.

———. "Polar-orbiting weather satellites." Colorado State University. Available on-line. URL: www.cira.colostate.edu/ramm/hillger/polar-wx.htm. Updated January 13, 2003.

"History of the Dustbowl." Available on-line. URL: www.ultranet.com/~gregjonz/dust/dustbowl.htm. Accessed October 24, 2002.

Hoare, Robert. "World Climate." Buttle and Tuttle Ltd. 2001. Available on-line. URL: www.worldclimate.com/worldclimate. Updated October 2, 2001.

Hoffman, Paul F., and Daniel P. Schrag. "The Snowball Earth." Harvard University. Available on-line. URL: www.eps.harvard.edu/people/faculty/hoffman/snowball_paper.html. August 8, 1999.

Holder, Gerald D., and P. R. Bishnoi, eds. *Challenges for the Future: Gas Hydrates*, vol. 912 of the *Annals of the New York Academy of Sciences*. New York: New York Academy of Sciences, 2000.

Houghton, J. T., Y. Ding, D. J. Griggs, M. Noguer, P. J. van der Linden, X. Dai, K. Maskell, and C. A. Johnson. *Climate Change 2001: The Scientific Basis*. Cambridge: Cambridge University Press for the Intergovernmental Panel on Climate Change, 2001.

"How Hurricanes Do Their Damage." Available on-line. URL: hpccsun.unl.edu/nebraska/damage.html. Accessed November 2, 2002.

"Hurricane." American Red Cross, 2001. Available on-line. URL: www.redcross.org/services/disaster/keepsafe/readyhurricane.html. Accessed November 2, 2002.

Hybrid Electric Vehicle Program, Department of Energy, 2002. "What Is an HEV?" Available on-line. URL: www.ott.doe.gov/hev/what.html. Accessed October 22, 2002.

Idso, Graig D., and Keith E. Idso. "There Has Been No Global Warming for the Past 70 Years," *World Climate Report*, vol. 3, no. 13, July 2000. www.co2science.org/edit/v3_edit/v3n13edit.htm.

Intergovernmental Panel on Climate Change (IPCC), Working Group II. "Summary for Policymakers: Climate Change 2001: Impacts, Adaptation, and Vulnerability." Available on-line. URL: www.ipcc.ch/pub/wg2SPMfinal.pdf. Accessed November 5, 2002.

International Institute for Applied Systems Research. "Cleaner Air for a Cleaner Future: Controlling Transboundary Air Pollution." Available on-line. URL: www.iiasa.ac.at/Admin/INF/OPT/Summer98/negotiations.htm. Accessed October 22, 2002.

Kaplan, George. "The Seasons and the Earth's Orbit—Milankovitch Cycles." U.S. Naval Observatory, Astronomical Applications Department. Available on-line. URL: http://aa.usno.navy.mil/faq/docs/seasons_orbit.html. Last modified on March 14, 2002.

Kennedy, Martin. "A Curve Ball into the Snowball Earth Hypothesis?" *Geology*, December 2001. Geological Society of America. Summary available on-line. URL: www.sciencedaily.com/releases/2001/12/011204072512.htm. December 4, 2001.

Kent, Michael. *Advanced Biology*. New York: Oxford University Press, 2000.

Kid's Cosmos. "Channeled Scablands." Available on-line. URL: www.kidscosmos.org/kid-stuff/mars-trip-scablands.html. Accessed November 20, 2002.

Knauss, John A. *Introduction to Physical Oceanography*. 2d ed. Upper Saddle River, N.J.: Prentice Hall, 1997.

Lamb, H. H. *Climate, History and the Modern World*. 2d ed. New York: Routledge, 1995.

Lash, Gary. "Thunderstorms and Tornadoes." Fredonia State University. Available on-line. URL: www.geocities.com/CapeCanaveral/Hall.6104/tstorms.html. Accessed November 29, 2002.

Leung, George. "Yellow River: Geographic and Historical Settings," from "Reclamation and Sediment Control in the Middle Yellow River Valley," *Water International*, vol. 21, no. 1, pp. 12–19, March 1996. Available on-line. URL: www.cis.umassd.edu/~gleung/geofo/geogren.html.

Libbrecht, Ken. "Snow Crystals: Snow Crystal Classifications." California Institute of Technology. Available on-line. URL: www.its.caltech.edu/~atomic/snowcrystals/class/class.htm. Accessed January 30, 2003.

Lomborg, Bjørn. *The Skeptical Environmentalist*. Cambridge: Cambridge University Press, 2001.

Lovelock, James E. *Gaia: A New Look at Life on Earth*. 2d ed. New York: Oxford University Press, 2000.

———. *The Ages of Gaia*. New York: Oxford University Press, 1989.

Lutgens, Frederick K., and Edward J. Tarbuck. *The Atmosphere*. 7th ed. Upper Saddle River, N.J.: Prentice-Hall, 1998.

Mantua, Nathan. "The Pacific Decadal Oscillation (PDO)." NOAA Climate Prediction Center. Available on-line. URL: http://tao.atmos.washington.edu/pdo. January 2000.

———. "The Pacific Decadal Oscillation and Climate Forecasting for North America." Joint Institute for the Study of the Atmosphere and Oceans, University of Washington, Seattle. Available on-line. URL: www.astmos.washington.edu/~mantua/REPORTS/PDO/PDO_cs.htm. August 1, 2000.

Mason, C. F. *Biology of Freshwater Pollution*. 2d ed. New York: John Wiley, 1991.

McCully, Patrick. "About Reservoir-Induced Seismicity." *World Rivers Review*, vol. 12, no. 3, June 1997. Available on-line. URL: www.irn.org/pubs/wrr/9706/ris/html. Accessed November 6, 2002.

McIlveen, Robin. *Fundamentals of Weather and Climate*. London: Chapman & Hall, 1992.

Mellanby, Kenneth. *Waste and Pollution: The Problem for Britain.* London: HarperCollins, 1992.

Michaels, Patrick J. "Carbon Dioxide: A Satanic Gas?" Testimony to the Subcommittee on National Economic Growth, Natural Resources and Regulatory Affairs, U.S. House of Representatives, October 6, 1999. Available on-line. URL: www.cato.org/testimony/ct-pm100699.html. Accessed November 2, 2002.

Michaels, Patrick J., and Robert C. Balling, Jr. *The Satanic Gases: Clearing the Air about Global Warming.* Washington, D.C.: Cato Institute, 2000.

Miller, Paul R. "Concept of Forest Decline in Relation to Western U.S. Forests." In MacKenzie, James J., and Mohamed T. El-Ashry, eds. *Air Pollution's Toll on Forests & Crops.* New Haven, Conn.: Yale University Press, 1989.

Moore, David M., ed. *Green Planet.* Cambridge: Cambridge University Press, 1982.

Moore, Peter D. *Wetlands.* New York: Facts On File, 2000.

Murray, Lucas. "Mesocyclone." Available on-line. URL: www.geo.arizona.edu/~/lmurray/g256/vocab/mesocyclone.html. Updated December 3, 2001.

NASA. "Earth's Fidgeting Climate." Science@NASA. Available on-line. URL: http://Science.nasa.gov/headlines/y2000/ast20oct_1.htm. Posted October 20, 2000.

———. "Hydrologic Cycle." NASA's Observatorium. Available on-line. URL: http://observe.arc.nasa.gov/nasa/earth/hydrocycle/hydro2.html. Accessed November 12, 2002.

National Oceanic and Atmospheric Administration. "Billion Dollar U.S. Weather Disasters, 1980–2001." Available on-line. URL: http://lwf.ncdc.noaa.gov/oa/reports/billionz.html. National Climatic Data Center, January 1, 2002.

———. "Impacts of El Niño and Benefits of El Niño Prediction." Available on-line. URL: www.pmel.noaa.gov/tao/elnino/impacts.html. Spring 1994.

National Science Foundation. "Lake Vostok." NSF Fact Sheet, Office of Legislative and Public Affairs. Available on-line. URL: www.nsf.gov/od/lpa/news/02/fslakevostok.htm. May 2002.

"Natural Air Pollution." Available on-line. URL: www.doc.mmu.ac.uk/aric/eae/Air_Quality/Older/Natural_Air_Pollution.html. Accessed October 21, 2002.

New Scientist. "Snowball Earth." Available on-line. URL: http://xgistor.ath.cx/files/ReadersDigest/snowballearth.html. *New Scientist*, November 6, 1999.

"Nuclear Fusion Basics." Available on-line. URL: www.jet.efda.org/pages/content/fusion1.html. Accessed October 22, 2002.

"Ocean Surface Currents: Introduction to Ocean Gyres." Available on-line. URL: http://oceancurrents.rsmas.miami.edu/ocean-gyres.html. Accessed November 12, 2002.

Oke, T. R. *Boundary Layer Climates.* 2d ed. New York: Routledge, 1987.

Oliver, John E., and John J. Hidore. *Climatology: An Atmospheric Science.* 2d ed. Upper Saddle River, N.J.: Prentice Hall, 2002.

O'Mara, Katrina, and Philip Jennings. "Ocean Thermal Energy Conversion." Australian CRC for Renewable Energy Ltd., June 1999. Available on-line. URL: http://acre.murdoch.edu.au/refiles/ocean/text.html.

Palmer, Chad. "How the Jet Stream Influences the Weather." *USA Today.* Available on-line. URL: www.usatoday.com/weather/wjet.htm. August 11, 1997.

Patel, Trupti. "Bhopal Disaster." The Online Ethics Center for Engineering and Science at Case Western Reserve University. Available on-line. URL: http://onlineethics.org/environment/bhopal.html. Updated September 6, 2001.

Peterken, George F. *Natural Woodland.* Cambridge: Cambridge University Press, 1996.

Pettit, Paul. "WeatherConsulting." Available on-line. URL: www.weatherconsultant.com/Feature10.html. Accessed January 14, 2003.

"The Ramsar Convention on Wetlands." Available on-line. URL: www.ramsar.org. Updated November 6, 2002.

Rekenthaler, Doug. "The Storm That Changed America: The Galveston Hurricane of 1900." DisasterRelief.org. Available on-line. URL: www.disasterrelief.org/Disasters/980813Galveston. Posted August 15, 1998.

Robinson, Peter J., and Ann Henderson-Sellers. *Contemporary Climatology.* 2d ed. New York: Prentice Hall, 1999.

Rosen, Harold A., and Deborah R. Castleman. "Flywheels in Hybrid Vehicles." *Scientific American,* October 1997. Available on-line. URL: www.sciam.com/1097issue/1097rosen.html.

Rosenberg, Matt. "Polders and Dykes of the Netherlands." About.com. Available on-line. URL: http://geography.about.com/library/weekly/aa033000a.htm. Accessed November 5, 2002.

Ruddiman, William F. *Earth's Climate, Past and Future.* New York: W. H. Freeman, 2001.

Schneider, Stephen H., ed. *Encyclopedia of Climate and Weather.* 2 vols. New York: Oxford University Press, 1996.

Science and Technology. "Structure and Dynamics of Supercell Thunderstorms." National Weather Service. Available on-line. URL: www.crh.noaa.gov/lmk/soo/docu/supercell.htm. Accessed December 9, 2002.

Seismology Research Centre. "Dams and Earthquakes." Available on-line. URL: www.seis.com.au/Basics/Dams.html. Last modified October 30, 2002.

Sloan, E. Dendy, Jr., John Happel, and Miguel A. Hnatow, eds. *International Conference on Natural Gas Hydrates,* vol. 715 of the *Annals of the New York Academy of Sciences.* New York: New York Academy of Sciences, 1994.

Sohl, Linda, and Mark Chandler. "Did the Snowball Earth Have a Slushball Ocean?" Goddard Institute for Space Studies. Available on-line. URL: www.giss.nasa.gov/research/intro/sohl_01. Last modified November 12, 2002.

Spokane Outdoors. "Channeled Scablands Theory." Available on-line. URL: www.spokaneoutdoors.com/scabland.htm. Accessed November 20, 2002.

Srinivasan, Margaret, and Kristy Kawasaki. "Science—El Niño/La Niña and PDO." Jet Propulsion Laboratory, NASA. Available on-line. URL: topex-www.jpl.nasa.gov/science/pdo.html. Updated May 14, 2002.

Thieler, E. Robert, and Erika S. Hammer-Klose. "National Assessment of Coastal Vulnerability to Sea-Level Rise." U.S. Geological Survey. Available on-line. URL: http://pubs.usgs.gov/of/of99-593.

Thomas, Keith. *Man and the Natural World: Changing Attitudes in England 1500–1800.* Harmondsworth, U.K.: Penguin Books, 1984.

"Three-Cell Model." Available on-line. URL: www.cimms.ou.edu/~cortinas/1014/125_html. October 2002.

"Trees and Air Pollution." *Science Daily Magazine.* Available on-line. URL: www.sciencedaily.com/releases/2001/01/010109223032.htm. November 1, 2001.

"The Tsunami Warning System." Available on-line. URL: www.geophys. washington.edu/tsunami/general/warning/warning.html. Accessed November 7, 2002.

U.N. Environment Programme. "The State of the Environment—Regional Synthesis," chapter 2 of *GEO–2000: Global Environment Outlook.* Available on-line. URL: www.unep.org/geo2000/english/0048.htm. Accessed October 21, 2002.

———. "Montreal Protocol." Available on-line. URL: www.unep.ch/ozone/mont_t.shtml and www.unep.ch/treaties.shtml. Accessed October 21, 2002.

USA Today. "Understanding Clouds and Fog." Available on-line. URL: www.usatoday.com/weather/wfog.htm. Updated April 22, 2002.

U.S. Department of Agriculture Forest Service. "American Semidesert and Desert Province." Available on-line. URL: www.fs.fed.us/colorimagemap/images/322.html. Accessed October 23, 2002.

U.S. Environmental Protection Agency. "About EPA." Available on-line. URL: www.epa.gov/epahome/aboutepa.htm. Updated August 8, 2002.

———. "Acid Rain." Available on-line. URL: www.epa.gov/airmarkets/acidrain. Updated October 17, 2002.

———. "Air." Available on-line. URL: www.epa.gov/ebtpages/air.html. Updated October 21, 2002.

———. "Air Toxics from Motor Vehicles." Fact Sheet OMS-2. Available on-line. URL: www.epa.gov/otaq/02-toxic.htm. Updated July 20, 1998.

———. "Clean Air Act." Available on-line. URL: www.epa.gov/oar/oaq_caa.html. Updated March 29, 2002.

———. "Emissions Summary." Office of Air Quality Planning and Standards. Available on-line. URL: www.epa.gov/oar/emtrnd94/em_summ.html. August 1, 2002.

———. "Environmental Laws that Establish the EPA's Authority." Available on-line. URL: www.epa.gov/history/org/origins/laws.htm. Updated August 12, 2002.

————. "Radioactive Waste Disposal: An Environmental Perspective." Available on-line. URL: www.epa.gov/radiation/radwaste/index.html. Updated October 21, 2002.

U.S. Geological Survey. Available on-line. URL: www.usgs.gov. Last modified November 1, 2002.

————. "The Cataclysmic 1991 Eruption of Mount Pinatubo, Philippines." Fact Sheet 113-97. Available on-line. URL: http://geopubs.wr.usgs.gov/fact-sheet/fs113-97. January 12, 2002.

————. "Drought Watch: Definitions of Drought." Available on-line. URL: http://md.water.usgs.gov/drought/define.html. Updated June 17, 2000.

————. "Flash Flood Laboratory." Available on-line. URL: www.cira.colostate.edu/fflab/international.htm. Accessed November 7, 2002.

————. "Prediction." Available on-line. URL: www.cira.colostate.edu/fflab/prediction.htm. Accessed November 7, 2002.

————. "Tsunamis and Earthquakes." Available on-line. URL: http://walrus.wr.usgs.gov/tsunami. Last modified August 3, 2001.

Visbeck, Martin. "North Atlantic Oscillation." Available on-line. URL: www.ldeo.columbia.edu/~visbeck/nao/presentation/html/img0.htm. Downloaded March 11, 2003.

Volk, Tyler. *Gaia's Body: Towards a Physiology of Earth*. New York: Copernicus, 1998.

Waggoner, Ben. "Louis Agassiz (1807–1873)." University of California, Berkeley. Available on-line. URL: www.ucmp.berkeley.edu/history/agassiz.html. Accessed November 19, 2002.

The Weather Channel. "Forecasting Floods." *Storm Encylopedia*. Available on-line. URL: www.weather.com/encyclopedia/flood./forecast.html. Accessed November 7, 2002.

"Weather Satellites." SpacePix. Available on-line. URL: www.spacepix.net/weather. Accessed January 14, 2003.

"Weather Satellites and Instruments." Boeing. Available on-line. URL: www.boeing.com/defense-space/space/bss/weather/weather.html. Accessed January 14, 2003.

"Weather Satellites—Types." University of Wisconsin, Stout. Available on-line. URL: http://physics.uwstout.edu/wx/wxsat/types.htm. Accessed January 14, 2003.

"What Is Drought? Understanding and Defining Drought." National Drought Mitigation Center. Available on-line. URL: http://drought.unl.edu/whatis/concept.htm. Accessed October 24, 2002.

Williams, Sara. "Soil Texture: From Sand to Clay." Available on-line. URL: www.ag.usask.ca/cofa/departments/hort/hortinfo/misc/soil.html. Accessed October 24, 2002.

Willis, Bill. "Weather Fronts." Available on-line. URL: www.wcscience.com/weather/fronts.html. Accessed November 26, 2002.

World Health Organization. "Air Pollution." *Fact Sheet No. 187*. Available on-line. URL: www.who.int/inf-fs/en/fact187.html. Revised September 2000.

World Meteorological Organization. Geneva: Secretariat (Home Page). Available on-line. URL: www.wmo.ch/index-en.html. Accessed April 23, 2003.

World Nuclear Association. "Safety of Nuclear Power Reactors." Available on-line. URL: www.world-nuclear.org/info/inf06appprint.htm. July 2002.

Wouk, Victor. "Hybrid Electric Vehicles." *Scientific American*, October 1997. Available on-line. URL: www.sciam.com/1097issue/1097wouk.html.

Zavisa, John. "How Lightning Works." Howstuffworks. Available on-line. URL: www.howstuffworks.com/lightning.htm. Accessed November 4, 2002.

Index

Page numbers in *italic* indicate illustrations.